MASTER OF PRECISION

MASTER OF PRECISION

Henry M. Leland

Ottilie M. Leland
with
Minnie Dubbs Millbrook

with an Introduction by
Allan Nevins and Frank E. Hill

 Wayne State University Press   Detroit

Copyright © 1966, 1996 by Wayne State University Press, Detroit, Michigan 48201. All rights are reserved. No part of this book may be reproduced without formal permission.

Library of Congress Catalog Card Number 66-10501

ISBN-13: 978-0-8143-2665-7   ISBN-10: 0-8143-2665-X (pbk.)

All photographs are courtesy of the National Automotive History Collection, Detroit Public Library.

Great Lakes Books

A complete listing of the books in this series can be found online at wsupress.wayne.edu

PHILIP P. MASON, Editor
Department of History, Wayne State University

DR. CHARLES K. HYDE, Associate Editor
Department of History, Wayne State University

Contents

Preface to the 1996 Edition		7
Preface		8
Introduction		11
Chapter I	Like a Giant	15
Chapter II	Apprentice	19
Chapter III	Master of His Craft	37
Chapter IV	A Shop of His Own	51
Chapter V	The Cadillac Is Born	65
Chapter VI	Recognition Abroad	79
Chapter VII	An Enlarged Vision	87
Chapter VIII	To the Rescue	98
Chapter IX	The Finance Committee Reigns	109
Chapter X	Making Mechanics	119
Chapter XI	The Self-Starter	128
Chapter XII	New Lines, More Power	140
Chapter XIII	His Civic Duty	155
Chapter XIV	A New Dedication	171
Chapter XV	Engines of War	182
Chapter XVI	Another Fine Car	195
Chapter XVII	Disagreement and Desperation	207
Chapter XVIII	Henry Ford Listens	223
Chapter XIX	Betrayed	237
Chapter XX	The End of Hope	252
Notes		267
Index		283

Illustrations

Frontispiece:
Henry M. Leland

Following p. 64
The Leland Farm home in Vermont
Leland and Faulconer plant in 1902
Morning consultation at Leland and Faulconer
Henry Leland, Robert Faulconer, Wilfred Leland, and stenographer
Interior of foundry at Leland and Faulconer
Wilfred Leland dictating to his secretary
First Cadillac on its first road trip
The car that began the Cadillac tradition
Cadillac carrying sixteen riders up Shelby Hill in Detroit
1902 Cadillac advertising stunt
Mr. and Mrs. Henry M. Leland in London in 1910
Wilfred Leland Jr. at age one
Baby Cadillac once belonging to Prince Olaf of Norway
Announcement of one of Leland's speeches
Cartoon appearing in the *Detroit News* June 13, 1919
Cartoon of 1909, when Durant was assembling General Motors
1902 Cadillac plant
1917 plant constructed by the Lincoln Motor Co.
Morning conference at the Lincoln Motor Co.
Lincoln employed large numbers of women during the war
The 6500th precision Liberty motor
The Lelands and the Fords at the Lincoln Motor Co.
Front page of *Pipp's Weekly*, July 7, 1923
Henry Leland with Osceola in 1930
Wilfred Leland on his thoroughbred Rigel
Henry Leland and his riding horse, about 1910
Henry Leland and his grandson
Henry Leland at 89, cranking a 1903 Cadillac
Wilfred Leland at 84, discussing Cadillacs with car enthusiasts
Motor assembling at Cadillac in 1902
Motor assembling at Cadillac in 1952
The Lincoln Motor plant at the time it was purchased by Henry Ford
Wilfred Leland and second wife, Ottilie Masey Leland

Preface to the 1996 Edition

HENRY MARTYN LELAND (1843-1932) is one of automotive history's most outstanding figures. In the early years of the twentieth century, he was in the forefront of those who set Detroit on its course as the automobile capital of the world. Trained in New England factories known for their precision manufacture, Henry Leland became known for his insistence on attaining the highest standards of workmanship and the best possible products. He was the developer of two automobiles whose names are still associated with high quality: the Cadillac and the Lincoln. Affectionately called both "Uncle Henry" and the "Grand Old Man of Detroit," he was a demanding but highly regarded employer and an idealistic, unusually dedicated citizen.

Master of Precision is an invaluable, firsthand account not only of the life and work of Henry Leland but also of the early days of the automobile industry in which he played such an important part. Wilfred C. Leland, Henry's only son who shared every aspect of the elder Leland's automotive career—its triumphs as well as its ultimate disappointment—began writing the book a few years before he died; it was finished by his widow, Ottilie. First published in 1966, it makes use of unpublished manuscripts and other original documents belonging to the Leland family, as well as some more readily available sources. Its republication in 1996, the centennial of the automobile industry, is a fitting tribute to the "master of precision" and his contribution to that industry in its fledgling days. Anyone who appreciates the drama and serendipity in the evolution of the motor car and the automobile industry will savor every page. No automotive history collection is complete without it.

Preface

SELDOM DOES A MAN live long enough for history to catch up with him. No matter how dramatic or meaningful the episodes of his youth, there comes a time during his maturity and older age when his children, his friends and the general public are unreceptive and uninterested in the story he could tell. His reminiscences are endured with wandering attention and polite yawns.

But let this man's history lie fallow for a time, let it be stored, neglected, in an attic. After the passage of half a century or so it will be rediscovered and proclaimed by historians. The Civil War and its veterans are a case in point. How many of us were bored by the tales of our grandfathers, only to return to them fifty years later with avid interest. By that time only a few of the old soldiers remained to retell their story. A man must live a long time for history to catch up with him.

Wilfred Leland lived a long time and, as he approached his eightieth year, the historians awoke to the value of the story he could tell. They sought him out and begged for his recollections of the beginnings of the automobile industry in Detroit. His last years were happily dedicated to recounting the tale of his father's long struggle, with his son by his side, to attain a unique place in that industry. Newspapermen, writers of books, historians—all sought Mr. Leland, asking information, incident and detail on the birth of the motor car.

No one was refused. Some of the seekers gave Wilfred Leland credit for the facts, others repeated his very words without reference to source. In time distortions appeared; anecdotes emerged that had no basis in fact. Mr. Leland decided to write a book telling the story as he knew it. With the aid of his wife, Ottilie M. Leland, he began to compile his material. He dictated page after page; he dug into the heaps of pamphlets and catalogs, the files of letters and memorabilia, that his family had accumulated. But time ran out. Wilfred Leland died at the age of eighty-eight with his task unfinished.

This story of Henry M. Leland is more than an account of the early automobile industry. As a man he differed from many of the mechanics, entrepreneurs and financiers who had a finger in the development of that most fascinating of machines, the motor car. His life is one chapter of a revolution which changed the American way of life. From early history Americans had as an ideal the free, independent man living on and owning his bit of land and getting his living from that land. The industrial revolution reformed this ideal into the image of an industrial man living by his skill in producing comforts and conveniences for other men.

Henry Leland, born on a farm into a family which clung persistently to the farm, had this transition to make. With him he brought into the constantly evolving world of the machine some of the personal virtues of that older, simpler world of his youth. In his eyes machines had a morality of their own, a rightness of conception, an exactness of execution and a precise and lasting usefulness. That in the end the business world failed him in no way dims the luster of his ideal or the inspiration of his belief that honor and faith may attend the machine age.

As the story unfolds, it becomes evident that the son, Wilfred, played an ever-expanding role in the Leland drama. He was the necessary complement that every aggressive, strongly opinionated genius needs. Gentler, more persuasive, he was always the arranger, the soother, the diplomat when Henry Leland's outspoken, hard-held ideas encountered opposition. Henry Leland's mastery of the machine and his ideas of perfection were the root and branch of the Leland achievement, but that achievement would have been much more difficult without the son's devoted aid.

The account in these pages has been based primarily upon the Leland papers and memoirs in the possession of Mrs. Wilfred C. Leland. It does not pretend to be a history of the automobile industry, only one man's contribution to that history. Other materials have been added only to give background and continuity to the story.

The authors owe a special debt to Dr. Allan Nevins and Frank Ernest Hill, who encouraged the writing of this book. Frank Ernest Hill not only read the whole manuscript but also took time to give a detailed criticism and many valuable suggestions. Miss Maud Payne and James J. Bradley of the Automotive History Collection of the Detroit Public Library gave helpful assistance on many topics. Our appreciation extends also to others of the Library, Robert R. Runser, Charles W. Morhardt and the staff of the Burton Historical Collection. Many others helped by contributing memories and letters or making records available, including Frederick S. Bennett, Lloyd Blunden, John Bourne, Leo Butzel, George Clement, Will Foltz, William Henry Gallagher, Ralph C. Getsinger, Ada Grimm, Sidney Handyside, Edward Johansson, W. A. P. John, Frank Johnson, Charles F. Kettering, William H. Layne, Harry LeDuc, Ralph Lewis, Pliny Marsh, Charlie Martens, William B. Mayo, Lot A. Merrill, Charles Nash, William H. O'Brien, Charles Oostdyke, Clair Owen, Arthur Pound, John B. Rae, Frederick E. Searle, George Stark, Kenneth M. Stevens, LeRoi Williams, Samuel E. Wilson, Miriam Woodbridge, William Guy, Henry D. Sharpe, and Clarence T. Wilson.

—Minnie Dubbs Millbrook

Introduction

"HENRY LELAND ALWAYS got deep satisfaction out of anything which was made right." This sentence in his biography strikes the keynote of his distinctive career as engineer, designer, businessman, and public servant. He had in high degree the pride of craftsmanship that has marked the master workman down the centuries. Originality of conception had to be matched with close attention to practical effectiveness, and both had to be crowned with artistry of form. He set new standards of precision in a factory that attained unusual harmony in the relations of worker and employer, and he gave the world a vehicle some of whose special values endure along with its name. Meanwhile, he was a model citizen and public servant, some of his qualities too fine for a rough world.

Europe gave mankind the automobile. The Austrian Siegfried Marcus developed a successful gasoline-powered car in 1875, and men like Otto, Daimler, and Benz in Germany made one advance after another in the employment of internal combustion engines to drive machines. They were pioneers in laying the foundations of the automobile industry while Americans remained onlookers.

However, a land dependent as few others on long-distance transportation soon asserted its interest in the "horseless carriage." In 1893 a car made by Charles and Frank Duryea made a successful run, and two years later an improved model won a widely publicized race arranged by a Chicago newspaper. In 1896, the year in which the first motor show was held in the British Isles, Frank Duryea invaded Europe, and won against some of the best competition the Old World could offer.

Henry M. Leland, then busy with his machine shop, was still more interested in bicycles than in motor cars, and till the close of the century had no idea that he would be concerned with making them. But his zeal was fired when he undertook the manufacture of an engine for Ransom E. Olds's car, the Oldsmobile, and designed an improved model of his own. By the latter part of 1902 he was preparing to use it in the Cadillac. This car leapt into prominence when a test at Brooklands, England, in 1908 was supervised by the Royal Automobile Club. Three Cadillac cars were to be disassembled, their parts mixed, a certain number withdrawn and replaced by others from stock, and three cars were then to be assembled from the materials. This was successfully done without the use of files or even sandpaper. Thus the high accuracy of machined elements for the car was proved, and their complete interchangeability, while possibilities for quantity production and reliable service were established. The world was amazed, the machine-industry of America (as represented by the Cadillac company) was shown to be more reliable than any hand work could be, and an infinite saver of time.

Henry M. Leland, who was awarded the Dewar trophy for this accomplishment, was undoubtedly at this time the most knowledgeable and best-trained man working with automobiles in the United States. At a bound he became one of the three great personalities in the American automobile industry, the other two being Henry Ford and William C. Durant. While Ford evolved quantity production and the cheap car, and Durant founded General Motors and became not only a great promoter but the creator of a family of cars and supporting-parts manufacturers, Leland stood for quality of product. His high standards influenced competitors and all types of suppliers. He went on to develop cars which for comfort, convenience, and speed anticipated the automobiles we know today.

Leland's preeminence has always been conceded, but until the appearance of the present volume there has never been an authoritative account of his life and work. I personally felt the lack of such a work, and when I discovered that his son, Wilfred C. Leland, had abundant materials in his possession, I urged him to undertake a full account of his father's background and accomplishments. He was ready to do so, but unfortunately death intervened to check his work, and Mrs. Leland and Mrs. Millbrook have completed the task. They deserve the thanks of the many Americans interested in the story of the automobile. Their book contains much original material—letters, records, memoranda—and they have worked with these records and with others of a less personal nature in libraries and automotive collections to produce the final book.

Leland's role was an inspiring and often a successful one. He developed the Cadillac, the self-starter, the Lincoln car; held up high standards of performance for the industry; and established the first notable school for automobile mechanics. Unfortunately, near the end of his life he saw his company (the Lincoln Motor Company) go into a receivership. Eventually it passed under the control of Henry Ford, who at first proposed to keep Leland and his son in the industry as a public service, but in the end failed to live up to his professions. The authors go fully into this painful episode, as they do into all phases of Leland's career.

They are to be commended for performing a difficult and interesting task. Henry M. Leland from his earliest to his latest experiences will belong to the public. His career takes us back to the early toolmakers, for he worked for Colt and Brown and Sharpe, and carries us on to the modern closed cars. This account of it will fill a gap in pre-automotive and automotive history, and will provide a deeper understanding of a great industrial adventure that has helped make modern America, and is still one of the most important and essential activities in the further growth of the nation.

ALLAN NEVINS
FRANK E. HILL

Chapter I

Like a Giant

ON FEBRUARY 29, 1908, the Royal Automobile Club of England began an unusual test on its new race track at Brooklands in Surrey, some twenty miles from the heart of London. The Standardization Test, as the event was called, had been open to all automobile companies, but there was only one entrant—the American Cadillac Motor Company.

The test was complicated. Three one-cylinder Cadillac cars were selected by a committee appointed by the club; actually they were chosen from the stock of the Anglo-American Motor Car Company (Cadillac) at 19/20 Hedden St. W., London. At Brooklands they were to be driven some miles to prove their operable condition. Then at a nearby garage all three were to be disassembled, and their parts thoroughly mixed up under the eyes of observers appointed by the club. These gentlemen were also to select as many parts as they chose, which they would present to Frederick S. Bennett, the English Cadillac representative, who would replace them with identical ones from stock. Three cars were then to be rebuilt under Bennett's supervision with only spanners and screwdrivers as tools, and without the use of a file, scraper, or even sandpaper. All three cars were then to be driven 500 miles to prove their complete fitness.[1]

If successful, the test would prove that all parts in Cadillac cars were interchangeable, and that parts of all automobiles, if properly manufactured, could be interchangeable. This would be a development of the first magnitude. Cadillacs were the product of machine tools, and if it could be demonstrated that they were so accurately made, this fact would smash the idea held by most Europeans that machine tools and quality do not go together, and that the finest car was one that in large part was handmade. It would also indicate that machine-made cars could be produced in larger numbers.[2]

The test was the result of a trip Bennett had made to Detroit in 1907, where he had seen the manufacture of Cadillac components by machine. A little later in England he watched his mechanic fitting a new steering knuckle into a Cadillac axle he was working on. The man said, "Here is a beautiful fit, sir." Thinking that the parts were made to an accuracy of 2000th of an inch,* Bennett replied, "If only we could tell the world this! It would then have the best reason for buying Cadillac cars."[3]

Bennett proposed to the Royal Automobile Club that they hold a test for accuracy, and the club agreed. Many manufacturers were claiming that they could easily supply new parts for broken or defective ones in their cars, and that the parts would fit. Actually some machining or filing was usually necessary, making quite a task of the operation. The Standardization Test was open to all automobile firms, but significantly Cadillac was the only one to attempt it. Experts freely predicted failure because, as one put it, "A uniform accuracy of fitting to the two-thousandth fraction of an inch would be indispensable to prevent failure." Such precision was deemed impossible.[4]

Before the three cars arrived at Brooklands a heavy fall of snow had made the new track a difficult area of operation. Nevertheless, the three cars all completed ten circuits (about seven miles), were pronounced operable, and were driven through two feet of snow into the garage. Here they were knocked down. The observers then

---

* Actually, they were made to 1/1000th of an inch.

removed 89 parts, and Bennett supplied identical ones from stock. The test then went forward.

Two weeks later three weird-looking cars emerged from the workshop. Someone dubbed them "Harlequins," and the name stuck, for the original three Cadillacs had been of different colors, and those that were reassembled represented studies in motley. None had four wheels of the same hue, and all the mudguards were of assorted shades, while the coachwork of the bodies and even the hoods varied, so that the total effect was comparable to the camouflaged trucks or tanks that men were to use later in war.[5]

Nevertheless, the motley three proceeded to give incontrovertible testimony to the quality of Cadillac workmanship. According to one account,

> The three Harlequins were then driven for 500 miles around Brooklands (track) and on official examination were found to be in perfect condition at the close of the run. Two of them were then returned to the salesroom for repainting, while the third was retained in the custody of the Royal Automobile Club as an entrant for the great event of the year, a 2000-mile trial to be held some four months later.[6]

In February 1909, on the basis of the standardization trial, the Cadillac motor car, "in recognition of the most noteworthy performance of the year," was awarded the Dewar Trophy, a prize set up a few years earlier by Sir Thomas Dewar. In the brash young automotive world it occupied a position comparable to the Nobel prizes in the fields of science and literature.[7]

The Cadillac performance had been supervised by Bennett, and he merited high commendation for its success. But he was only the English agent for the car, and had contributed nothing to its design or workmanship. The man who had developed it was Henry M. Leland, president of the company that bore its name, and already known in the Detroit area and indeed throughout the United States. But with the Dewar award for a feat that literally had startled the world he ceased to be merely an eminent motor-car manufacturer and stood out like a giant on the automotive scene.

Charles and Frank Duryea had built the first operable motor vehicle in the United States, Ransom E. Olds had launched in his

Oldsmobile the most popular car of the early period. But Leland had now laid the foundation for the future American industry. He had established manufacturing procedures (generously implemented by machine tools) never previously so effectively employed and, at a bound, took a position of leadership. He was to maintain it, and in the next decades would be comparable in stature with (although quite different from) William C. Durant, Henry Ford, and Alfred P. Sloan, Jr.

In comparing Leland with Durant and Ford it should be pointed out that Leland's contribution to the development of the motor car was the establishment of high standards of manufacture. Ford, of course, through the moving assembly line also developed standards, but for the manufacture of a cheap car. He himself recognized Leland's great contribution. Durant as the founder of General Motors was a promoter, but made contributions as the head of an organization offering a variety of cars, and the establishment (or acquisition) of companies supplying parts. Sloan reorganized General Motors (with Du Pont aid) on a sounder basis, and established its highly successful system of financial controls. The Dodge Brothers would be included by some experts as a major force in the period 1908–1922, and in the 1920's Walter P. Chrysler took a prominent place in the industry. Leland's period of eminence might be set as 1908–1922.

How had he reached this eminence? Let us go back and follow the Leland story from its beginnings. It takes us first into an earlier industrial era, goes hand-in-hand with the steady rise of American manufacturing through the bicycle and the pioneer automotive stages, enables us to understand more fully the maturing of the motor car in the United States, and still has relevance to the developments that are taking place today.

Chapter II
Apprentice

1

IN 1843 NORTHERN NEW ENGLAND was almost as rugged an area as Iowa Territory on the far side of the Mississippi or the distant lands of Oregon and California that were soon to be the El Dorado of tens of thousands of adventurous Americans. Near Barton, Vermont, the land had been cleared for farms, but dense wooded areas still remained edging the cultivated tracts carved from the wilderness, and most of the roads were rough tracks negotiated by sleighs in the icy winters and by lurching wagons and horsemen in the summer when the ways wound between boulders and swamps, and were pocked with mud or dust holes. On a farm in this rugged country on February 16, an eighth child was born to Leander Leland and his wife.[1]

It was a boy. Quite in character, the parents did not name him for the father's idol Commodore Perry, or for Prince Albert, lately married to Queen Victoria of England, or for John Tyler, then President of the United States. His given names were Henry Martyn. They were those of an English missionary who had carried the gospel to darkest India. Lord Macaulay, whose poems the couple may have known, had briefly celebrated the peaceful accomplishments of the brave preacher:

> Eternal trophies! Not with carnage red,
> Not stained with tears of hapless captives shed,

which would take the zealot

> to a happier shore
> Where danger, death, and shame assault no more! [2]

Thus Henry Martyn Leland was launched in life with a push toward the hereafter rather than the here; and considering the circumstances of the family this was not surprising. Leander was indeed the owner of a farm, but it was heavily mortgaged. He earned a living less from it than from the bone-bruising occupation of driving an eight-horse wagon between Boston and Montreal. In Massachusetts the highway he traversed was straight and good for its day, but farther north much of his route wound over mountains or through forest where bogs, steeps and half-cleared brush tried the resources of the most skillful driver. Henry Leland told of his father's hard life:

> The teams at times could go but a short distance every day. In bad weather at night there would be as many as 150 horses at one of the small frame inns which were not more than five or eight miles apart. Each driver had to care for his eight horses, feed, clean, card, harness and unharness. For all this work my father received the wages of $15 per month.[3]

Leland had been forced into this hazardous occupation through sheer folly. When on coming of age he had inherited his farm, he had promptly mortgaged it to engage with a little-known partner in the cattle trade. He had given the money to this man, and soon both man and money had disappeared. Leland had then taken on the punishing Boston–Montreal route to get cash for his mortgage payments. He often stayed overnight at an inn in Glover, Vermont, not far from his farm, where he met the innkeeper's daughter, Zylpha Tifft. Within a year or two he married her and took her to the mortgaged farm, where she managed as best she could the farm and the children as they came along.

APPRENTICE

Leander Leland was of old New England stock: the first Henry Leland arrived in America in 1652. Through the generations the family had shifted from Massachusetts to Maine and Rhode Island, and in 1810 Joseph Leland, Leander's father, had exchanged his farm there for a large tract of land in what is now Orleans County in northeastern Vermont.[4] Thus he hoped to provide homes for his seven sons and one daughter. Leander had inherited a portion of this property, only to lose it after years of struggle to keep it.

In person Leander Leland was a wiry, sturdy man, reticent in speech and devoted to his horses. He handled them with surpassing skill, often guiding his team by voice alone. A member of the militia, he drilled with his company when he could, was a good shot, and was expert at sword play. He bequeathed a singularly trustful disposition to his youngest son, who could never believe that other men were not inherently as good and honorable as he himself, and was several times to pay a stiff penalty for this faith in human nature.

Soon after Henry's birth the rigors of the cruel freight route proved too much for Leander Leland and he retired to the farm to recuperate. Even with his help the payments on the mortgage could not be squeezed from the stony acres, and foreclosure compelled the family to occupy a farm owned by another "on halves." That is, the arrangement gave them a roof and half the profit they could make from the place; the owner got the rest. It was barely enough to enable them to exist. Though the food was plain and the clothing sparse Zylpha Leland brought up her boys and girls firmly according to the precepts of her Quaker faith.[5] All were taught religion and morality, and her instructions even went beyond to more practical values. Henry M. Leland later recalled an incident of his early childhood which illustrates his mother's care.

Although but six years of age at the time, he already had a few duties. One was to drive the cows in from the woods to the barn lot to be milked. He had a small boy's fear that one of the bears might come out of the woods at twilight. Full of dread one evening, he threw down the poles of the gate in haste, scattering them helter-skelter. Before he could drive the cows in, his mother appeared and called him back. She showed him how to place the bars neatly to one side, so that the cows would not break them, or be injured by them. "There is a right way and a wrong way to do everything," she told him. "Hunt for the right way and then go ahead."

Although he did not know it then, this simple admonition was to become a creed that would govern all his actions later as he rose from position to higher position in industry.

However, there was no suggestion of industry in the remote Vermont where he passed his childhood. Here was only a country life so bare and wild that it had to be fought unremittingly and desperately to make it yield the barest livelihood. For the boy there were additional handicaps. School was kept for only a few months in the summer, and while he attended it, an accident soon impaired his hearing (it became normal again when he was fifteen) and he learned little. Furthermore, another unhappy condition shadowed his early years. The Lelands shared the farmhouse with a second family—distant cousins of Leander's. The father was an habitual drunkard. When sober he was a thoughtful kind-hearted man, but often came home from the tavern two miles away "merry drunk," and in this condition was feared by his wife and children, Henry Leland remembered, "as much as a hungry wolf." Often the little ones would watch from the top of a nearby hill as their father approached, and at the cry, "Yes, see, he staggers!" all would run and hide until the mother had got the tipsy man to bed. This was not always an easy task. "I have seen the wife, with her nose and face bleeding, being dragged about the house by the hair of her head," recalled Leland years afterward. "It made an impression upon me which all the years since have not effaced from my memory." [6]

Despite these grim conditions the boy had time for play in the green New England summer, and in the winter used his jumper (a box with two barrel staves nailed to the bottom for runners) to slide on the hard crest of the snow. There was enough to eat, although barely enough, and the free, wild country with its quiet pure air must have had an invigorating effect upon him, for he grew to be a tall and powerful man.

He enjoyed also an inner peace rooted in his religious convictions. This was intensified by an event which occurred one night when he was about seven. He was awakened from a deep sleep by hearing someone call his name. Three times he was summoned. Thinking it was his mother he answered, "Yes, mother, what is it?" The voice replied: "I want you always to be good." The boy promised, and went to sleep again. But the next morning when he spoke to his mother about the occurrence, she denied having called him. Then she burst into tears and exclaimed that it was surely the voice of God. All through their lives the two firmly believed that Henry had had a supernatural visitation, and from the time of the event onward it had a sobering and uplifting effect upon the growing boy.[7]

Soon afterward the family again faced a crisis. The Lelands were barely existing on the halves system, and desperately cast about for a means of escape from the farm. Through friends and relatives they heard that work was to be had near Worcester, Massachusetts. Once before they had sought to establish themselves in that vicinity and had been forced to return defeated. But the promise of success seemed to be brighter now, and they had nothing to lose through a second attempt. Mary Ann and Henry were left with relatives in Vermont while the parents and the two older boys proposed to find work. The decision once taken the Lelands quickly put it to the test. The event was a turning point in the life of Henry M. Leland.

2

The venture was successful. Leander Leland soon found employment in a grist mill; the mother took a position as nurse in the family of the head farmer on the large Merrifield estate. Frank got work in a shoe-making shop, while Edson went to school and did odd jobs. Undoubtedly the fact that four instead of two were working made the experiment happier than the earlier one. Mary Ann and Henry were summoned. The daughter, now fifteen, soon obtained a position and added her small earnings to the family income. Henry was to live with his mother on the farm and go to school. But even he found a small job. He was given the task of feeding and watering the 400 chickens on the estate, and of keeping separately the eggs of several fancy breeds of poultry. It was a happy time. The family was reunited under one roof, and Henry found time to fish and hunt. When he was eleven he learned to peg shoes (heavy brogans for slaves in the South) when such work would be put out by the factories. He developed a special system which saved time and enabled him to earn $1.50 a day. Even the most skillful man could make no more than $1.75.[8]

As he entered his 'teens he blossomed out in many ways. He learned to dance and became a skillful ballplayer. He was a regular attendant at church, where he met a girl named Ellen Hull. One evening, while attending an illustrated lecture on the life of Christ, he was startled when, as a picture of the Ascension was shown, a man in the audience rose and repeated in a clear voice some verses from the *Bible:* "Ye men of Galilee, why stand ye gazing up into heaven? This same Jesus, which is taken up from you into heaven, shall so come in like manner as ye have seen Him go into heaven." (Acts I, 11) Henry was deeply impressed. Later he learned that the man was Elias Hull, an assiduous student of the *Bible* and the father of Ellen.

Henry too was a student of the *Bible* and, seriously pondering the teachings of the Book, he came to believe in the Second Advent, or Second Coming of Christ. William Miller had been first to proclaim this prophecy in America and he had calculated that Christ would come down to earth again in 1843 to pass judgment on the people. The belief had attracted many followers and although the prophecy was not fulfilled in 1843 and a church was not organized at the time, still many continued to believe that Christ would come again though no one could tell the day or the hour. In Worcester these believers banded together and formed a church organization in 1850 and eventually the Leland family as well as the Hulls became members.[9] Henry's acquaintance with the motherless Ellen Hull ripened into a friendship cemented by similar interests and religious convictions.

Henry was now sixteen. His family had moved into the city of Worcester. Both his sisters were married and his mother kept a boarding house. Leander Leland was employed at the George Crompton Loom Works. Frank ran a planer in a machine shop, while Edson and Henry found work in a wheel factory.

Worcester had benefited from the growing textile industry, which had its inception early in the 19th century. The population had more than tripled from 1830 to 1850, increasing from 7,497 to 24,983. Small shops manufacturing machinery and other textile equipment had multiplied, bringing increased job opportunities for laborers. The Lelands, when they arrived in the Worcester vicinity, had found work on farms or in agricultural pursuits. They had even tried to acquire land and operate a farm again. As one historian stated the situation:

> Americans of the 18th century understood how to till fields, sail ships, fell forests and run sawmills but they knew little of complex machinery or factory operations. . . . Native manufacturing skill, therefore, was scarce and the first concern of all new undertakings was to procure experienced operatives. These usually came, in spite of hostile legislation from abroad." [10]

However, as the industrial revolution thus introduced accelerated, the Lelands, like thousands of other New Englanders who had no land and no hope of continuing in their traditional farm life, began entering these rudimentary factories and shops, some forced by the necessity of making a living and others attracted by a broadening opportunity to exercise their latent Yankee ingenuity. By 1857, as stated, the Lelands, father and sons were working in one shop or another. Henry Leland in the wheel factory of the Crompton Works was having his first contact with American industry.

This establishment manufactured a power loom originally invented by William Crompton in England in 1836. He and his son George had brought it to the United States in 1839, and found a ready sale for it because it wove fabrics of complicated designs which earlier looms could not produce. By 1851 George Crompton was making looms in Worcester, and in 1857 constructed and patented a better machine than his father had designed. The works were now manufacturing these new looms for use throughout New England. The work in the wheel factory was routine; all day Henry cut wood to the proper length for wheel spokes. But it happened that the minister of the Second Adventist congregation, the Reverend Jerald, was acquainted with Mr. Gordon, the superintendent of the Crompton Works. The Rev. Jerald recommended Henry to Mr. Gordon as a potential mechanic, and Gordon offered the youth an apprenticeship at the works.

It was an opportunity, but Henry Leland was not sure that he wanted to become an apprentice machinist. The hours were long (at least 10 a day for a 6-day week), and most factories did not pay high wages. Moreover, farming was still the traditional American occupation, which offered a possibility of independence, and did not shut a man indoors with noisy machinery. However, in his work clothes Henry went to the loom factory with his tools in a bucket. He waited there but no one paid the slightest attention to him, and finally he returned to the wheel factory and asked to be taken back. But Mr. Gordon learned what had happened, came to him with the assurance that there had been a mistake, explained that the opportunity was a good one, and persuaded the youth to return for a two-week trial. He was to receive 50 cents a day for a ten-hour day. Considering his inexperience and the cost of living at that time, this was good pay.[11]

Once in his new position, the young man perceived that it offered many possibilities. He was learning something all the time, and he saw that in comparison with the wheel factory his new job held promise for the future. Even the gibes of his older shopmates merely fired him with a determination to master his craft and become a real mechanic.

The carping and witticisms to which he was subjected were the usual initiation of apprentices. They underwent a kind of hazing in all shops. But at Crompton Works the mechanics were all English, who viewed the new world from a self-created summit of superiority. "What can you expect of a Yankee?" they demanded. "Thou'lt never be a mechanic, lad." It was simply impossible, they smugly pointed out, for any American to achieve real competence in mechanics. America had no really skilled workmen, inventors, writers, statesmen. In fact there were no great men but Englishmen. Had Henry been aware of the work of John Fitch, Eli Whitney, Robert Fulton, and Cyrus McCormick; had he known of Thomas Jefferson, James Fenimore Cooper, Ralph Waldo Emerson and other distinguished compatriots, he would have been able to defend his countrymen. But while he resented the chaffing, he lacked the background of reading and experience that would have afforded him effective rebuttal. Actually, in the weaving industry the impetus had been English and in industrial growth England was still ahead of the United States, and her skilled workmen were everywhere in demand.[12]

However, Henry was already discovering the education that could be mined from books. At first, though fond of reading, he had been attracted by cheap adventure novels which he borrowed from the local library. One night a stranger there, seeing what he was taking out, exclaimed, "Surely you don't read that trash!" Henry replied, "What better use can I make of my time than to read?" The stranger answered, "It makes a lot of difference *what* you read," and suggested some better books.

The episode was a revelation to young Leland and he was soon reading volumes that acquainted him with American genius in literature, government, and invention and was able to argue spiritedly with, if he could not confound, his English shopmates.[13]

In 1861, on the eve of the Civil War, while Henry had still to complete his training, there came a lull in which industry sagged. The Cromptons discharged practically all their men except the apprentices, whom they were legally obliged to retain. Young Leland, about to become eighteen, had worked hard and won the confidence of Gordon, who now gave him a higher grade of work (although no higher pay) than he would have had if the master mechanics had all been working. He would soon become a full-fledged mechanic himself, and could handle more difficult assignments.

When war came, he was caught up in the excitement that followed the firing on Fort Sumter. His reading and his feeling of the necessity to defend his country had made him deeply patriotic. Abraham Lincoln was his idol. His brother Edson had enlisted, and although Henry was under age and his parents had refused their permission for him to become a soldier, he determined that he would join up. Now a tall stalwart young man, he doubtless would have been accepted, but his mother guessed his intention, followed him to the recruiting office, had his name removed from the roll of eligibles, and sent him back to work.

He accepted the situation, the more so because he was soon able to serve the government directly. The Crompton Works had taken a contract to make the Blanchard lathe, used in the federal armories to turn out gun stocks.* It was a piece of delicate precision work, and the task of making it was assigned to Henry Leland. When finished, it was inspected and approved by Army officers from the Springfield Armory. This was a matter of no small pride to the young man, and he determined that when he had completed his apprenticeship he would get more such work to do.

About this time he joined the Machinists' Union. He was now able to express himself well, and at one of the first meetings he attended he spoke forcefully against a proposed strike for which he felt there was no justification. He was hissed, but renewed his protest at the next meeting. Again he found no supporters. At a third meeting he won some adherents, but became convinced that he could not find harmony in the union, and resigned. Another apprentice, Jill Backson, had jeered at him for his sentiments, and for working on special jobs for only $12 a month. "He was a disturber in the shop," said Leland later. "He kept telling me that I was too careful, that I was turning out too much work, and that I ought to get more money for what I was doing. Now do you think Backson and I spent much time holding hands? No, sir, it was a constant fight."

His apprenticeship completed, Henry was approached by Gordon with a proposal that he take on important work at higher pay. Mr. Crompton wanted to do less, and there was a good opportunity for a young man. The offer was flattering, but the nineteen-year-old machinist refused it. His brother Edson had already become a casualty in the great war, and Henry wanted to work where he could render the greatest service to his country.** He had learned that the U.S. Armory at Springfield needed expert mechanics, and he had

* Thomas Blanchard, born near Worcester was one of the early American inventor mechanics who contributed greatly to the machine-tool industry. In 1818 he invented the lathe for turning irregular forms which was used for turning gun-stocks at the Springfield Armory. He also invented or improved mortising and turning machines. Joseph Wickham Roe, *English and American Tool Builders*, New Haven, 1916, pp. 220–21.

** Edson Leland contracted swamp fever on the Chickahominy, was captured and sent to Libby prison in the South. Released to the New York City Hospital, he died there September 12, 1862.

APPRENTICE 29

determined to help there with war production. He did so, and remained at the Armory until hostilities ceased in April 1865.[14] As he said afterward the particular lesson he learned in the Armory was the value of order and neatness in a work shop. Everything was clean and systematic, a state of affairs not common in the early cluttered factories and machine shops at other places.

3

With Lee's surrender at Appomattox, the Springfield plant was no longer called upon to equip armies, and Leland, with numerous other workmen, was discharged. He found employment next day at the Colt Revolver Factory in Hartford, Connecticut. He now had a background of experience which included textile machinery and all phases of the manufacture of firearms. During the war he had reached his majority, had cast his first vote—for Abraham Lincoln —and had acquired a foundation in what was to become an important life work.

The times were crucial for anyone interested in the production of machines and machine tools. While making important contributions in this field—Eli Whitney had demonstrated the interchangeability of parts as early as 1798—Americans up to the 1850's had followed the lead of the English in industry.[15] At the same time native artisans were developing the mechanical skill and inventive mind which were steadily reshaping and adapting the English methods and tools as well as developing a distinctive American mode of machine manufacture. While Whitney had early formulated the concept of making uniform parts and fittings so they might be readily interchangeable, the full implementation of this concept awaited better and more accurate fabrication of parts. In Whitney's day, uniformity meant to the one-thirty-secondth of an inch and when the parts were put together much filing was necessary and uneven joints were common. By 1880 the standard of uniformity had risen to one-half-thousandth of an inch. The improvement was achieved by the steady invention and perfecting of machine tools, those basic devices, such as cutters, borers and milling machines, which made the parts before they were put together into the final product or machine. These tools, steadily becoming more capable and more accurate, made possible what came to be called "American industry" or quantity manufacture.

By 1861 manufacturers of firearms, textile machinery, water wheels, steam engines, locomotives and sewing machines were building lathes, jigs and gauges for their own processes and finding the sale of these tools to others a profitable side line. For some, toolmaking would soon become the main line.[16]

The Civil War gave great impetus to the fast-developing machine age. The machines and tools to implement and support an ever-increasing industrial volume would be produced by men trained, ready and able in 1866. Joseph R. Brown, a clock maker, had designed in 1851 the *vernier caliper,* an instrument which permitted measurement to one-thousandth of an inch. Though in 1858, with his partner Lucian Sharpe, he began manufacturing sewing machines, his enduring fame came later from his invention of the micrometer, wire gauges, gear cutters and turret screw machines. Others were also active. Francis A. Whitney and Amos Pratt were both machinists who had been employed at the Colt Armory. In 1860 they began working on their own account, manufacturing a small winder for a linen company. Frederick H. Howe had designed an advanced milling machine in 1852 and was superintendent of the Providence Tool Company manufacturing muskets during the war. He would design other machines. All of these men and other American toolmakers were poised at the war's end for advances that would make them indisputable leaders in their field throughout the world.[17]

Considering his abilities as revealed up to that time, and his later accomplishments, one would expect Henry M. Leland to have joined enthusiastically in the exhilarating movement for the development of American industry. Actually it seems not to have fired his imagination. He was only twenty-two in 1865, and it is questionable whether he recognized then, for example, the dynamic possibilities of the interchangeability of machine parts. To be sure, precision was already his god, and his personal work was outstanding, but apparently he lacked any soaring industrial vision. That would come with further experience. It is significant that later, in his recollections, he tended to de-emphasize this period.

The truth was that he had not yet accepted factory life as his permanent and passionate concern. "The discipline and subordination of factory life ran counter to American individualism."[18] Probably he still toyed with the idea of eventually owning a farm. He had also an intense religious preoccupation. One of its manifestations was his practice of reading the *Bible* in the yard at lunch time at the Springfield Armory. Soon a group was gathering around every day to hear him read. This custom he continued at Hartford when he worked at the Colt Armory. He was also drawn to the Worcester community that he knew, where Ellen Hull, now his fiancee, had her home. The long separation from Nelle, as he called her, was wearing on him. They had corresponded ardently but, as Leland later put it, when he took up his *Bible* for study "it too often led me to Jacob, who had to wait twenty-one years for his wife." Nelle would soon complete her normal-school training and return to Worcester. When his job with Colt was finished he set out for Massachusetts, prepared to take the best job he could get in the city where Ellen Hull had her home.[19]

Back in Worcester he found himself working for Augustus B. Prouty, a manufacturer of card-setting machinery for weaving. Letters between the lovers at this time show their faith in each other, and the expectations they shared. He feared that once she was his wife she might look back regretfully upon the happy days before her marriage. "Of course [and here we see the shadow of his hard early life falling over him] I can promise nothing certain." But he added: "I am in hopes that our home will itself have so many attractions for us that there will never be a possibility of wishing for the pleasures of the past." (Ellen, one reads between the lines, was sure of it.) He referred perfunctorily to his work: "I like some things very well and others not," but "it is a very clean pretty shop." He looked forward to her arrival in Worcester for her vacation.[20]

His skill and diligence were evidently not lost upon his employer, for when Prouty decided that he would visit the World's

Fair in Europe to promote personally his card-setting machine, he left George H. Noble in charge of the shop and made Henry M. Leland responsible for the office. There was money in the bank, and more would presumably come in regularly from the sale of machines, so that there seemed to be no difficulties in prospect.

For some reason the income from sales was negligible. Eventually Leland discovered that a trust had won control of the marketing of textile machinery and opposed all new devices, putting pressure on potential customers to discourage buying. By this time the money in the bank had been exhausted, and Henry Leland, determined that the shop should be kept going, had dipped into his own savings to pay the workmen. Prouty returned, but had no money to repay his manager, and proceeded to liquidate the business.[21] It was a heavy blow to the young executive, for the date of his wedding had now been set. But probably Ellen Hull insisted that it be kept, for on September 25, 1867, she and Leland were married. They bought furniture on the installment plan, and Leland took a succession of jobs—with the Loring Coes Wrench Works, the Lucius W. Pond Tool Company, and finally the Charles H. Ballard Rifle Company.[22]

He soon became the father of two children, Gertrude and Wilfred; and, through the birth of a son to his brother Frank, Uncle Henry as well.[23] "Uncle Henry" seemed a suitable designation for the tall young man with a gleam in his eye and a keen interest in his fellow men. It was to follow him through life. His associates, his partners, and his workmen all felt a special kinship with him which the term seemed to express.

4

There now followed a period in which Leland was active in church and town affairs but seemed to lack a sure sense of his purpose in life. Soon after his marriage he joined the Worcester Fire Department and, as tongue man on Rapid No. 2 Volunteer Fire Company, shared in the fierce rivalry that was characteristic of all the city brigades. His uniform was gorgeous: a flaming red blouse, a shining patent leather belt with an enormous brass buckle, and dark trousers with red stripes running down the sides.

The work was a fascinating and competitive activity. The companies, forty men strong, pulled the engines themselves for a fee of $4.00 if horses were not immediately ready, and used hydrants in the central portion of the city, and wells, ponds, and cisterns in the outskirts. The men pumped the water themselves, sometimes having to relay it. Every company strove to get to the fire first, and each sought to "wash out" its closest rival.*

After every fire there was likely to be a rough and tumble fist fight between companies. "Tiger Company No. 6," Leland recalled later, "was a pugnacious, fighting organization, and was conspicuously aggressive both at the fire and in the disputes afterward. No matter how strenuously the Rapid No. 2 had worked at the fire, we counted it only preliminary to the after meeting with Tiger Company No. 6."

Leland was active in the fire department for about five years. Then a nervous breakdown drove him from the shop to the Hull farm for a rest. There someone was needed to run the sawmill, and the convalescent mechanic undertook this task. He learned not a little from it.

A crack had started to develop in one of the forty-eight inch saws. Henry cut out a piece and patched the saw, riveting the patch and filing it down. This was wholly successful so he took in hand another saw which had become overheated and had buckled. He had seen men repair such defects by pounding the saw with a hammer, and decided that he would try this remedy. It did not restore the saw, and after several days, somewhat crestfallen, he took it to a sawsmith. For about ten minutes this man studied the blade to see where the steel had been stretched then, with a much smaller hammer than Henry had used, hit it lightly about six times and handed it back as good as new. Leland made a mental note that knowing how, or fully understanding a job, was a prerequisite to any accomplishment.

* "Washing out" consisted in pumping so much water into another company's tub that it overflowed. This was a great humiliation.

The machinist was now ready to return to work, but decided to try something other than the factory. One of his friends had become a policeman, studied law at night, and finally risen to the position of judge. Henry was tall and strong, and physically equipped for police service; he wrote and spoke well, and might apply these talents to the law. Who could tell how far he might go?

He was accepted for the police force, was given night duty, and could study law during the day. It seemed a happy combination. But the new officer soon found that he was losing too much sleep and, once when he was pacing his beat and awakened himself by stumbling over a large stone, he realized that he was attempting too much. The doctor concurred, and forbade him to continue this kind of double duty.[24]

Leland now took a long, hard look at his future. His mind, independent and teeming with ideas, made it difficult for him to work with others. He longed for a business in which he might put his theories to work. But he had no money, with a family to support, and his father and mother in need of aid. It would be years before he could save the necessary capital to launch a business. But, he reflected, he could prepare himself for the time when he might; accordingly he decided to go into the best factory he could find and learn all that was to be learned there. At the Springfield Armory he had become familiar with the machine tools made by Brown & Sharpe, and since then he had read about the firm in scientific magazines. With them, he felt, he would get the best possible training. He applied for a position, was accepted, and moved his family to Providence, R.I., where his new employer was located. He arrived to begin work on July 1, 1872, in a policeman's uniform—the only suit he possessed. He had set his foot on the rung of the right ladder, yet some time must still pass before he could put his whole effort into it.[25]

The firm with which Leland had cast his lot was an old but prosperous manufactory. Founded in 1833 by Joseph R. Brown and his father, in 1853 it had fourteen employees. During that year Brown took into partnership Lucian Sharpe, a former apprentice and shrewd businessman. The firm expanded and, in 1872, Brown & Sharpe Manufacturing Company built a great new building, providing 6600 feet of space to accommodate its various departments and 300 employees.[26]

At first Leland's duties were varied, while the company was moving into the new building. He was shunted from place to place but worked particularly at the installation for the counter-shafting. When the move had been completed he became a tool-maker in the gear and cutter departments. Here he replaced a man who had relatives holding responsible positions in the company, and he feared that he would encounter resentment and trouble. He did; and although he had the backing of the management he had to fight a number of skirmishes himself.

Mild in disposition and an earnest Christian, when convinced that he was right Leland could show plenty of fire and determination. For example, he had continuous trouble with the toolroom attendant, who apparently had been encouraged to make things disagreeable for him. Leland never went to the tool room without having an argument, or without having difficulty getting what he wanted. He endured this for a time. But one day he asked the man for a center rest, and was told there was no such tool. Leland pointed at the part hanging on the wall. "That's a back rest," the attendant blandly informed him.

This absurdity triggered an explosion. Henry leapt over the counter, grabbed the center rest and the man, and stormed, "You have been deliberately making trouble. This will be the last time that I endure any more nonsense from you. The next time you open your mouth for anything but a courteous response, I shall take you by the neck and throw you through the window, whether it is open or closed!" He gave the fellow a shake that convinced him he could do what he threatened, and from that moment his difficulties with the toolroom attendant ceased.[27]

Leland had been preceded at Brown & Sharpe by George Noble who, it will be recalled, had run the shop at the Prouty factory in Worcester. Noble had been in charge of the screw-machine department of the sewing-machine division but was going out on a special assignment. Leland, by that time transferred to the screw-machine department, was given Noble's place. Here he encountered opposition just as he had in the gear and cutter department. The inspector, who checked the output, rejected thousands of screws which Leland thought fully met specifications. He studied his machines and even scraped some of them, but could find nothing to account for inaccuracy. He then examined the gauges used in inspection and was able to demonstrate that a number of these were worn and inaccurate, so that the rejected screws actually met qualifications.

He noted that a number of parts were being made on lathes, which he felt could be turned out better and cheaper on the screw machines. Indeed, he thought that on some items he could produce as much a day on the screw machine as the lathe could put out in a week or more. Accordingly, he proposed certain shifts to the superintendent, who authorized him to go ahead. The shift was made, and so successfully that by the time he left the department he was supervising sixty machines where at first he had but six. And for the first time he felt the thrill of real accomplishment in his chosen life work.

Chapter III
Master of His Craft

1

LELAND'S SUCCESS EMBOLDENED him to suggest other improvements. The steady and ever-increasing demand for sewing machines had been one of the main factors in the dramatic growth of Brown & Sharpe. Though the number of workers had increased enormously the organization and routing of the work seemed to have altered but little from the earlier days. Leland came to believe that his department could be operated in a more efficient fashion. Specifically he noted that the work was subject to orders and that on one day six parts might be required for one machine and ten for another, and that a day later a similar order might arrive. Each time the machine tools had to be set up for the required work, which took several hours. Leland pointed out that the system was wasteful. "Why can't we carry screws and small parts in stock?"

The idea seems obvious today, but at the time it was so revolutionary that it took some time to put it into operation. Another department head was appointed to investigate. When he made a favorable report, L. D. Burlingame was assigned to work out the details. But once accepted the new system was so successful that it was expanded to include many other parts. Years afterward when Mr. Leland came back to visit Brown & Sharpe, Mr. Richmond Viall showed him the screw cases and how the work was organized, and how the orders were being filled.[1] He remarked, "We all know, Mr. Leland, that this is a monument to you, and to your foresight." [2]

As may be seen, Henry Leland had many ideas. Some were approved, others were not. However, as time went on he was asked to take other small departments under his supervision, and thereby hangs another story. There are many versions of this tale, but Leland himself told it in this wise.

An order for horse clippers came in and was assigned to one of Leland's departments for manufacture. As a farmboy he had a warm place in his heart for horses and he did not like the idea of clipping them because he thought it would be cruel to leave them shivering. So he went to the superintendent and told him he would not make the clippers. After some argument Leland was persuaded that if the clippers were not made at Brown & Sharpe they would be made elsewhere—the practice could not be stopped by refusing the order. When he finally agreed to make the clippers, he went into the matter thoroughly, obtaining calf hides on which to test the clippers to see whether they would cut full length without pulling. He found that there had to be a good deal of cut and try and resharpening to make them do this. In fact, before he was through with the job Leland had some ideas on how a grinder might be improved to grind clipper plates and other like parts.

A barber brought one pair of the clippers to Mr. Leland, asking if he could not adapt it for cutting human hair. A spring in the center and a few alterations in the design made it satisfactory to him. "They were clumsy enough then," said Mr. Leland, "and I kept at the problem of making them lighter and more efficient. When I had perfected the design I had to convince my employers that there was a market for them. It took two years to induce the Brown & Sharpe Company to take my proposition seriously, Mr. Sharpe in particular being blind to it."

"Eventually," continued Leland, "I went to Boston with the clippers and showed a pair to Mr. Dame, of the hardware firm of

Dame, Stoddard and Kendall, and his enthusiastic commendation opened Mr. Sharpe's eyes. The manufacture of the clippers was started and rose quickly to an output as much as three hundred daily. For this I received a 'Thank you' and fifty cents a day more in my pay envelope. That was one of the times I thought I ought to quit making other men rich and go to work for myself." [3]

The sewing machine department in which Leland worked was the largest and most profitable one in the whole factory. Lucian Sharpe, junior partner of the firm, had been instrumental in 1858 in securing the manufacturing contract with the Wilcox & Gibbs Sewing Machine Company, which led not only to the great expansion of the firm, but also to a change in the direction of its development. "From first making machinery and devices for their own [sewing machine] demands, they were led to making for others also and gradually the machine tool business became the more important end. . . ." [4] Joseph R. Brown, the inventive genius of the combination, turned his interest from gauges and measuring devices to milling machines, grinders and automatic gear cutters.

Although Mr. Brown's time was short after Leland came to work at the plant—he died suddenly in 1876—the supervisor of the screw division in the sewing-machine department had an idea for a better grinder which he wished to suggest to the inventor. The shafts, needle bars and foot bars of the sewing machines were being ground in his department on lathes. The process was very difficult since the grinding grit destroyed the alignment of the work with the lathe spindles and centers. Leland became convinced "that instead of the live spindle revolving as in the ordinary lathe, the spindle could remain stationary and the shafts and other pieces to be ground could turn upon two dead centers." * Since he was not familiar enough with Mr. Brown at this time to take up the matter with him, he talked instead to Mr. Viall. Ever helpful, Mr. Viall arranged an interview with Mr. Brown, who was not enthusiastic about a grinder

---

* Among the Leland Papers is a manuscript on "Grinding Machines," written by Henry Leland. It contains material apparently used in speeches before various groups and also submitted in 1926 to Alfred D. Flynn, director of the Engineering Foundation in New York when that gentleman was gathering information on the invention of grinders.

because he was absorbed in other work. Still, running the risk of offending, Leland embraced every opportunity to describe the machine to Mr. Brown.

At length Mr. Brown did design a new grinder which he finished the year of his sudden death. Named the Universal Grinder, it was put on the market a year or so later and served the trade for twenty years.[5] Useful and popular as this machine was, Leland did not quite approve of it.

> Mr. Brown's machine designing was too light. This fault was almost characteristic of his designing and it is not surprising when one remembers that he was originally a watch maker. Then he made the small tools, vernier calipers, etc. . . . then sewing machines and a large line of milling machines and other machinery for use in the manufacture of sewing machines and other work equally light. Since he had only had experience on light work it would be reasonable for him to design his new machine very light.[6]

Ten years later, with Leland again giving advice, Charles H. Norton re-designed this grinder, making certain parts heavier, providing for the use of more coolant and increasing its speed and power. This grinder was called the No. 1 Surface Grinder.

2

On February 16, 1878, Richmond Viall was made general superintendent over all the Brown & Sharpe plant and Henry Leland succeeded him as head of the sewing-machine department. Thus in less than six years the machinist from Worcester had made a notable advance. One would expect such a promotion to be accepted with pride; rather it was accepted with reservations. Leland decided that he must refuse the position unless he could be independent in carrying out several policies which he felt were important. Mr. Viall bristled at this intimation that the department needed improvement. Leland replied that there were three important features he would insist on changing if he were to take charge: he would abandon the contract system, adopt piece work prices, and determine the wages of the men coming under his supervision. These ideas seemed so radical to Mr. Viall that he tried to argue Leland out of them, but instead the discussion resulted in the general manager's becoming at least partially convinced. Mr. Viall took the matter to Mr. Sharpe who, as Mr. Viall later reported, "went up in the air" and wanted to know if Leland expected him to give him the key to his safe.

After considerable discussion back and forth, with Mr. Viall as intermediary, the terms were agreed to and Leland became superintendent of the sewing-machine division. The agreement was brought about partly by the assurance Leland gave that if he had his own way he would cut the labor cost of sewing machines within a year's time.

Previous to this the department had had four contractors, each hiring his own help, mostly boys or unskilled workers, paying starvation wages and making all possible profit on the job.[7] Under the reorganization one of these contractors was appointed foreman and three transferred to other work.

There was also opposition to the plan of setting piece-work prices for each operation. One of the opponents held up a sewing-machine hook and said, "There are 80 operations on this piece. You don't mean to fix a separate price on each?"

Leland replied that he would give prices—so much for 10, so much for 100 and so much for 1000 pieces for each of these operations—and he had his own way in the matter. The next difficulty was the claim of the workmen that they could not make good on the prices set. Leland, being a practical mechanic, would then ask the mechanic to hold his watch while he, himself, performed the operation and showed how much profit could be made above wages without strain or overwork.

Mr. Ripley, the office manager, a special friend of Leland's, agreed to have a careful cost record kept during the last month before the transfer, and then again at the end of the year after the transfer had been made. This audit showed that the labor cost of sewing-machines at the end of the year was just 47% of what it had been before Leland took the job.*

* It should be remembered that this occurred long before there was any such thing as detailed cost accounting or motion studies. Also this was Leland's own remembrance. When presented with Leland's story of these innovations, Henry Sharpe Jr. wrote, "In some respects my recollections do not accord with Mr. Leland's." Letter to L. D. Burlingame, September 10, 1929.

It seems that such an achievement should have merited some special recognition from the company, but if it did Leland forgot to mention it and it seems unlikely. There is no record of Henry Leland's salary during this period, but it seems never to have exceeded $100 a month. Nelle tried to make a contribution by teaching in the Providence schools but her health suffered, extra help was needed in the home and doctor bills were heavy. Then Leander Leland came to live with them after his wife's death in 1876, and the third Leland child, Miriam, was born in 1882. Henry's dream of a shop of his own faded.

In 1880 the farm near Worcester, which had belonged to the Hulls but had passed into other hands, came up for sale. The Lelands had always loved it, and now determined to buy it. The down payment was small. The family hoped that with care the land itself could produce enough to meet the annual payments. The plan was this: Leander Leland and Nelle and her children would all move to the farm. Leander could do some work, and Henry, while keeping his post at Brown & Sharpe, would commute back and forth weekends, and give some assistance. It seemed a reasonable plan, almost a necessary one, although perhaps it represented the lingering dream on the part of Henry and Nelle that he might find a happier life than he had in the factory.[8]

Wilfred Leland, by this time a boy of eleven, later recalled the days on the farm with pleasure. He led the horse while his grandfather guided the plow to make a garden. But Leander, now in his seventies, could not do as much as he once had, so that the farm management devolved upon Nelle. It was a many-sided task. Wilfred remembered that they had an orchard of Baldwin and Greening apples. These had to be picked and prepared for sale. "The two top rows," he said, "had to be carefully set in with the stem side up to make a fine appearance when the top of the barrel was taken off." At $1.00 a barrel they packed and sold hundreds of barrels.[9]

There was also berry-picking, in which Henry Leland joined, and of course the cows, chickens, grain and hay crops. It was a man's full-time job, and Nelle had to do it with irregular and insufficient help, and at the same time care for the house and the children. She did not scant that task. In the evenings she read aloud to them, sometimes from the *Youth's Companion*, often from volumes of poetry. "She read them so impressively that I memorized the choicest of them and repeated them often," her son recalled. All the Lelands remembered and quoted easily except Henry. But even he had one poem of Lord Macaulay's which he never forgot and which seemed to fit the circumstances of his life. At the end of a hard week at the plant he would enter the farmhouse declaiming from "Horatius,"

> And how can man die better
> Than facing fearful odds
> For the ashes of his fathers
> And the temples of his gods.[10]

But the happy period ended soon. It became evident that the large farm was a greater burden than Nelle could carry. Also, the long trips between Worcester and the plant at Providence wore on the father. The annual payment could not be met. Sadly, even rebelliously, the Lelands were forced to face the facts and give up the farm.

Before leaving, Henry M. Leland walked about the place that was so dear to him and yet beyond his reach. Greatly disturbed, he sought comfort in the woods. There he prayed, and he felt that God spoke to him and walked by his side. He came out of the forest comforted, and sure at last of one thing: he had never been intended for a farm. He was convinced now that the factory was his destined place of work. The conviction brought him peace, and a sense of uplifting change. When he went back to the shop he did what he always had done, but what he did met with greater success. When he spoke now, he was conscious of an authority he had never known before. It carried him forward, and he was sure that he faced a future of power and accomplishment.[11]

3

Henry Leland went back to work with vigor, his mind and ambition dedicated to making his department more efficient and more productive. His future lay among machines, and he would master them. Whether it related to the method of manufacturing, the utility of an old or proposed new machine, or the design and construction of some device which a customer had brought in to be made, he sought continuous improvement. All in one he was engineer, designer, production man, efficiency expert, employment man, timekeeper, stock chaser, inspector, and manager, for the time was not yet when manufacturers delegated their varied responsibilities to specialized men, skilled in but one line. Actually this was a magnificent opportunity to learn the business of manufacturing.

Henry Leland formed many theories on the management of men and the work in factories. Like all ideas which he found good, he propounded them at every opportunity.

> Too many men depend upon the inspector. It is the foreman's place to know that every piece turned out by his department is RIGHT, and it is his work to teach his men how to make them RIGHT. I hired every man who was employed in my department, and I showed every man what I wanted. I had an eighteen-year-old boy and I asked him, "Would you like to be a good mechanic, get promoted and have a better job?" When he answered in the affirmative, I said, "Then do just as I show you." Then I showed him.
>
> I would take him to some simple job and make some pieces while he watched me use the machine. When he said he understood, I told him to make some, and I went away to avoid embarrassing him. He was to stay at it until he had made several pieces exactly right and bring them to me. Soon he would come along, happy because his pieces were finished. I would test them with the gauge and perhaps find them as I wanted them. Then I would tell him there was no reason why he could not make a thousand right. Now if he knows when they are right, and then makes them that way, what more is necessary? Don't you see that scrapers and fitters and finishers are eliminated and that there is little need for inspection? And never forget this: It doesn't cost as much to have the work done right the first time as it does to have it done poorly and then hire a number of men to make it right afterwards.

All this logic may sound self-evident and simple but to Henry Leland it was basic. The workman must know his job. However, there was more to manufacturing and, having advanced to the position of a department head, he had learned it.

The art of manufacturing consists first in knowing thoroughly what one is to make, its materials, its parts and their function; and second is the ability to select the most advantageous machines and tools for speedy operation, fewest cuts and fastest feed. Yet nothing is more important as far as shop expense is concerned, and as far as having the completed machine perform its functions properly, than judiciously placing the tolerances or limits. One *must* study and learn the work that each piece is to perform and adapt the operating tolerances to match. There is a reason for fineness in some work, while to grind off a thousandth part of an inch on other parts is ruinous to profits; and it calls for the soundest judgment to determine and set the limits. Then if one piece can be made true to the requirements, a million can be made in the same way and they will all be exactly alike.

This matter of establishing limits and manufacturing to the precisely set tolerances was emphasized at Brown & Sharpe. Their fine machine tools were made with great precision, a precision that set their products above the average level and earned them a unique reputation.

To illustrate, if one is making a wheel barrow with its one wheel, it is of no importance whatever whether the wheels are the same size on each wheelbarrow or whether they vary half an inch in diameter. On the other hand, if for instance one is making a wristpin to go into a piston in an internal combustion engine, he must make it to a close fit or it will be an absolute failure. So in making the piston-pin we set the limit as close as one-tenth of a thousandth of an inch in diameter.

But it is very expensive to make parts to these close limits, and the *art* consists in always setting the limit as large as the best practice will permit. Hence, on a high grade machine the limits on some parts may be one-thousandth of an inch or less, but one should always allow three or more thousandths of an inch when the nature of the work and conditions will permit, because the larger the limit the less will be the cost of manufacture and the less the scrap.[12]

Even as he advanced in the knowledge and understanding of his work, Mr. Leland advanced in his other activities. He read the *Bible* at noon to a circle of men in the yard; he became a deacon in his church and taught a *Bible* class. As he had done at Worcester he affiliated himself with a church, the Church of the Jahveh, which followed the doctrine of the Second Advent.[13] Henry believed in the Second Coming—that Christ would come again to earth at some time unknown to man, to judge the quick and the dead—for the *Bible* said so. But it was perhaps the attitude of this church towards other religious practices that most attracted his logical, inquiring mind. It had no established creed or disciplines; its adherents read the *Bible* and construed its precepts individually. Each agreed "to receive the Scriptures of the Old and New Testaments as the rule of our faith and practice, believing that reference to their sacred teachings will be sufficient to guide us in all the duties of life, as members of the body of our Lord Jesus Christ." [14] Of course not everybody interpreted the Scriptures in the same way and each devoted interpreter studied the *Bible* intensively to determine for himself his proper practice.

The churches that followed the second-advent teaching were mostly small and struggling. There was no central organization, each congregation standing alone. But after years of discussion other denominations began to consider and approve its validity.

Around 1880 Henry Leland and his pastor, Rev. Lemuel Osler, attended a large gathering at Chicago, composed of prominent pastors and laymen of leading churches, called to study the Second Coming. The attendance of such men was felt to be a recognition of the Adventist position, and much agreement was found among them. It was then that Henry Leland asked his pastor, "What further need is there for a sect which was brought into existence to emphasize a particular truth, after the truth has been admitted by the Christian world?"

"The present need," he declared, "is to preach Christianity, giving due heed to all truths." So on the return of the deacon and the pastor to Providence a church meeting was called and as a result the Church of Jahveh went out of existence as an Adventist body and was reorganized as the Pearl Street Baptist. The Baptist denomination was chosen as a successor because of its traditional adherence to Biblical practice and because the Baptists in particular were friendly to the teaching of the Second Coming.

In 1883 Leland had a desperate bout with typhoid fever after which his physicians advised a change of air and release from his numerous responsibilities. He found a position with Jordan &

Meehan, manufacturers of roller casters in Columbus, Ohio. Taking his family with him he went to live at the Neal House, a boarding house near the state capitol where politicians gathered.

This was a momentous experience for Leland. He found in the Neal House an open forum for the discussion of economic and political questions. All shades of opinion from the radical socialist on were represented among the boarders. To their discussion Leland brought his own conservative New England views. Among the boarders was the secretary of the Ohio Republican committee, a young man who took a fancy to Henry Leland and piloted him to party councils, where he met such state leaders as Hayes and McKinley. This introduction to the inner circles of practical politics opened up a new world to Leland. In particular it convinced him of the necessity of partisanship in politics and, more important, he learned how through political action citizens could secure whatever kind of government they desired.[15]

The significance of these political and economic discussions might not have gripped him so firmly had it not been that in Columbus he listened regularly to the preaching of Dr. Washington Gladden, the powerful advocate of practical Christianity.[16] Leland never had sat under a man of his caliber, and his whole nature expanded as his vision enlarged. The social message of the gospel immediately appealed to him. From then on he recognized that as a Christian he had an obligation to society and political institutions. He set forth enthusiastically to discover and discharge this obligation and was for the remainder of his life devoted to the cause of social and civic righteousness.

Within a year fire swept through the factory where he was employed, wiping out the entire plant and terminating the Leland job. There was nothing to do but go back to Brown & Sharpe. It is not clear in just what capacity he was re-employed when he returned to his old firm. Very soon, however, he became a traveling representative of the company, and it was said to have occurred in this wise. When on vacation it had been his custom to visit other shops and talk with the mechanics and foremen, during the conversation explaining how Brown & Sharpe machine tools could be used to advantage on the particular work in hand. Later when he returned to his work after his vacation, orders for machinery would come, orders whose origin was unaccountable to Mr. Viall or Mr. Sharpe. Mr. Viall would ask Leland if he had visited such and such a plant, and often he had. As a consequence Leland was sent out to represent Brown & Sharpe. Remembering Columbus and the vigor and enterprise of the west he asked for the territory from Pittsburgh west to the Pacific. Here he traveled, going no farther west than St. Louis but visiting in all the industrial towns of the mid-west. He claimed he never was a salesman and never expected to bring home orders—he just talked about jobs and machines. When he found a tool or a machine not being used in the most advantageous manner he would stop and give proper instructions. In some shops his advice led to a change in the whole system of manufacture. One day he was roundly criticized by another salesman, who heard him recommend a Pratt & Whitney machine to do a certain job. Surely this was disloyalty, this helping to sell a competitor's machine instead of his own. But a year later the manager to whom he had recommended the rival machine sent for him. A new building had been erected and was to be equipped with new tools and he wanted Leland's advice and recommendations for the installation. Many Brown and Sharpe machines were ordered.

One of the plants where Leland called was the Westinghouse Air Brake Company. The air brake was a new device and far from perfect. Though its principle was correct, it was so crudely made that under high pressure all the air leaked out. Consequently the first trains equipped with these air brakes did not stop promptly.

When Leland reached the Westinghouse plant he found in the yard a long train of cars which the men were testing. They would start the train and then put on the air brakes. Instead of stopping abruptly the train kept on going because the air leaked out of the brakes. After each test a crew would take off the leaky pistons, fuss around scraping them, then replace them on the cars for another trial.

This interested Leland, who finally explained to the mechanics that for such precision work the cylinders and pistons should be ground; and he so convinced them that they sent him to Mr. Welch, the deaf superintendent. He was received with a great deal of skepticism but was allowed to take some rough castings back to Providence where on an improvised apparatus he finished a complete set of parts by the grinding process.

It was a tense moment when his cylinders and pistons were attached to the system for their first trial. But the air held and the cars pulled up short. The salesman got an order for a number of grinding machines. When the machines were ready for delivery Leland, knowing that grinding machines were not well understood, offered to send along some mechanics experienced in their operation. The Westinghouse people thought this unnecessary, with the result that within three months the machines were condemned as useless. Mr. Leland then went himself and within a few days had all the machines in successful operation. Thus was it demonstrated that parts accurately made could hold air under pressure, and the air brake has been a reliable safety device ever since.[17]

Besides the special grinding machines Leland had many other tools and machines to offer to the small manufacturer where he often visited. He listed some of these:

> Brown & Sharpe produced the Universal and plain milling machines, a line of small lathes which used a split tapered chuck for making small pins, screws and other parts. They also made screw slotting machines, surface grinding machines and many other types. Besides all this they made small tools such as vernier calipers, micrometer calipers in large volume and a great variety of dimensions. They also made accurate beam squares, straight edges, center gauges, etc., etc. All these were designed and perfected by Joseph R. Brown, and they enabled the high grade mechanic who was ambitious to achieve results which had hitherto been impossible because they enabled him to divide an inch in 1000 or more parts and to use one or a fraction of one of these fine measurements, an achievement unknown to the industrial world until Mr. Brown brought out these instruments.[18]

A letter of this period, written from Chicago to his son, gives little information on Leland's work but records his longing for the folks at home and the activities of a Sunday on the road.

> I have had thee much in mind these days of our separation and have often wondered what you and Sisters and Mama were doing at that particular time. So you work in the laboratory as

much this term as formerly? Are you racing around with those deadhead bills of Dr. Stone's as of old? I shall be in Milwaukee next Sunday I expect, shall from there feel that every move brings me nearer home.

I went out on the cable road to 23rd and Michigan Ave. to hear Dr. Geo. Lormer today. He is one of the brightest men in the Baptist denomination, and preached one of the *best* sermons I ever heard. It was one of those original and impressive kind that fasten themselves upon one's memory for all time.

From there he went on to give the text and a detailed explanation of every verse. In fact the remaining four pages of the letter were devoted to the sermon, and the writer ended by saying he must get a letter off to his pastor at home.[19]

Wilfred was already at this time looking forward to a career in medicine, doing errands and collecting bills for Dr. Stone. He had also taken over the family accounts. He later wrote, "The month's end with its march of bills depressed Father, so I asked him to let me do the budgeting and dispensing. Mother's continued ill health brought in large doctor's bills. Father sent his wages home and I added my small earnings and paid the bills."

As usual there was little money left over for saving. And yet at this very time Henry Leland was more hopeful of going into business for himself than ever before. He had brought his skill and experience to the service of the ambitious industrialists of the west and they had shown him in return the financial method that had put them in business. With a background of experience and only a little money as a nucleus, each had organized a company and by selling stock secured the further capital needed. "Eureka," said Henry Leland to himself, "I have found it," for he had great experience and he was sure he could raise a little money. His dream of an independent business might come true, after all.

Chapter IV
A Shop of His Own

As HE TRAVELED through the Middle West, Leland kept looking for a city in which he could establish himself in business. One version has it that he cast a receptive eye upon Chicago, but got off the train there the morning after the Haymarket riots and stood on the spot where eight policemen had been killed. "Shuddering with horror . . . and contemplating the effect of this sort of labor in a new organization," ran one account, "he made a sudden and firm decision to go elsewhere."[1] He was supposed to have come on immediately to Detroit, stopping over on Sunday to get relief from the long train ride. While he was dining at the Russell House someone exchanged a cast-iron derby, which Leland abhorred, for his hat. He took the offending headpiece to the foot of Woodward and threw it into the river. Then, as it was Sunday and he had nothing to do, he spent the afternoon riding back and forth on the Belle Isle Ferry. From that vantage point Detroit looked so inviting that he decided to become a citizen of the town.[2]

A fine story but the truth is not in it. The Haymarket riots took place in May 1886 and Leland did not come to Detroit until 1890. Undoubtedly the behavior of labor in Chicago turned him against that city while Detroit, as a firm open-shop town, attracted him. In addition, Detroit's gracious tree-lined streets and water panoramas offered a happy location for a home. But Leland located in Detroit because in that city he found the financial backing he needed. He had to have a partner who would supply most of the necessary cash and yet be able to see that the Leland experience and knowledge was an equal contribution.

Charles Strelinger, who sold tools and hardware in Detroit, knew and had confidence in Leland and introduced him to Robert C. Faulconer of Alpena, Michigan.[3] Faulconer was looking for an opportunity to invest the money he had made in lumbering. Leland's compelling arguments persuaded him to put up most of the money for a machine shop.

In 1890 Detroit was a thriving town. In the previous decade only Chicago of the mid-western cities had exceeded it in rate of growth. It had 206,896 people living in a four-mile square extending roughly from the river to the railroad on the north and from 24th Street to Elmwood east and west. Anticipating the need for more room, the limits had been extended to enclose 29 square miles, and the plan for a Grand Boulevard around the city was a topic of hot discussion.[4] Manufacturing investment had more than doubled in the decade, increasing from 30 million to 77 million. Other signs of urban enterprise were the new Belle Isle Bridge and the first tall building—ten stories high—downtown.[5]

Though lake-shipping had long been the city's traditional concern, it had turned readily to railroads and by 1890 had eight lines running into it. Both means of transportation had joined in servicing the great lumbering industry of Michigan which was now moving on westward. Detroit was still building ships, marine boilers and engines, but its factories made a great variety of other products. The largest business in Detroit was the Michigan Car Company which, "close to iron and lumber," made railroad freight cars in numbers exceeding the "output of any city on the continent." Four factories made stoves, two produced pharmaceutical products and a great scattering of smaller concerns made doors, barrels, furniture, carriages and wagons. The Ferry Seed Company was already well-known throughout the country and Berry Brothers claimed "the most extensive varnish works in the world." [6]

Like the rest of the United States, Detroit was much taken with the bicycle craze. Salesrooms and repair stations were numerous. In 1890 the Detroit Bicycle Club was incorporated and more than a hundred of its members rode their wheels to Niagara Falls to the national convention. Races were held on Belle Isle and more and more workers pedalled to work every day leaving the horse-propelled streetcars far behind.[7]

All in all Detroit was a lively expanding town with a variety of industry, with some lumber money seeking investment and with an active interest in its prospects for the future. The increasing industrial development of the mid-west augured well that not only the present manufacturers but also others to come would need a variety of tools and mechanical helps to service their processes. There were not many machine shops in Detroit; in 1887 directories listed six; in 1890, nine.

The new firm, Leland, Faulconer & Norton, was formally organized on September 19, 1890. The corporation was capitalized at $50,000 and of this $40,000 was supplied by Robert Faulconer. Into it also went Henry Leland's savings of $1600, together with $2000 loaned by Lucian Sharpe through the intercession of Richmond Viall.[8] Charles F. Norton, who had been for some years a machine designer at Brown & Sharpe, was brought out from Providence to design such new machinery as would be necessary. Norton was given a small amount of the $10-per-share stock as was Charles Strelinger. Faulconer was made president; Leland, vice-president; and Strelinger, secretary. Leland was also the general manager at a salary of $2000 a year. His first action was to get out a form letter and send it to a list of all the prospects in Michigan, northern Ohio and northern Indiana. With some little help from Strelinger's clerks in addressing envelopes, he carried these announcements out in market baskets and filled all the post boxes in the neighborhood.[9] The fourth floor of the Strelinger building at Bates and Congress streets was rented, some machinery bought and the shop opened for business. So quickly did Detroit and the mid-west make use of this new facility that within three months the labor force had to be increased from the original dozen to sixty employees.

Mr. Leland was anxious to have his son come into the business with him and invited him to try it for a year. Wilfred was then in his second year of the pre-medical course at Brown University preparing to become a physician. He had worked at Brown & Sharpe during his school vacations but thought his future lay in the medical profession. Nevertheless, he agreed to come to his father for a year and arrived in Detroit on November 7, 1890, on his twenty-first birthday. After his preliminary year, feeling his father's need of him, he elected to stay in the machine-manufacturing business and agreed to go to Brown & Sharpe for some special training.

With the cooperation of the ever-helpful Mr. Viall, the general superintendent, Wilfred was able to cover in a year most of the operations which the usual apprentice did in three years. When he had finished, Mr. Viall asked the foreman to have the young man make by himself a standard one-inch plug and a standard one-inch ring. When these pieces were completed, the foreman put them through the required tests in the presence of Mr. Viall and pronounced them to be within the required limits of accuracy of one-hundred thousandth of an inch. The plug and ring were then given to Wilfred as the symbols of his competence in the mechanical field and his certificate of graduation from the course. Upon his return to Detroit and Leland, Faulconer & Norton, he was put in charge of the gear-cutting department, where he was able to demonstrate to the employees the intricacies of making spiral gears which he had just learned in Providence. Now there were two Lelands in the shop and the men referred to them as H. M. and W. C.

With his own shop, Henry Leland was able to organize his work in what was to him the best way. From the beginning there was a daily conference of department heads in which general problems were discussed and the work laid out. The general manager strove to inculcate into his co-workers his standards of precise and planned production, in the process of which he spoke often of Brown & Sharpe. So often, in fact, that the wags about the place insisted that the boss often inadvertently ended the blessing and other prayers with "Brown & Sharpe" instead of "Amen." Many a man learned practical engineering as Henry Leland had learned it—starting out with nothing more than his own natural aptitude and some mechanical training, to be progressively developed, taught and encouraged by the old pro from Brown & Sharpe. After two years in that pioneer machine shop one of the workmen went on to a rather fabulous career of his own. His name was Horace Dodge. He and his brother John established a machine shop of their own, furnished the first motors for Henry Ford and went on to manufacture a motor car which still carries the Dodge name.

When they first opened up, Leland, Faulconer & Norton, tool manufacturers, announced that their facilities were available for general jobbing work. For a long time their chief dependence was on general gear grinding and special toolmaking though they hoped that some product might be found which could be manufactured in profitable quantity. A double-wheel wet tool grinder was the first new design, then a lathe center grinder and a riveting machine. A newly designed milling machine also proved successful. Some of these machines were still working in Detroit factories thirty-five years later.

For many years, pattern shops had used a wood-trimming machine known as the Fox trimmer. It was crudely made and fell short of performing the work the pattern maker needed. James W. Oliver, who had been selling the Fox Trimmer to the pattern industry, brought one in to Leland and asked him to design a more substantial and more accurate machine. Mr. Leland called a conference and, pointing out the faults of the trimmer, set his men to work to rectify them. When the new machine was ready, Wilfred Leland went out with Mr. Oliver to demonstrate the new product. Evidently the elder Leland thought some selling experience would be valuable to his son, as it had been to him. So Wilfred traveled to cities up and down the Mississippi, through the mid-west, to the east and finally to England, France and Germany.[10] He never forgot the demonstration which began his trimmer sales-talk.

> The procedure was to hire an express wagon and its driver, who would help me carry the heavy trimmer into the pattern shop. There I would, with one stroke of the lever, cut an 8×5 inch surface on each of two blocks, leaving each surface so smooth

and flat that when those surfaces were placed together they adhered so closely that the top block would lift the lower one although it might be four or five inches thick. This would make a great impression and secure undivided attention for the more important later demonstration.[11]

One of the very first orders that came in to the company was for construction of an elaborate machine to set type. This device was the invention of Earle V. Beale, and it was financed by Col. Frank J. Hecker of Detroit. The idea was to perforate paper like the rolls of a player piano, each perforation representing a different character or letter of the alphabet. When this perforated paper was passed through the machine, called the "Subtyposer," electrically controlled fingers formed a contact at each perforation which mechanically brought a corresponding type character into the line-up. This character was impressed on the matrix after which it returned to its original position for further use. The Subtyposer was entirely automatic and seemed to be a good thing—if any print shop had room to house a machine of its size. When completed it was sent to Boston by its inventor, but never became popular.

The other construction work was interesting in its variety. It included a typewriter, a repeating rifle, a motorcycle, an automatic chicken feeder, a pencil sharpener, a milk condenser and a thousand other miscellaneous articles, large and small, simple and intricate.[12] Within three years the company outgrew its downtown quarters and orders had to be refused because there was not room for more machinery. In 1893 a factory, specially designed for the firm, was built on Trombly Avenue near Dequindre and Widman on the east side of Detroit. Mr. Norton withdrew from the firm in 1894 and rejoined his family in the east. The name of the company was thereupon shortened to Leland & Faulconer and became generally known as L&F.

Because of the small capitalization and the need for more and more shop equipment and material, there were times when, after the men were paid, not much money was left for Mr. Leland. The building up of a business, which expands rapidly and must be financed primarily from its own earnings, is often a discouraging process. In 1895 the capitalization was increased to $70,000 and

A SHOP OF HIS OWN 57

other stockholders were added, among them William H. Strong, R. W. Gillette, William K. Anderson and still later E. Y. Swift and H. K. Lathrop Jr.[13] In scarcely more than a year, May 29, 1896, capital was increased to $100,000 and again to $175,000 in 1902. By 1897 the income exceeded the out-go by $5434, though the directors refrained from declaring a dividend. In 1901 the profits had grown to $14,518.[14]

Leland's salary, set at $2000 annually in the beginning, was advanced to $2400, though he could not always draw it. When he could not pay his loan to the impatient Mr. Sharpe, Mr. Viall took it over. When in 1901 the general manager asked for a raise in salary to $5000, he was given a $1000 loan at 6% and 10% of the profits of the company.[14] Through this latter provision he would finally become debt-free and start buying out some of the small stockholders.

In one of the periods of capital expansion when it was hoped that Mr. Faulconer could double his original investment and keep the controlling interest between him and Henry Leland, Mr. Faulconer had trouble locating so large a sum of money. Wilfred recalled how the difficulty was met.

> One of my father's dearest life-long friendships was formed with Joseph Boyer of St. Louis in the days when H.M. traveled as sales representative for Brown & Sharpe. Father talked with Mr. Boyer, convincing him of the soundness of Leland & Faulconer, with the result that Mr. Boyer loaned Mr. Faulconer the $40,000.

The friendship with Mr. Boyer continued. By 1902 the Lelands were well established in Detroit where labor conditions were excellent; in St. Louis Mr. Boyer was experiencing labor difficulties. Again H. M. consulted his friend, with the result that Mr. Boyer moved his business, the Chicago Pneumatic Machine Tool Co., to Detroit in 1904. Eventually this firm grew into the Burroughs Adding Machine Co., one of the city's great enterprises.

After his experience in selling, Wilfred Leland gradually became more concerned with the financial end of the business. This shift of responsibility was quite natural, as his father's interest was mainly in design, production and high standards of performance. Wilfred later recalled how he was first entrusted with the payroll.

Mr. Faulconer was a fine gentleman, but he was not in good health and he knew little about manufacturing. One thing he did was to check the payroll to make sure it was correct. His health demanded a vacation but he felt he could not go away lest the payroll be neglected in his absence. Mr. William Strong, a close friend, persuaded him that I would serve as checker in his place.

On my first round of checking, I went through the process exactly as directed by Mr. Faulconer. Then I went back the next day, a Sunday, to re-check and found a discrepancy of $200 between the payroll and the amount drawn from the bank, and the company was the loser. Going back to previous payrolls, the same discrepancy appeared. When the findings were reported to Mr. Strong and my father, the bookkeeper was discharged. After that Mr. Faulconer felt I had demonstrated my financial acuity and he felt free to take vacations more frequently.

One of the problems that handicapped L&F in its first years was the difficulty of securing in Detroit iron castings of satisfactory quality. After trying out castings made by several local firms, Henry Leland settled on a foundry which seemed most capable and most willing to cooperate. Steps were taken to install in this foundry improved methods, such as were used in the better foundries of New England. Some study of proper mixtures for different grades of castings resulted in steadily improving quality. Inevitably the time came when other progressive Detroit manufacturers also insisted on having their important castings made in this foundry, which made it more difficult for L&F to get the quantity it needed.

So in 1896 L&F erected a large, well-equipped foundry adjacent to the machine shop on Trombly Avenue. This foundry embodied every feature necessary to make castings equal to those of Brown & Sharpe in Providence, and it was soon working to capacity supplying the needs not only of L&F but also of other mid-western manufacturers. One of the first pieces of advertising literature for the new foundry stated, "We appeal for business only to those who want the best. We do not attempt to compete with the average foundry as concerns price. We believe no other foundry can successfully compete with us as concerns quality."

But shortly the new foundry superintendent began to fall below the Leland standard of quality. For months Mr. Leland personally inspected every wagon load of castings delivered; and in the effort to get workmen and foremen educated to his own critical viewpoint, he would throw out piece after piece for any slight deviation from pattern or form. Or he would go through the foundry, pick up a casting and throw it with force onto the floor. If it broke it was defective, if it remained whole it was satisfactory. For a time perhaps half the product, although fully up to the commercial standard of most foundries, went back for remelting. This went on until it began to be whispered around the works, "The old man is going crazy," and Mr. Faulconer received bitter complaints from foundrymen, foremen and stockholders.

Alarmed, Mr. Faulconer, as kindly a man as ever lived, would plead with Leland for compromise, but the general manager stuck by his standards and predicted that after the quality of his castings had become recognized people would come begging for them even at the higher price. Said Leland, "There always was and there always will be conflict between Good and Good Enough, and in opening up a new business or a new department one can count upon meeting this resistance to a high standard of workmanship. It is easy to get cooperation for mediocre work, but one must sweat blood for a chance to produce a superior product." [15]

Time upheld his judgment, for when he himself needed all his foundry output and had to drop his outside customers, Pierce Arrow begged for another year's supply, and offered to pay 20 cents a pound for Leland castings when they could be bought elsewhere for eight cents.

In the 1890's the demand for bicycles reached its height and some of the manufacturers began making chainless wheels. They soon learned, however, that because of weather conditions and dust the bevel gears wore out too fast. When they tried to overcome the difficulty by hardening the steel gears, the process of heating them to a high temperature then plunging them into cold water or oil introduced strains which pulled the teeth in different directions and resulted in unsatisfactory gears. Leland conceived a remedy:

> When cutting the teeth in the bevel gears, instead of making each tooth the correct finished thickness on the pitch line, each was left four or five thousandths of an inch thicker than it should be. This thickness on each tooth overcame the distortions result-

ing from hardening. Then the engineers created a device for grinding off each side of each tooth with a very thin emery wheel running at high speed. When a gear had been passed through that specially constructed grinding device, every tooth was restored to its exact proper thickness at the pitch line and to the proper shape or form for a bevel gear of that pitch and number of teeth.[16]

This device for grinding gears was said to have been invented by Henry Leland and Frank E. Ferris, one of the engineers, for the Pope Manufacturing Company. It was based on the known fact that there is no more sensitive or accurate indicator than the free cutting, rapidly revolving, rigidly mounted abrasive wheel. It will detect inaccuracies and variations of dimension so minute that they are almost beyond the discernment of the vernier or micrometer caliper. An automatic mechanism designed about such a wheel produced a gear generator which for its work reached "a degree of finish, refinement and accuracy never attained in lathe practice."[17] While not so revolutionary, L&F designed other machines for making gears accurately. One was a generator for producing gears when in the soft state, and a gasher for roughing out the stock for the soft generator.

The chainless bicycle makers were delighted. Colonel Pope bought ten machines for his factory at Hartford; the George N. Pierce Company of Buffalo also ordered a number. Gears were made by the thousands for many other firms, and through this concentration on gear grinding Leland and Faulconer became manufacturers.

Along with its renown for gear manufacturing, L&F managed also to establish a reputation as manufacturers of engines. One of the first orders along this line was a rotary steam engine of original design for Mr. Charles Fisher of Petersburg, Illinois, which when completed was installed in the Cadillac Hotel in Detroit. Then there were the steam motors made for Mr. John Healey, several hundred in number and used on Detroit streetcars. L&F also made the motor for the clock in the old city hall. About 1896 came an order for internal combustion engines for the motor-propelled boats called "naphtha launches." The first of these were small marines for Mr. Frank J. Dimmer, who had a boat shop at Wayne and

A SHOP OF HIS OWN

Woodbridge streets in Detroit. Later, large marines were built upon the request of Charles Strelinger for the retail trade. These motors ranged from five to twenty horsepower. In developing these motors Henry Leland and his helpers gained valuable experience in producing maximum power from an internal-combustion engine. Endless testing adjusted the timing so as to get the most out of a given quantity of gasoline. These motors, produced for launches on the lakes, became stepping stones to gasoline motors for automobiles.[18]

Mr. Ransom E. Olds had moved his business from Lansing to Detroit in September 1899, occupying a factory building on East Jefferson Avenue near the Belle Isle bridge, where the U.S. Rubber plant now stands. He advertised that the Olds Vehicle Company was going to manufacture automobiles in large quantities. He used a small single-cylinder engine, and his second model—the small, curved-dash runabout, selling for $650—became popular. But he had one difficulty in his car which he seemed unable to cure: the transmission made an intolerable racket.

After wasting months of valuable time trying to overcome this difficulty, Mr. Olds called upon Henry Leland, who was known as a specialist in gear work, and arranged to have L&F make the transmissions for him. Contracts for motors were given to John and Horace Dodge. Thus Olds was responsible for first drawing both the Dodges and the Lelands into the automobile industry.

Mr. Leland succeeded in making the transmissions so they were quiet and, because of exacting standards, were also interchangeable. This was more than Mr. Olds had expected, confessing that it was necessary for the assemblers of his car to do a good deal of scraping and fitting to get the machine together. Meanwhile a wonderful demand developed for the Oldsmobile. People fairly stood in line to buy.

Olds had just gotten into full production and was making large shipments when on March 9, 1901, the engine department of the Olds factory was destroyed by fire. Although the Dodges had been making motors for Olds, they could not now hope to keep up and make motors to replace those which had been destroyed. Once more Olds appealed to L&F for assistance and the firm took on a contract to make 2000 motors. The contract was signed June 27, 1901. It was an enormous contract; up to that time no three makers had turned out so many engines in a year. Henry Leland said, "At first we were of necessity slow in putting out those motors, but after we had gotten under way we delivered them so rapidly that Mr. Olds said we must have a motor incubator at our place."

Charlie Martens, newly made head of the motor-testing department at L&F, remembered how he worked on these motors.

> I was sent to the Oldsmobile plant to get *educated* in their testing department. If the engine was no good, the Olds boys threw it away and fixed it at night. I asked the superintendent if I could come in at night to work on the broken down engines. I wanted to see the part that wouldn't work. But even the general manager said I couldn't come.
>
> H.M. got tired of waiting for specifications. He told me, "I'm just wasting my time." So he bought an Olds car, his first car. He asked me to come and take the engine out of the chassis. I disassembled it, marking each piece. Then I put it back together again and it ran.*

Dodge Brothers and L&F were making motors from the same design but turning out motors which were quite different. This was revealed to Wilfred and his father at the first Detroit automobile show held in the old Armory Building on Larned Street in 1901. The most interesting part of the Olds exhibit was a display of two motors on a platform with two large dials indicating that the two motors were running neck and neck in speed.

> My father and I went down on the second day of the show and as we were watching the motors running at a seeming equal pace, a grinning bystander suggested that we go up on the platform behind the motors. Here he pointed out the fact that a brake load had been applied to the fly wheel of one of the motors to hold its speed down to equal that of the slower motor. My father and I were somewhat amused and interested to find that the motor on which the brake load had been placed had been manufactured by us, while the other motor had been built by Dodge Bros. The higher craftsmanship embodied in our motor

---

* Charlie Martens, who died in 1960, always took great pride in the fact that he had presided over every motor-testing department in all the Leland-managed plants. In 1959–60 he told Mrs. Wilfred C. Leland many stories concerning his work under Henry Leland.

A SHOP OF HIS OWN   63

enabled it to run faster. The Dodge-made motor delivered three horse power; the Leland-made motor delivered three and $7/10$ths horse power

As the Lelands would find out several years later, the interested by-stander was Henry Ford, an acute observer of everything pertaining to automobiles.

Although careful workmanship had increased the power of the Olds-designed motor, the Lelands felt that the design also could be improved. Therefore they proceeded to create a motor of the same bore and stroke and the same cubic-inch displacement but with certain improvements.

> We made large valves, held the valves open longer, instituted the efficient timing we had learned on the marine motors, and found that the motor we developed delivered 10.25 horse power. We offered this motor to the Olds Company, taking it down personally to Mr. Fred L. Smith, the business manager of the company. We emphasized that this motor, the same size as the other, manufactured at the same cost, would develop nearly three times the horse power. Mr. Smith considered the improved motor momentarily but turned it down. He was unwilling to bear the cost of the re-tooling that would be necessary should the design of the engine be changed.[19]

The Olds Company moved back to Lansing and after a few years converted the Oldsmobile into a large and much more expensive car which was not so popular. But Ransom E. Olds will always occupy an important niche in the automobile hall of fame, for he demonstrated that the motor car was a practical vehicle which could be manufactured in quantity and would attract buyers by the thousand.

It now seemed likely that the automobile industry might grow to considerable proportions. Henry Leland believed that it had a great future, yet he had no idea of entering the business himself. The engine intrigued him as did any complicated machine which he thought could be improved. He had put all his engineers on this first model—Ernest E. Sweet, Frank Johnson, Walter Schwartz, Lyle Snell, Walter H. Phipps, Fred Hawes and Clair Owen—men who were to contribute their ideas and spend the rest of their lives on automobile motors. But none of them could foresee the magnitude of future production. Together with Henry Leland and his son, they pictured the role of L&F as helping the new industry with designs, machine tools and parts, all carefully, expertly, precisely made.

Illustrations

The Leland Farm home in Vermont.

The Leland and Faulconer plant in 1902.

Morning consultation at Leland and Faulconer: *from left*, Frank Johnson, Walter Phipps, Ernest Sweet, Wilfred Leland (*back to camera*), Henry Leland.

Henry Leland, Robert Faulconer, Wilfred Leland, and stenographer, about 1900.

Interior of foundry at Leland and Faulconer, about 1900.

Wilfred Leland dictating to his secretary at Leland and Faulconer, about 1902.

The first Cadillac on its first road trip. Alanson Brush drove and Wilfred Leland was the passenger. The car was finished at the Leland and Faulconer plant in September 1902. Also in the picture are Joe Johnson, Harry Teagan, Frank Johnson, and Ernest Sweet.

The Cadillac tradition began with this car, in October 1902. Selling for about $750, this model-A roadster weighed 1300 pounds, had a 76-inch wheelbase, and was driven by a one-cylinder, ten-horsepower engine at speeds from five to twenty-five miles an hour.

The Cadillac carrying sixteen riders up Shelby Hill in Detroit, April 1904.

As an advertising stunt, Alanson Brush drove the Cadillac up the steps of the Wayne County building in 1902.

Mr. and Mrs. Henry M. Leland in London in 1910. Frederick S. Bennett is at the wheel of the Cadillac.

Wilfred Leland Jr. in the Dewar Trophy at age one in 1909.

Powered by a Cadillac starter, this baby Cadillac once belonged to Prince Olaf of Norway. It was built by Frederick Bennett, and later was sent to Wilfred Leland Jr. on his fifth birthday.

Henry M. Leland

Founder and Manager of the Cadillac Auto

Is the next Speaker

in the

Westminster Lecture Course

(Admission Free)

He has always been a factory man and knows what a factory man is up against. The working man has no stronger friend. In this Sunday evening address he specially invites the men from the automobile plants. It's a warm, home-like church, too, and if you want one fine evening, with a hearty welcome, be on hand Sunday next, October 30, at 7.30. The best seat is yours if you get around early enough. The place is on the corner of Woodward and Parsons, 20 minutes easy walk from the factory. Make this date for Sunday evening. Save this as a reminder.

An announcement of one of Henry Leland's many speeches made in churches and clubs.

MUM'S THE WORD, IF MR. LELAND'S LAW IS PASSED

"I wish a law could be passed prohibiting anybody from criticizing the street car company in the future."—Henry M. Leland.

This cartoon appeared in the *Detroit News* June 13, 1919. Henry Leland opposed municipal ownership of the city streetcar system. Frank Couzens and the *News* favored it, and when Couzens became mayor the city purchased the Detroit United Railway.

THE GLEANER.
A cartoon of 1909 when Durant was assembling General Motors.
From the Leland scrapbook.

In 1902 all machines in the Cadillac plant were operated from a main overhead shaft powered by a single steam engine. Oil and electric lamps were used.

The large plant constructed by the Lincoln Motor Co. in 1917 for the manufacture of the Liberty motor.

The same group that gathered about the table at Leland and Faulconer fifteen years before (*see photo above*) meet for a morning conference at the Lincoln Motor Co.: *from left*, Frank Johnson, Walter Phipps, Wilfred Leland (*back to camera*), Ernest Sweet, and Henry Leland.

During the war, Lincoln employed women in large numbers to offset the shortage of men.

A duplicate of this, the 6500th precision Liberty motor, is in the Smithsonian Institution. Some of the men in the picture had been associates for as long as twenty-seven years. *From left:* Henry Leland, Charles Martens, William H. Ebelhare, William Guy, Paul Abbott, Ernest E. Sweet, Wilfred Leland, William T. Nash, LeRoi J. Williams.

The Lelands and the Fords at the Lincoln Motor Co.: *from left*, Henry Leland, Mrs. and Mr. Wilfred Leland, Mrs. and Mr. Edsel Ford, Mrs. and Mr. Henry Ford.

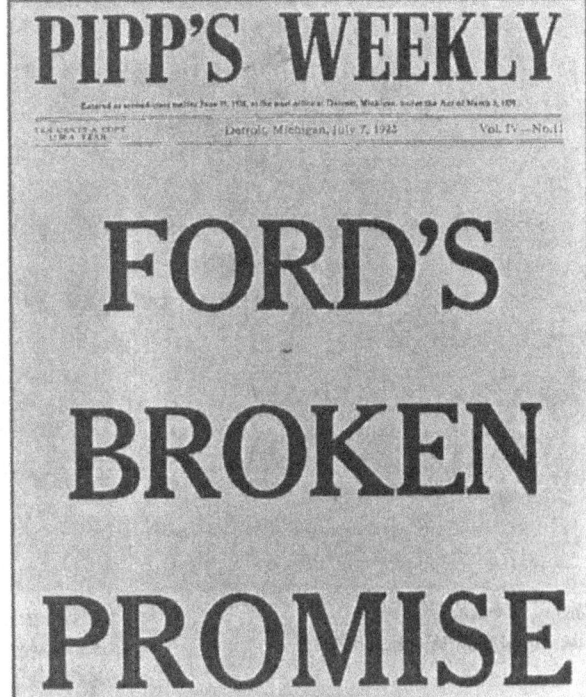

Front page of *Pipp's Weekly*, July 7, 1923, which excoriated Ford for breaking his promise to the Lelands.

Henry Leland with Osceola in 1930, when Leland was 87 years old.

Wilfred Leland on his thoroughbred Rigel, 1920.

This picture of Henry Leland and his riding horse, taken about 1910, appeared on the front page of the employees' magazine the *Lincolnian*.

Henry Leland and his grandson, Wilfred Leland Jr., about 1915.

When this picture was taken in 1932, Henry Leland was 89 years old. He is cranking a 1903 Cadillac.

Wilfred Leland, at 84, discussing Cadillacs with car enthusiasts.

Motor assembling at Cadillac in 1902.

Motor assembling at Cadillac in 1952.

The Lincoln Motor plant on February 4, 1922, at the time when it was purchased by Henry Ford.

Wilfred Leland, at 82, explaining the acetylene lamp in the first Cadillac (1903) to his second wife, Ottilie Masey Leland.

Chapter V
The Cadillac Is Born

IN 1901 LELAND & FAULCONER and their products were well known through the United States and in several countries in Europe. Customers were satisfied with the machinery built; stockholders were getting gratifying profits. Years of patient training of craftsmen in the shops had established a body of highly skilled, loyal and cooperative laborers.

The Lelands themselves owned an automobile. "Our car was an Oldsmobile," Wilfred Leland said later, "delivered to our home by Mr. Olds himself. I recall how our family went out to the street curb to look at it. Mr. Olds worked quite a while cranking it, muttering something about each car having an individuality of its own. But after we began to make motors for him, father took the *individuality* out of them. After our own little Oldsmobile was properly equipped, it acted in quite an exemplary fashion."

It was some satisfaction to put the more powerful, more reliable motor into their own personal car, but the Lelands thought that the improved motor they had created ought to have a wider use. Nevertheless, it did not occur to either of them that they themselves might build a car for that motor. They were too comfortable in their own business. But a change was coming and the memory of it would always remain in Wilfred's mind.

Our status as manufacturers of fine machine tools was never the same after a warm August day in 1902. I worked wall to wall with my father and only an open door separated our offices. On that day I heard strange voices through the open door, and father's secretary called to me to come in.

I was introduced to Mr. William Murphy and Mr. Lemuel W. Bowen, both men that neither I nor my father had seen or met before.* The spokesman, Mr. Murphy, explained that they had come to ask my father to appraise their automobile plant and its equipment since they had decided to go out of business. H.M.'s reputation in a machine tool line had brought them to him.

It is doubtful that at the time of this visit Mr. Murphy went into any detail of his experiences in automobile manufacturing. The Lelands in their memoirs did not touch further on this matter. But we know from other historians of the automobile industry that as early as 1899 Murphy and associates had financed an attempt to make motor cars under the supervision of Henry Ford. The Detroit Automobile Company was organized August 5, 1899, but apparently proved unsuccessful and surrendered its charter in November 1900. Ford then went to work to develop a racing car, again financed by Murphy. The car was successful in racing and led the earlier group to resume the manufacture of cars. The Henry Ford Company was incorporated November 30, 1901, and Henry Ford again took his place as engineer. Difficulties and disagreements en-

---

*William H. Murphy (1855–1929) was the son of Simon J. Murphy, a native of Maine who had made a great fortune lumbering the pine forests of Michigan. William Murphy was active in the management of the Murphy estate, which was invested in extensive realty holdings and early Detroit corporations such as the Detroit Edison. The Murphys built the Penobscot Building in downtown Detroit. Besides his enthusiasm for automobiles, William Murphy had a great interest in music and was an early supporter of the Detroit Symphony Orchestra. He was the major contributor in the gift of organs to the First Congregational Church, the Church of Our Father (Universalist) and the Art Institute.

Lemuel W. Bowen was treasurer and general manager of the D. M. Ferry Seed Company. He was also at one time president of the Standard Life and Accident Insurance Company.

THE CADILLAC IS BORN

sued and though some cars were built Ford left the company by March 10, 1902.* Succeeding superintendents had not proved satisfactory and by August 1902 the directors had decided on liquidation.

When approached, Henry Leland promised he would go to the plant at 1363 Cass and look over the machinery. The fact that this young automobile concern had failed to survive did not surprise him. The auto craze had fallen upon Detroit and half the mechanics of the city were concocting cars in their home workshops.

When father accepted the job of appraising the automobile company's equipment, he must have had a further flash of inspiration. Some days later he appeared in our common doorway at the office with the higher-powered motor, rejected by the Olds people, under his arm. He said he had the appraisal figures ready for the automobile people and he wanted me to drive him over there.

Parking our Oldsmobile at a hitching post on Amsterdam Avenue, we walked through the Cass Avenue entrance of Mr. Murphy's company. There Mr. Murphy and Mr. Bowen were waiting to introduce the other directors to us. Father placed his appraisal sheet on the table and the motor beside it. But he wasted no time telling the men before him what values he had found in their equipment. "I have done what you asked me to do, but gentlemen, I believe that you are making a great mistake in going out of business." And from there he launched into an exposition of faith in the future development of the motor car industry.

As he went on to the motor he had laid on the table his enthusiasm grew, "I have brought you a motor which we worked out at Leland & Faulconer. It has three times the power of the Olds motor. Its parts are interchangeable and it is not temperamental. (Laughter from the audience.) I can make these motors for you at less cost than I make the others for the Olds works.

Sold on both the motor and the salesman, the wealthy men decided to stay in business if Mr. Leland would join them in the reorganization of their firm. He agreed; he wanted his motor to find

* A detailed account of the Detroit Automobile Company and the Henry Ford Company has been written by Allan Nevins and Frank Ernest Hill, *Ford, The Times, The Man, The Company*, New York, 1954, pp. 174–215. Since the Lelands knew neither Henry Ford nor his financial backers during the life of these companies, the Leland papers and memoirs add nothing to the history of these projects.

a place to work. On the way back to his office H.M.'s eyes twinkled, "I'm nearly sixty years old but I believe I could get a job as a salesman yet."

It is entirely possible, even probable, that in Leland's visit to Mr. Murphy's factory he not only appraised the machinery but also observed some layouts and methods that he would consider awkward and inefficient. After all he was an authority on mechanical fittings and factory procedures while Ford and the other superintendents were still amateurs.* Henry Leland was never one to withhold advice. Ford and the other men were gone; such criticism would not harm them and it might help the company. A resumé of possibilities for improvement might also inspire the directors to continue the work.

Some twenty years afterward reporters and other observers telescoped these events of 1902 and decided that Henry Leland's criticisms of Ford's work had discredited Ford with his backers and caused his dismissal. This chronologically impossible tale has become firmly entrenched in the folklore of Detroit automobile history. Writers and historians have continued to repeat it and a workman who knew both Ford and Leland included it in his memoirs some fifty years later, adding further credence to the story.[1] This workman, W. W. Pring, whose memories of early automobile days were interesting and helpful, erred in another small detail. He stated that Murphy became acquainted with Leland when they were members of the same church.[2] Leland belonged to the Westminster Presbyterian Church and Murphy was a Congregationalist or a Universalist. (Both the First Congregational Church and the Church of Our Father claim Murphy was a member of that church in the early 1900's.)

His motor accepted, Henry Leland now embarked on the great adventure of his life; he would play an important role in the organ-

* One writer states that Henry Ford was followed by Otto Barthel and Alanson Brush. Theodore F. McManus, *Men, Money & Motors*, New York, 1929, p. 2. Wilfred Leland insisted that Alanson Brush never worked for the Murphy company, nor is there any record that Brush ever mentioned such a position.

THE CADILLAC IS BORN   69

ization of Detroit's first successful automobile company.* At a special meeting, the directors, Murphy, Bowen, Clarence A. Black and A. E. F. White, on August 27, 1902, agreed that the new company would be called the Cadillac Automobile Company after that French adventurer, Antoine de la Mothe Cadillac, who had founded Detroit some two hundred years before. The capitalization was increased to $300,000 and Leland was given a small block of stock, made a director and awarded the contracts for making the motors, transmissions and steering mechanisms of the new car.

The first Cadillac car, a sample or model, was completed on October 20, 1902, at the L&F factory. According to the plan set up by the board of management, the chassis, body, wheels, *et cetera*, together with the parts manufactured by L&F, were to be assembled into the complete car at the old factory headquarters on Cass Avenue at Amsterdam. However, the three cars completed in 1902 were all finished at L&F. Two of these were turned over to William E. Metzger, the sales manager, for his display at the automobile show in New York in January 1903.** The car was an immediate success. At that show Metzger took orders and deposits for over 1000 cars and, by September, forty-eight Cadillac agencies had been established throughout the country.

The features of that first Cadillac car are to be found in the pictures and copy of the early advertisements. The run-about, Model A, sold for $750 and a larger Model B, four-passenger with a tonneau, entrance in the rear, was $900. Both models had a steering wheel instead of a tiller like the Oldsmobile. There was no windshield; the brass carriage lamps and the horn attachable to the steering post were extra equipment and not included in the quoted cost. Fenders were nothing more nor less than the old mudguards of the family surrey. Also copied from that same vehicle was the small round iron step giving access to the front seat. The steering wheel

* The Oldsmobile had moved back to Lansing where it had originated.
** William Metzger was one of the early automobile enthusiasts and a promoter of automobile racing. Besides the Cadillac he sold the Pope Waverly, Pope Toledo, Columbia, Packard and Autocar. Detroit *Free Press*, February 16, 1904.

was on the right side and the starting crank on the left side where the single-cylinder, air-cooled motor was installed under the front seat.

A commentator said of that first Cadillac:

> Not only was the Cadillac born for the production class, but it was also born in the interchangeability class because the engine built by Leland & Faulconer Mfg. Co. of which Henry M. Leland was president, made all parts of the engine interchangeable. The five h.p. engine was located about the middle of the chassis. Accessibility as well as interchangeability was a feature evidenced by the fact that the engine was readily detachable from the frame, and also the body was attached to the chassis, so that by the removal of six bolts it could be removed without disturbing a lever or wire on the chassis. Reliability was a factor as shown by the unusually large size of the crankshaft bearings, and accessibility by the fact that these bearings could be removed from the engine and changed without taking the crankshaft out. The fact that a safety device was provided, making it impossible to crank the engine with a too early spark as it was described in those days, indicates that the necessity for a self-starter was subconsciously in mind.[3]

The design of this first car could be credited to no one person. It was built by engineers and men who had been trained and accustomed to transform the most complex ideas or plans into mechanical reality. It was built under Henry Leland whose experience and knowledge of materials, methods and tools was equal to the best in the country at that time. The car came forth, a simple, straightforward machine, well-made, sturdy and reliable, to set a standard that would not be matched at once by all the amateur geniuses with their cut-and-try experiments.

The year of 1903 has been generally regarded as the date of the real beginning of the automobile industry in Michigan. Olds was well established by that time. Cadillac had made its start in 1902. In 1903 Henry Ford found another backer and made his successful debut. Henry B. Joy, infected by the auto craze, went down to Warren, Ohio, and bought into the Packard Company, removing it to Detroit in 1903. Buick was also chartered in that year.

Although Cadillac started off with a bang, all was not rosy for the Lelands at Amsterdam and Cass. As ever, there was at least one critical director who thought things could be better. He was not sold on the L&F engine, and he thought Cadillac was paying much more for it than it was worth. Of this he partially convinced Mr. Black, the president. As he was on the board of directors, Henry Leland could not help but be aware of this situation. His stock interest was small; it was entirely possible that the contract for L&F motors might not be renewed another year. H.M. resolved to put out an anchor to windward. Shortly before Cadillac's annual meeting he packed his grip and started out to see if he could find another market for his engine.

He called on the Columbus Buggy Company at Columbus, Ohio; Parry Brothers at Indianapolis; and Frederick S. Fish, son-in-law of John M. Studebaker, at South Bend, Indiana. He told them what had been accomplished at Olds, showed cuts of the L&F engine and pointed out that they could get into the automobile business if they so desired. All were interested; the Studebakers were enthusiastic. Known widely as vehicle-makers, that company had already experimented with an electrically propelled car. Leland made clear to them that if he got a renewal contract from Cadillac he would stay with that company but, that failing, he would make motors for Studebaker. The offer that came from Studebaker was $15 more per motor with a contract for 3000 of them. Almost before Leland had returned to Detroit the Studebaker firm had its representative after him to urge the merits of the contract.

The annual meeting at the Cadillac factory was clamorous and contentious. When his time came Henry Leland defended his motor, pointing out all its fine points. Then he waxed sarcastic and told the assembled directors that he did not blame them for not wanting a *poor* engine or for not wanting to pay *two prices for them*. He bade them good-by and left the room indignantly, yet not so quickly but that Mr. Black could catch up with him before he reached the sidewalk. At the appeal of Black he returned to the meeting and was offered the contract for another year at the same price. Only then did he tell the board of the Studebaker offer. Speaking of that crisis later, H.M. said: "That extra $45,000 looked big to me then and it was quite a temptation. But I had promised Murphy and Bowen, who were both in Europe at the time of the meeting, that I would stick to them. So I did it." [4]

All had not run smoothly in the factory either. New buildings had to be built and much new equipment installed. Still production that year was substantial, with an output of 1895 cars, exceeding that of every other company except Olds. The second year opened with high hopes. Production had risen to fifty cars a day and shipping had just begun on that basis when the enlarged Cadillac plant was gutted by fire on April 13, 1904. This disaster put the company temporarily out of business.

The fire, said to have been started by a bursting cap in the rivet room, spread, igniting varnish and gasoline and causing several minor explosions. It burned through portions of the main factory and partly demolished the new south wing not yet turned over to the company by the contractors. The damage deprived the company of its big assembly room, the department most needed during that period of rush orders. Much stock was burned, but 500 completed machines and 2000 engines were in the warehouse across from the main buildings. The management hastily rented new quarters, the sales-manager wired the dealers to hold their orders for thirty days, and in a very short time the 600 workmen were back at work.[5]

Detroit was now automobile mad. In 1904 twelve new companies were incorporated, none of which survived for more than a few years. A similar fate met the ten incorporated in 1905. Meanwhile, sales for producing companies were no problem. The difficulty was to get the parts manufactured, brought together in the factory, and assembled into a complete car. None of the early manufacturers really manufactured. They designed and ordered the parts and then put them together, hoping that each part would be there when it was needed in the regular order of assembly. The failure of one supplier could stop the whole process, and often did. The Cadillac Automobile Company was no exception; the bodies and chassis were seldom ready for the engines and transmissions. Remembering those days Mr. Leland would say, "I never intended to get into the automobile business; there was too much trouble in it."

But to the directors it seemed reasonable that if the Lelands could do such a good job on their part of the process, they could probably handle the whole operation much better than it was being done. Finally, as the difficulties multiplied Murphy and Bowen came again to call at Leland and Faulconer. They were very definite, "Either you fellows come and run the factory for us or we will go out of business." So the Lelands became automobile manufacturers. Other men had built cars for many reasons—for the fascination of creation, for the profits in it—but Henry Leland agreed to build a car because he did not want to see a pet engine unappreciated and unused.

The new management came to the Cadillac factory to take over on December 26, 1904. The workmen in the windows watched as the little one-lunger car drove up and parked across the street. All eyes were on the three men who got down and walked toward the door. Then the inevitable wit made his observation, "Well, boys our troubles are all over now. Here comes the father, the son and the holy ghost." The irreverent phrase was apt in several ways. The father and son were always together; both Henry Leland and his consulting engineer, Ernest Sweet, wore patriarchal beards; and H.M.'s mechanical reputation as well as his prowess in Biblical dissertation was formidable.

The Lelands had agreed that they would assume general direction of the Cadillac operation and would spend at least two or three hours there every day though still giving the major part of their time to L&F. Yet from the first day they found themselves devoting more and more attention to Cadillac and less and less to their own establishment. To meet the exigencies of the situation, they also transferred their first-level engineers to Cadillac, leaving the others at L&F to carry on the work there.

As has been said, the early automobile manufacturers were merely assemblers, farming out the construction of parts to dozens of small shops and factories. While this system required smaller investment and less of an operation to supervise, it also meant that the assembler had less control over his supplies, and the failure or delay of any consignment could paralyze or even shut down the automobile factory right in the midst of the rush season. Hence as time went on the automobile manufacturer, exasperated by the omissions, imperfections and unreliability of a myriad of suppliers, began fabricating certain parts himself to have better control over the quality of the parts as well as their delivery. The Cadillac Automobile Company having taken the Lelands as managers or consultants, soon saw the advantages of also taking over the L&F plant which was already making the Cadillac motors, transmissions and steering gears and could, if relieved of other work, make yet other parts. The advantages of consolidation were so plain that the board of directors soon went to work on the project.

The Lelands, too, were happy at Cadillac. Henry went to work at once systematizing the operation and winning the friendship of the personnel, as he introduced his way of efficiency and ideal of precision. Before long a group came in to ask him to read the *Bible* to them at the noon hour as had been his custom at L&F. Throughout the plant, the men began to speak of the new manager as "H.M." or "Uncle Henry" and he knew the loyalty of the men had been won. Wilfred became assistant treasurer under William Murphy and as such was given authority to sign the checks. His position would expand mightily in a few years.

Representatives of the Cadillac stockholders visited all the L&F stockholders except the Lelands, and bought their stock. Mr. Faulconer, now almost an invalid, was glad to liquidate his investment and repay his Boyer loan in full. The name of the new combination was changed to the Cadillac Motor Car Company and the organization was re-capitalized at $1,500,000, the assets of Cadillac valued at $1,000,000, L&F at $500,000. A number of new stockholders were added. Of the personnel of 1000, 600 worked at Cadillac and 400 at L&F.[6] The value of the Leland team was recognized; each of them was to draw a salary of $750 a month and at the end of the year divide between them five per cent of the Cadillac profits.

All this time, Cadillac cars were pouring out of the factory faster and faster. During the year May 1904 to May 1905, 3863 cars were delivered, making a grand total of 8000 cars up to August 1, 1905.[7] The demand was insatiable. A noted authority on the automobile industry said:

> On a dollar-for-dollar basis, the Cadillac was in all probability the best car on the market. It appeared at a time when there was

THE CADILLAC IS BORN 75

still a marked premium upon reliable performance and Leland was an expert in a field where experts were still uncommon.[8] Competitors would learn, they would find out by trial and error, the ways Henry Leland had learned through a lifetime spent in factories among machines. But it would take time for them to catch up.

At this early time, with the exception of Ford, the automobile companies were paying the royalty exacted by the holders of the Selden patent. George Selden had invented a "horseless carriage" in

	Royalties Paid	Cars Built
Cadillac Motor Car Co.	$140,918.56	12,212
Olds Motor Works	111,599.74	11,011
Winton Motor Carriage Co.	109,128.75	3,554
Pope Motor Car Co.	87,595.00	2,121
Packard Motor Car Co.	87,439.74	1,682
H. H. Franklin Mfg. Co.	76,853.34	3,474
Geo. N. Pierce Co.	68,231.26	1,682
Autocar Company	67,121.25	3,794
Stevens-Duryea Co.	58,895.11	2,242
E. R. Thomas Car Co.	56,280.31	1,526
Peerless Motor Car Co.	54,343.10	1,176
Locomobile Co. of America	54,342.80	1,146
Buick Motor Co.	46,496.70	3,019
Knox Automobile Co.	37,967.83	1,702

1879 and obtained a patent on it in 1895. Though a car never was manufactured under the patent, a company was formed to enforce the patent priority and exact royalty from all automobile manufacturers. In 1911 courts declared the patent inapplicable but until that year the royalty was paid. In opposition to what was considered an exorbitant demand, the Association of Licensed Automobile Manufacturers was organized to protect the rights of its members, and to regulate and collect the royalty. Through the efforts of the Association the royalty was reduced from 5% to 1.25% and then later to .08%.[9] Because the royalties were paid through the Association, there remains a record of the production of the member manufacturers during those early years, 1903, 1904, 1905 and 1906, when there are few statistics from other sources. The figures are accumulated for the four years.[10]

Through this same four-year period Ford seems to have made 7500 to 8000 cars, though exact figures are not available.[11] This was before the days of the Model T, but Ford too was able to sell all the cars he could produce. Hence the figures seem to underline Cadillac's claim of its ability to produce more cars than any other company.

The early automobile was looked upon as exclusively a pleasure or sports car. News concerning automobiles was invariably placed on the sport page of the newspaper and cars were advertised through races or stunts of various kinds. A *Free Press* item of February 9, 1904, states that the Cadillac was one of the most versatile cars at the automobile show if judged by what it had done. It had drawn a five-ton-truck load of railroad iron up a four-per-cent grade after a two-cylinder car had failed to move the load an inch. It had climbed the capitol steps at Washington and chugged easily up the steps of the county building in Detroit. Alanson Brush was the driver and he remembered:

> It was back in 1902 that I drove a one-cylinder Cadillac up the front steps of the Wayne County Building and down again. I'd never made it, if the car hadn't had a wheel base shorter than a frog's chassis. Thousands of people stood in Cadillac Square and cheered.[12]

Finally the Cadillac was shackled to an ensilage cutter that ordinarily required an eight-horsepower stationary engine and ran it without a hitch. On April 3, 1904, a picture of a Cadillac with sixteen persons aboard, ascending Shelby Hill in Detroit, was published in the *Free Press*.

Along with its power, the reliability of the car was stressed. In a day when cars frequently broke down or got stuck every time they went out, Cadillac advertised, "When you buy a Cadillac you buy a round trip." [13] Much was made of that motor. "When a competitor tells you that we are going to remodel our motor and increase the cylinder capacity in order to get greater power, he don't know what he's talking about. We're going to do nothing of the kind. We don't need to. We have more power in that little 5x5 engine of last year than was needed for ordinary work." [14]

In 1908 the Cadillac company was still advertising the car with the same motor,* the same transmission, the same carburetor. It was boasting that no Cadillac car had been cast aside because worn out or unfit, although a number of them had been driven 50,000 miles, twice the distance around the earth. There was a little hedging as to speed.

> It is not offered as a car that will equal the speed of the high-powered machines over good roads, but it is easily capable of 25 to 30 miles per hour. This is faster than most persons care to ride, is faster than the law allows and faster than is driven nine-tenths of the time even by users of speedier cars.[15]

Henry Leland had a soft spot in his heart for that first model with its sturdy little motor. Experimenting on glass-enclosed models in 1905, the factory made one for his use. Like all cars which the Lelands owned it had a name, Osceola, after the great leader of the Seminole Indians. Fifty years later, Bill Foltz, one of the Cadillac engineers recalled:

> Uncle Henry drove Osceola . . . on evenings up the Avenue of Poplars, (LaSalle Blvd.), not far from his Boulevard home. He used it even after we put self-starters into our four cylinder Cadillacs, and after we powered them with V-8 type cylinders. The little car was high and somewhat top heavy. He drove it at high speed often tipping it over into a snow bank in the winter time, or while rounding a corner too fast. Then he would telephone the company for help to put Osceola on her wheels again. Uncle Henry used to tear around at 28 miles an hour when Osceola was new. Once he hit a street car on his way to the office. Going home the same night, he ran into a coal wagon. And whenever he went out of town, his daughter would call me and ask me to lower Osceola's speed by changing the sprockets. I'd be called on the carpet for doing it as soon as the boss returned. His family worried about his fast driving. He was not a speedster, actually, but he forgot himself and drove to keep up with his speeding thoughts.

* There are indications that the original Cadillac motor was gradually improved. A brochure in the Automotive History Collection, undated, but probably of 1904 or 1905, features a motor called the little Hercules, credited to Alanson Brush. Brush worked on the original engine and is remembered to have had some ideas on the pistons. However of all the engineers who worked on the engine, Frank Johnson had the greater part in its creation. Letter from Lloyd Blunden to Mrs. Wilfred C. Leland, February 14, 1964.

That Osceola was top heavy is evident to the most casual observer who might pause to look at the car in the Detroit Historical Museum. She stands seven feet, three inches tall on a wheel base of six feet, four inches. But she still runs and is capable of 23 miles an hour. Restored by Miriam Woodbridge, the only one of H.M.'s grandchildren to inherit his mechanical bent, Osceola came into the Museum in 1954 under her own power.* The original little motor chugged along as faithfully as in the first days when the Lelands wagered their future on its soundly conceived, precisely machined design.

* Miriam Woodbridge was assisted in the restoration of the car by her brother-in-law, Lawrence Hope, and a cousin, Jean Turner.

Chapter VI
Recognition Abroad

A 1903 ADVERTISEMENT in the *Cycle and Automobile Trade Journal* attracted the attention of Frederick S. Bennett of London, England. The ad pictured a Cadillac with this copy beneath it:

> Early orders are necessary if you desire to possess a Cadillac. It is as good as it looks. . . . The agent who doesn't secure it NOW is apt to hie himself to the woodshed a little later, and gently kick himself all over the place. Will you be one of the unfortunates? Now is the time to decide.

Bennett decided at once he liked the picture and persuaded his company to buy the car. In time the purchase led to the establishment of a Cadillac sales agency in London and a long association between the Cadillac and Mr. Bennett, which he himself called the Romance of the Cadillac Car.[1] As Bennett pointed out some twenty years later, the early history of American cars in Europe was the history of the Cadillac, the first car to establish itself overseas. While in this statement there is a hint of the salesman's pride in his own product, there is no denying that with Bennett's handling the Cadillac gained quick recognition in Britain and on the continent.

Some earlier indiscriminate dumping abroad of American bicycles had created a prejudice against American machines. Several poorly made American cars that followed only confirmed the world belief that English, French and German workmanship stood superior to American. While Bennett never faltered in his belief in and promotion of the Cadillac he admitted that for a time he plowed a lonely furrow.

The Anglo-American Motor Co., the company for which Bennett worked, bought in New York retail, as a sample, Cadillac car No. 530. The young British salesman set forth at once to try out the car which from the beginning had earned his respect. The ebullient Bennett tells the story most effectively in his own words.

> In the Summer of 1903 a hill-climbing contest up Sunrising Hill was organized by the Midland Automobile Club. Among the competitors was a dark horse, a little unknown car and an equally unknown driver, a dinky little American car and a tall spare young man, the character of unknown being further accentuated as car and driver resembled nothing so much as an interrogation mark on wheels.
>
> But the performance of both was so much of a surprise to everyone that even the staid judges, who rarely allow anything like enthusiasm to creep into their official report, pronounced the feat of act and driver as "Best Yet." The car was a 6 h.p. Single Cylinder Cadillac. The driver was Mr. Frederick Stanley Bennett. The Award, "The Best Yet," while never adopted as a trade mark of the Cadillac, has remained none the less the comment of all who have watched the progress of both car and driver.[2]

The car averaged 8.09 miles per hour on the steep gradient, described by some as the worst hill in England. Again the same year the Automobile Club of Great Britain and Ireland (later the Royal Automobile Club) organized a 1000-mile reliability trial. And again Cadillac No. 530, with Bennett at the wheel, was an entrant for its class—cars selling for £200 or less. The 1000 miles were covered in eight daily runs and the Cadillac received the highest number of marks for reliability, 2976 out of a possible 3000. For hill-climbing capability it secured third place with 461 points, while for engine power and re-starting on hills it was awarded the maximum number of points. This success was achieved notwithstanding the ill luck which resulted in its being abandoned by its official observer. Bennett managed, however, to keep it in competition.

The reminiscence of this trial which stands out most in my recollection, apart from the success of the car through the whole test, was the unfortunate collision just beyond the foot of River Hill, when a large steam bus ran into me, smashing my steering gear, bending the front axle and breaking one of the back wheels. I was shot across the road into the ditch. Things looked somewhat hopeless and I think that everybody who saw the wreck shared my first thought that the trial was over as far as the Cadillac was concerned.

It must be remembered that this was the only car of the type in Great Britain; there was no agency in operation and no spare parts were available. The back wheel was smashed to atoms. Bennett made a quick examination and found that the steering gear and axle could possibly be repaired, but for the moment the wheel looked hopeless. Then he remembered an acquaintance, Mr. W. H. Wells, to whom he had exhibited the little Cadillac while extolling its virtues. Wells, a representative of the South British Trading Company which was the agent for Fiske tires, remarked that he had a sample wheel mounting Fiske tires that looked like those on the Cadillac.

It was my one and only chance, so I left my mechanic to do his best with the steering gear while I bolted for the nearest railway station, several miles away. Luckily there was a train shortly due and I arrived in London. I had time to figure out the train back and found that I had eleven minutes, as far as I can remember, to get from Cannon Street Station to Finsbury Pavement and back. Thinking I could do it quicker on foot than by cab, I ran the distance. I saw a wheel of the right size on the premises of the South British Trading Co., seized it—much to the bewilderment of those in charge—and bolted with the fewest possible words of explanation.

Bennett arrived at Cannon Street as the train was moving out, sprang aboard and fell flat on the floor with his wheel. Fellow passengers picked him up and brushed him off. He examined his wheel and found it was not a Cadillac, but was of the same outside diameter and took a tire of the same size.

The difficulty was that the Cadillac wheel was fitted with unusually large hubs, and the wheel I had got had only a very small hole in the center. From that day to this I have had great faith in second growth hickory for wood wheel construction and so would anyone else who tried to enlarge a 2-inch hole to 3¼ inches without a wood-cutting tool of any description. There was nothing to do but to burn out the hole.

With the kindly help of the good lady who lives at River Hill, near Sevenoaks, at the cottage on the right-hand side of the road going south, I proceeded. She made a big fire and procured all the pokers and other pieces of iron that could be found and heated them red hot. After several hours effort we succeeded in making the wheel fit the Cadillac. The mechanic had disappeared with the front axle and the steering gear, but about the time I had finished my wheel he reappeared with a successful repair to this important part of the car. His joy at seeing me with the wheel was not less than mine at seeing him with his portion of the work done.[3]

Bennett then hired a conveyance and drove into Sevenoaks, wired the club and secured from the motor agent at Sevenoaks a responsible person for an observer. Just at dusk they went on to finish the set course of their trial journey.

Bennett never regretted the smash-up that day because it brought the car into the lime-light of publicity. This led to sales of some cars and for Bennett an agency of his own at 24–27 Orchard St., London W. In 1907 Bennett made his first trip to Detroit, where he was deeply impressed with the methods employed in the Cadillac factories. The experience led directly to the standardization test at Brooklands early in 1908 and the award of the Dewar trophy to the Cadillac Motor Car Company in February 1909.[4] (*See* Chapter I) Never before had this trophy passed into the possession of an American manufacturer, and there was particular gratification because the award was given, not for a spectacular or sensational innovation, but in recognition of a serious and fundamental development in automobile construction.

While the world was hailing the winning of the Dewar Challenge Cup as an American triumph, Henry Leland took pains to show the cup to his workmen and left it on display for a long period in the factory itself. A small leaflet, *To the Men in the Shop,* relating the circumstances of the test which had brought the cup to

Cadillac, was given to each man. It was emphasized that the three disassembled cars were put back together with spanners and screwdrivers and that no part was touched by file or emery paper. Wrote Henry Leland, "The honor belongs equally to every honest, sincere and conscientious member of this organization, no matter what his position, who has striven constantly and patiently to acquire and maintain in the work he is doing each day that fine accuracy which has made possible the absolute interchangeability of parts in Cadillac cars." [5]

The silver cup, sometimes called the 100 Guinea Cup, was itself a magnificent trophy, approaching in size a wash basin. The Wilfred Lelands dramatized the size by putting their baby into it and taking his picture. Mrs. Leland was born Blanche Dewey,* so Wilfred called the picture, "The Dewey Trophy in the Dewar Trophy," and sent a copy of it to Sir Thomas Dewar.

A sequel to the standardization test came four months later when one of the three cars employed in that trial was taken from the Royal Automobile Club garage where it had been locked up and sent to the starting point for an international touring-car trial run of 2000 miles.

> It is only fair to "Compote de Trois" as the competing Cadillac was dubbed, to say that owing to the fact of the car's being held in bondage for so many months before the trial, it was seriously handicapped as against others of its class, inasmuch as they were able to be fitted with special tanks, etc., whereas the Cadillac was of the recognized standard type and had already undergone an exacting test of its standardization. However, having filled up and cleaned up, it started off on the most strenuous trial to which cars have ever been put in Great Britain. To make a long story short, Harlequin 3 or Compote de Trois, as the Frenchmen called it, arrived at Brooklands at the end of a ten days' run well ahead of its class as far as marks were concerned. Other small cars were much faster, it is true, and it was felt that the speed trial of Brooklands over 150 miles might be the undoing of the sturdy little Cadillac.

The sequel in the shape of the race at Brooklands was perhaps

* Wilfred Leland married first, June 27, 1907, Blanche Molyneaux Dewey. Their son and only child, Wilfred Chester Leland Jr., was born April 6, 1908. Blanche Leland died in 1929. Wilfred married Ottilie Masey in 1946.

the most exciting sporting event the famous track has ever witnessed. The only competitor within reach of the Cadillac's chances was the famous French car of more than thrice its speed. On level terms, and barring mishaps on the track, it was odds on the French car reaching the post first. For the little Cadillac never professed to be a fast car under the best of conditions. And certainly the Harlequin 3, after doing some 2000 miles over the toughest country in the British Isles, was hardly in racing trim. Luckily neither was its nearest competitor. And the last run of 150 miles at top speed was a gruelling experience which took it out of both to the last ounce of endurance. Time and again the French car licked up the intervening handicap, involving a most costly delay, while the little Cadillac, with Mr. Bennett up, trudged along as it had done over the hills of Scotland and the Lake District, cheered at every lap as it passed the grandstand, and finally arriving after a most exciting last lap, the winner of the R.A.C. Silver Cup for its Class.[6]

As time went on the Cadillac also went on to more cylinders in its motor and more speed on the road. But in spite of this advance, Fred Bennett, like Henry Leland, forever retained a soft spot in his heart for that first little car which, by its steady reliable performance, earned the respect of the world and a life career for Bennett. He fought determinedly and constantly the British prejudice that American mass manufacture was a cheap and "nasty" method which resulted in an inferior product.[7] He continued to demonstrate the contrary at every opportunity.

In 1913 he sought out that original Cadillac No. 530, and found it in Slough, owned by a chemist, who had fitted it with a light van body and used it as a delivery truck. It was estimated that the car had covered at least 50,000 miles since it had been unpacked from its crate in July 1903. Here was a chance to refute the saying that American cars were useful today and fit for the scrap heap tomorrow. Bennett offered to submit the car to a repetition of the 1000-mile trial it had undergone in 1903 with Royal Automobile club supervision. As for the matter of repairs and maintenance during the ten years, an examination of the car showed that these had been largely limited to matters which require attention on all vehicles, such as renewal of bearings, driving chains, tires, etc., for once the floor boards were raised all the original Cadillac features were there just as they had been originally built.

As the car was taken over directly by the observer from the owner at Slough, it had no conditioning prior to its start on its anniversary itinerary. True it suffered several stoppages, a burst tire occasioned by running into a water butt left near the pavement by road repairmen, a fractured petrol pipe and a "perished rubber connection in the water circulation system—the latter naturally occurring miles from anywhere, where it was not easy to procure a supply of water." [8] These delays spoiled its schedule of up hill and down dale, so Bennett himself decided to take over the task of driving it the last day.

It did not take him many moments to ascertain that the engine was not developing its full power. In those days of magneto ignition, it is only older motorists who remember the vagaries of the "make and break" and "wipe" contacts used with accumulator ignition, and Mr. Bennett was not long in discovering that the car must for a long period have been running with a "late" spark. It was the work of but a few moments to effect an adjustment. And what a change! Against a speed of about 15 miles an hour at which it had been jogging along, an average of 20 miles an hour was easily maintained, while the improvement on the hills was even more noticeable. There is no doubt that the car responded to the call of its old master.[9]

So great was Bennett's gratitude toward the car that he kept it and, as Providence extended long life to both him and Cadillac 530, he decided in 1953 to stage a sentimental repetition of that same 1000-mile trial in that same car, this time under the supervision of the Veteran Car Club of Great Britain. His average speed throughout the whole distance of 1094 miles was 21.2 m.p.h., an improvement on his time of 1903 and 1913. And this in spite of modern traffic, though of course he was in some degree helped by better road conditions. He was stopped only once, to remove some dirt from the carburetor.[10]

Fred Bennett remained with Cadillac throughout his life, and came to know Henry Leland well. When in 1953 his affection for the Cadillac and the Lelands was a summation of a lifelong acquaintance he wrote Wilfred, "There is one thing which I always tell present day manufacturers and that is, the real basis of the modern standardized car can be put down to the strong religious sense of your father. He insisted on complete accuracy in manufacturing for the reason that it would be wrong to put fine limits on to blue prints and not carry them out into the manufactured article." [11]

Historians have continued to find a profound significance in the facts revealed by the early British tests on the American automobile.

> The Brooklands demonstration revealed a great new mechanical truth. Men had behind them centuries of the hand craft era. While they acknowledged the possibilities of mass production, they none the less believed that quantity production and quality production were irreconcilable, that quality in a product could be achieved only by hand work or by closely operated machines under the supervision of expert workmen. Leland showed that the highest standards of precision could be secured by a factory working on a mass production basis, that the workmen in charge of the machine need not be men of the highest skill, that they could make parts accurate to one-one-thousandths of an inch without sacrificing speed of output. This was a revelation of the most profound importance whose effect would be felt wherever men used machines. It opened the way to thoroughly dependable cars on a mass production basis, selling at prices which millions of men could afford. Thus it did much to bring about what might be called the automobile civilization of our times.[12]

Chapter VII
An Enlarged Vision

HENRY LELAND ALWAYS got deep satisfaction out of anything which was made right. On a Sunday afternoon when he displayed his 1903 Cadillac with its one-cylinder motor to his guests he called attention to the steady purring smoothness of the motor. "It is perfect now as we can make it. There is nothing more we can do." He, as well as Fred Bennett, had a special affection for that motor. Nor were they the only ones.

Cadillac still displays in its front office No. 2163, one of the 1903 motors.[1] Fifty years after that motor was finished a group of old timers visited the Cadillac plant to see it.[2] Will Guy ran his hand over it. "She hasn't changed. I ought to know, because I assembled her. How do I remember? Well, I was so excited that I smashed my thumb with a hammer."

Charlie Martens remembered, "I had to design a motor-testing room and it had to be just so for Uncle Henry. We really tested those motors."

Frank Johnson, eighty-one years old, looked lovingly at the old one-cylinder, admiringly at the later V-8 beside it. "I had a hand in creating them both."

It was all true, many people in the new company had contributed their ideas and earnest labor. The brochure that the Cadillac Company gave away with its first cars read:

> Cadillac cars are not the exclusive design of any one person. They represent the composite ideas of a number of inventors, designers, and engineers, each skilled by many years of experience in his special branch of work. Every feature of Cadillac cars is thoroughly considered by a special committee of mechanical experts. No feature is adopted until it has been passed upon by them and its worth fully proven by long and severe test.

Satisfied though the engineers were with their first motor, the public would not be long content. Though the motor lasted five years, the cars changed their appearance from year to year as shown by the sales brochures in the Automotive History Collection in the Detroit Public Library. The first model of 1903 had only a token dash, and needed no hood, for the motor was stowed under the seat. In 1904 a flat square box in front of the dash showed a tentative approach to a hood. This evolved rather quickly into a proper bonnet with the motor under it and a radiator screen in front. Though the first models were painted black with wine-colored running gear, this color was soon abandoned for a body finish of Brewster green with a hairline red stripe. Fashion intruded in 1906 when, in addition to the regular body styles, a Victorian or "tulip-bodied" design was offered in both roadster and touring cars. This featured extravagantly curved lines on seat backs and doors and was to be had in a new color called purple lake (a rich wine color). The first enclosed coupe was also offered in 1906.

To all appearances Cadillac was entirely satisfied with its one-cylinder engine, and yet it began looking to the future as early as 1905 when it offered Model D, a four-cylinder car at the price of $2800. In 1906 there were models K and M at $2500; in 1907 model G, a 4-cylinder, 20 h.p. motor, price $2000 and model H, 30 h.p. motor, price $2400. The limousine was priced at $3600. The four-cylinder cars had 20-gallon gas tanks, a sharp contrast to the seven-gallon tanks of the one-cylinder. Thus did Cadillac approach a higher-powered, higher-priced car and thus was mirrored the growing demands of the motorist. While in the beginning he was well satisfied and even boastful if he got back from his trip without much difficulty or delay, pretty soon he wanted to travel farther and go faster. The larger, more rugged cars stood up better and rode better, for roads were still very poor. However, auto clubs were springing up all over the nation and their main objective was better highways.

The automotive industry was settling down. Every year new companies sprang up, failed and disappeared, and yet a number of companies seemed to have built their operations into stable businesses. The better-known names were Packard, Buick, Olds, Ford, Northern, Reo, Pierce-Arrow, Stearns and Thomas. The trend toward higher-priced cars was evident elsewhere as well as at Cadillac. Malcomson at the Ford Motor Co. wanted to make a high-powered car; Olds had discontinued its first great success, the curved dash run-about, and was turning out a heavier, high-priced car.

The trend was plain at the 1907 automobile shows.[3] A census of the cars displayed at the show of the Association of Licensed Automobile Manufacturers in New York showed four models of one-cylinder, eight of two-cylinder and 97 of four-cylinder cars. Presumably the four one-cylinder cars were all Cadillacs as the company had four such cars on display. Henry Leland had resisted the trend longer than most.

The financial panic of 1907 caused some dismay in the automobile market and although the crisis was short-lived the industry was sharply reminded that it operated on insufficient capital and as soon as demand abated trouble loomed.

Things began to go rather badly for the owners of the Cadillac company. When Wilfred Leland returned from his wedding tour in June 1907, he was greeted with the doleful announcement by Mr. Bowen, "We are bankrupt; all our money is lost." For four years the sales of Cadillac cars had increased steadily but in 1907 they slipped badly. The lack of demand was already apparent in June. The production in 1906 had been 4307 cars; in 1907 it fell to 2696 cars. The demand for the popular one-cylinder had weakened and none of the newer, larger cars had caught the public fancy.

Cadillac had, of course, suffered growing pains. The directors had declared a dividend of 25% on its capital stock of $250,000 in 1904, based on the profits of 1903.[4] But dividends had been foregone in the next two years, in spite of the fact that sales had burgeoned steadily. The rapid increase in sales had necessitated an equally rapid increase in machinery and facilities. Leland & Faulconer had been brought into the company. Henry Leland must have the best and most up-to-date machinery.

> No one in the country . . . had a firmer committment to the principle that economy demanded the steady scrapping of machine tools and their replacement by better devices. No matter how much a multiple drill or other tool cost, the Cadillac plant was quick to sell it at second hand the minute an improved type appeared.[5]

Much use had been made of short-term bank credit; large sums were borrowed at the beginning of the season and the notes paid off at the end when the cars had been sold. As long as sales kept on going up credit was available, but at the threat of panic that credit might be abruptly withdrawn and the notes called.

These notes were guaranteed by the personal signatures of the major stockholders. They were wealthy men but they had already had two failures in their automobile venture and they did not want to stake their financial solvency exclusively on the Cadillac company, promising though it had been. The four men underwriting the Cadillac debt of $1,000,000 in the early months of 1907 were afraid that the company might be on the verge of bankruptcy.[6]

The Lelands did not feel this stringency as sharply as the other directors. Although everything the Lelands owned was invested in the Cadillac, they had found the growth of the Cadillac Motor Car Co. less painful than that of L&F had been. Protected by salaries much more generous than any they had received from L&F and entirely absorbed in the engineering and administration of the business and the challenge and excitement of constant technical improvement, they more or less left the financial problems to the men who had furnished the money in the beginning.

However, they were confident that given a product of worth and solid value the company could not but make good on its debts. Henry and his engineers set to work on a new model. Wilfred carefully prepared a schedule of production and possible sales which showed that conditions, even with reduced sales, were neither impossible nor dangerous. This presentation was so convincing to the company's loyal banker friend, Mr. John T. Shaw, president of the First National Bank, that the director took heart. On the basis of Wilfred Leland's schedule of supplies, production and sales, Shaw advanced the needed funds as payments became due. So accurate a forecast was this schedule that month by month its specifications were met and before the year ended some of the indebtedness had been wiped out.[7]

As has been stated Cadillac had been working on four-cylinder cars since 1905 and had produced several different models, all much higher in price, none of which seemed to attract much attention. In 1908, the last year that the one-cylinder car was offered, everything was laid aside to devote the whole effort to a completely new four-cylinder car. The result was a 1909 model called the Cadillac "30" which, introduced at the auto shows in the fall of 1908, made an instant hit with automobile buyers. It was announced as "the dream of the age—a multi-cylinder car of tremendous strength." And it sold for $1400. In the material which entered into its composition, and also in its design and workmanship, it was not inferior to any car. Yet, though much more expensive than the little one-lunger, it in no way approached in price the luxury models of other manufacturers. Leland wanted to make a really good car at a moderate price and this he had done.

It was a step presaging the course that Cadillac would take. Based primarily on the Leland ever-watchful effort for quality and precision, the Cadillac was destined to gravitate into the higher-price class. With Henry Leland quality came first and then price.

At this same time other manufacturers made choices of direction. Henry B. Joy with his Packard fixed himself in the luxury market where the margins were greater and sales possibilites more restricted but steadier.[8] Henry Ford went into the low-priced field where he developed a new and ever-widening market for a single adequate but limited vehicle.[9] Other men considered the advantages of a combination of several companies, bringing the security of larger capital and the attraction of a variety of cars to offer a choosey and fickle public. William C. Durant was the man to put this idea into practice.

It may be well to pause here and consider why Leland took the course he did in the development of the Cadillac car. As he grew older his purpose in maintaining standards seemed sometimes to overshadow the necessity of making motor cars which would compete with those of dozens of other eager, pushing auto makers. In retrospect his way seems inevitable considering the mold of the man. But in those days of scramble for position in the industry, Leland was a man apart—"a crack-pot," an "autocrat" and a "scold." Even latter-day writers differ greatly in their estimate of his methods. Wrote one: "The white-bearded Leland was a holy terror to automobile suppliers. One of them, who fancied he put out a pretty good roller bearing, never forgot a wigging he received from the old man." [10]

> The white beard of Henry M. Leland seemed to wag at me, he spoke with such long faced emphasis. "Mr. Sloan, Cadillacs are made to run, not just to sell."
> On his desk were some of our roller bearings, like culprits before a judge. . . . Under Mr. Leland's brown hand with its broad thumb was a micrometer. He had measured the diameters of several specimen bearings. Then he had drawn lines and written down the variations from the agreed tolerance. I listened humbly as he went on talking.
> "Your Mr. Steenstrup told me these bearings would be accurate, one like another, to one-thousandth of an inch. But look here!" I heard the click of his ridged fingernail as he tapped it against a guilty bearing. "There's nothing like that uniformity."
> To Mr. Leland I spoke as softly as I could . . . that pressure had been put upon us by another customer to make fast deliveries. Nothing else had mattered.
> But Mr. Leland interrupted, "You must grind your bearings. Even though you make thousands, the first and the last should be precisely alike." We discussed interchangeability of parts. A genuine conception of what mass production should mean really grew in me with that conversation.[11]

In this interview with Alfred P. Sloan Jr., Mr. Leland had scored in his effort to teach men to do better work, and he had scored in obtaining for his own car a more dependable source of roller bearings. Incidentally, he had spread a little farther the Cadillac's reputation for excellence. And when Mr. Sloan bought a car for his own personal use he bought a Cadillac.

Uncle Henry wanted excellence and he was willing to argue and explain to get it, but he did not want it at someone else's expense. One time his purchasing agent brought him a contract for a certain part from a company Cadillac had not bought from before. The contract price was very advantageous; the purchasing agent was well pleased with himself and expected some word of appreciation. But the big boss was not pleased.

"They can't afford to make it for that price," he said. "Bring that fellow in here; I'll tell him. A man who agrees to accept work at a loss is tempted to crowd shoddy into his goods."

The astonished salesman came in. "You can't afford to sell this for so little," said Leland.

"You don't understand," answered the man. "Don't you realize that once you adopt this as standard equipment other motor-car manufacturers will do likewise. We can afford to give it to you for less if we can advertise that we supply Cadillac."

To which Leland retorted, "We buy the best parts we can find. We are not looking for cheapness or trading on our reputation to buy cheap. I have always contended price should be considered last by a manufacturer in selecting material for his product." [12]

As was perhaps implicit in this "quality first, price second" procedure, the price of Cadillac motor cars went up. For five years the Cadillac "30" was the mainstay of the Cadillac line and, though its price went up several hundred dollars a year, the sales manual could always cite new improvements and added equipment. Building on that basic model, however, the special body styles and limousines gathered steadily a greater and greater share of the sales volume. Although Cadillac was not known in those days as an expensive car, it then began that steady climb in the estimation of a discriminating clientele.

Richmond Viall of Brown & Sharpe had one of the 30 horsepower Cadillacs and he wrote Henry Leland about it on September 30, 1909. The letter details some of the difficulties that might have been experienced but were not.

> I arrived home last Saturday night from a seventeen day's touring trip with your car. When we got here there was not a scratch on it, neither had we laid one cent out upon it; and there was not a bruise nor a scratch on any of the parties in the car, which consisted of my wife and Mrs. Ball, the driver and myself. So far as the car is concerned, I don't see what I could ask for that would be any better than the way we were treated by your Cadillac.
>
> There was a man from Providence where we were with a $5000 Peerless. The water was boiling in the cooler, and there were other troubles with it all the time. The man had it new last April, about the same time we had ours; he tried to get a Cadillac in the first place, as that was what he wanted, but he could not get one under six or eight months, and he wanted it at once and so he bought this one that he had. If he had made me a square offer to swap even I would not have looked at it at all, as we were traveling smoothly and with no trouble.
>
> I thought that some of the hills that we attempted to climb, with a high water-bar at the top almost as high as the wheel, would fetch the machine up; but she kept chugging on all safe, so that I made up my mind after that that we could travel over anything that came our way, which we did, and some of it was almost as rough as a stone wall.

The public liked the "30" and there was immediately a brisk business in them. Within six months after the advent of the model, 4500 cars were delivered and the whole year's (1909) out-put of 6000 was sold before August. As a consequence the old indebtedness was almost entirely liquidated. Thus within the space of two years the Cadillac Motor Car Co. went from the edge of bankruptcy to affluence and a 45% dividend to the stockholders.[13]

Shortly after the advent of the new Cadillac model, a representative of the General Motors Company, which was then in the process of organization, had appeared with a proposition to buy the Cadillac company. Despite their present success the principal stockholders thought it would be a blessed relief to be quit of the worry in connection with this business they had built up after so many years of anxiety and uncertainty, and were willing to sell if they could liquidate their investment with some profit. They determined on $3,500,000 as a proper price. When the General Motors representative came in, Wilfred Leland, who had been delegated to carry on the negotiations, named the price. On the following day, Arnold Goss, the G.M. negotiator returned and offered $3,000,000. After lengthy discussion he went further and offered Wilfred something on the side if he could arrange the sale at the lower figure. Wilfred argued that the property was well worth the price asked, and he firmly rejected any side profits on the deal. Also rejected were terms including only a transfer of stock and no cash.

The story of the organization of General Motors in 1908 has been written many times. William Durant, promoter and super-salesman, set out to put together a combination of companies in the automobile field. He had started with the Buick Motor Company of Flint which, from the beginning, had been one of the fastest-growing companies in the industry. Such was its affluence and reputation in 1908 that Durant was able to bring several smaller companies into combination by an exchange of stock. General Motors Company was organized and, by an adroit continued addition of equities and stock issues, Durant was able to find the credit with which to finance his deals even where stock exchanges were not sufficient and some cash had to be used.[14]

When Wilfred Leland refused to listen to any deal without cash, the master promoter was presumably unable to close the deal. The first ten-day option lapsed without further contact. Yet the emissary came back six months later to inquire if the Cadillac company was still for sale.

In the interval Cadillac had received the immense advertising occasioned by the award of the Dewar trophy. The new Cadillac model "30" was breaking sales records, and the stockholders were not sure that they should let their company go so cheaply. The sales price was raised to $4,125,000 with a ten-day option, in which time the would-be purchaser must make up his mind. Again the ten days passed without any further sign of interest.

What sort of a game was this, all put and no take? Well, it was no matter! Though the price advanced each time, yet the man came back with his question, "What will you take for the Cadillac Motor Car Company?" The third time Mr. Goss returned to ask a quotation from Wilfred Leland the price had again increased—this time to $4,500,000, a good round figure of $300 per share. And this time the offer was taken, and the entire purchase price laid on the line before the ten days had gone.

The following Cadillac stockholders were notified in advance to assemble for the payment at the old Detroit National Bank on July 29, 1909: Lem W. Bowen 2840 shares, Clarence A. Black 2840 shares, William H. Murphy 3055, Wilfred C. Leland 1340, Henry M. Leland 1340, Albert E. F. White 1607, Everett A. Leonard 179 Ernest E. Sweet 107, Harry H. Pettee 50, Arthur C. Leonard 35. The Union Trust Company as trustee also held 1607 shares.[15]

Huge as the sale price might seem—it was the largest financial transaction that had taken place in the Detroit stock exchange up to that time—still it was not an exorbitant price. The net worth of Cadillac at the time was carried at $2,868,709; the rest was the good will the company had built up in its seven years of life. Certainly this good-will figure was not exaggerated. It showed up strongly in the report of August 31, 1909, where the annual net earnings were shown as $1,969,382. A concern that earned almost two million in a year was not over-priced at four and a half million. Actually the company was a tremendous bargain which only William Durant appreciated.

Only two dividends had been paid by the Cadillac company, $25 in 1904 and a modest $1.00 in 1907. But in 1909 on May 1 a $10 dividend was paid; on June 1 another $10 per share; and lastly on June 28 a final $25. Hence in the summer of 1909 the stockholders not only sold their stock for $300 a share, but they also received dividends of $45.[16]

Mr. Durant wanted something more from the Lelands than their stock. At the pay-off, $100,000 of Wilfred Leland's share was withheld and a phone call requested that he come to see Mr. Durant at the Russell House immediately after the transaction at the bank was completed. He was to bring his father along. The summons could not have been a complete surprise to either. When they arrived at Durant's hotel room he told them at once that it was his desire that they remain as managers of the Cadillac Motor Car Company.

To this request they answered that in their management of Cadillac they had established certain standards and had been guided by certain ideals and would not be interested in continuing to manage Cadillac unless they had a free hand to maintain those standards and live up to their ideals.

Durant slapped his knee and said, "That is exactly what I want. I want you to continue to run the Cadillac exactly as though it were still your own. You will receive no directions from anyone." And so it was agreed.

For his part in the sale of Cadillac, Wilfred Leland, at that time assistant general manager, received from the Cadillac board of directors a valuable Swiss watch with this letter of commendation.

> In the old ordeal by fire, a man's body shriveled, while his soul remained unscathed. In the modern ordeal, the crucible of high finance blackens and stains the soul, while the body remains uninjured. Happy the man who comes through both ordeals with body and soul unharmed.
>
> May this watch be as true and faithful and loyal to you, as you have been to your associates, in this entire Cadillac transaction.

Chapter VIII

To the Rescue

ONE OF THE fascinating features of the early automobile business was that it was possible to make so much money on a small initial investment. However, it was not so easy to get that first initial investment together. The banks, of course, were not interested in such visionary speculations. It was left to a few wealthy men with some loose cash to found the industry. They listened when mechanical geniuses with dreams came to solicit help. Oldsmobile went into production with not more than $200,000; in less than three years it had paid 105 per cent in cash dividends, and the capital stock had risen to a value of $2,000,000.[1] Ford's third venture started with much less—not more than $29,500 cash—and in four years the net profit was over a million.[2] It cost Cadillac backers $178,000 for three attempts and two failures at the game before they finally got into successful production and the company sold seven years later for $4,500,000.[3]

The ability of the automobile manufacturer to make so great a return on a minimum investment was due to the fact that in the beginning he was an assembler rather than a manufacturer. He bought parts hither and yon on thirty, sixty or ninety days' credit, put these parts together and sold the cars for cash. His main expenses after tooling up were rent and payroll. If men could assemble cars fast enough and sales managers sell them at once, the money from the sale could be in the bank before the bill from the parts-maker came due. Hence the automobile manufacturer operated in a way on the credit of his dealer and his supplier. His markup too was high, perhaps twenty per cent of sales. The profits plowed back into the company enabled him to put out more and more cars. Of course, this process was a rat race, run always on the thin edge of disaster, and more fell over than held on.

Besides the perils of difficulties and delays, there was also the necessity of attracting public acceptance and building a reputation. In the early period the cars which were able to maintain steady production and create a market were the ones that increased their output as fast as their finances would allow. Then as the demand mounted the temptation was to pour profits into plants and equipment instead of accumulating financial reserves. When a crisis came the producer went down not because he was not technically proficient but because he could not find the credit to tide him over.[4] This was the kind of hazard which had faced Cadillac in 1907-8 and the fundamental reason that the stockholders were glad to sell Cadillac in 1909.

The time was ripe for consolidation or combination in the auto industry which would give it a broader financial base. William Durant was not the first to see the advantages of concentration financially and operationally, but he was the man who went ahead and put the idea into practice.[5] Durant entered the auto business through the Buick Motor Company.

As early as 1900 David D. Buick and associates began working on a motor which they hoped to adapt to a carriage. The expense was so great that in time the suppliers refused further accommodation and one of them, the Briscoe Brothers, took control of the Buick business as a creditor. Unable themselves to carry the load, the brothers sold Buick to James H. Whiting of Flint, Michigan. In Flint production increased with great difficulty. Eleven cars were built in 1903, 37 in 1904. His money leaching away, Whiting looked about for a man of vigor and vision to get the business functioning. William Crapo Durant was recommended as such a man.[6]

Durant, slightly over forty, had already made his fortune. He had first engaged in selling insurance and then "cut his entrepreneurial teeth in the carriage business."[7] He had bought a special patent for a two-wheel cart and, by mass-producing it, sold the vehicle for $12.50 while older builders were asking $50 for such carts. Thus Durant made his first million. When solicited by Whiting, Durant came back to Flint and made a thorough test of the Buick car, finding it to his liking.

Buick had been capitalized at $75,000, but in November 1904 when Durant took charge the capital was increased to $300,000 and a year later increased again, to $1,500,000. This stock, instead of being held within a tight group of stockholders, was promoted and sold widely to Durant's friends and neighbors as well as to others farther afield. Thus Durant demonstrated that automobile stock could be sold to the general public if a master salesman went out and pushed it. A great many people were willing to take a small chance on the alluring automobile industry.

At the same time, the Buick car was building up in public favor. Within four years its manufacture occupied the largest automobile plant in the world, and an annual production of 8487—the largest output of any factory—and a net worth of $3,417,142.[8] The expansion went beyond Buick itself. In 1906 Weston-Mott, makers of wheels and axles for both Olds and Cadillac as well as Buick, was persuaded to move to Flint, Buick taking over half its stock. With Durant's help Albert Champion came to Flint and organized the Champion Ignition Co. The W. F. Stewart Body plant was bought. All this expansion was noteworthy but almost from the beginning Durant had an even bigger plan in mind.

On September 8, 1908, he organized the General Motors Company, a holding company, incorporated in New Jersey at a nominal capitalization which was soon increased to $12,500,000. Immediately General Motors began acquiring, through an exchange of shares, the stock of the Buick Motor Co. By the end of the year 90% of the Buick shares had been exchanged for General Motors stock. In like manner Durant through General Motors had also acquired the Olds Motor Works of Lansing.[9]

In 1909 the shopping about for companies accelerated. The

Oakland Motor Car Co. of Pontiac was bought, as was the Cadillac. Other companies brought in during the year were the Marquette Motor Co. of Saginaw; Reliance Motor Truck of Owosso; Carter-car Co. of Pontiac; Elmore Mfg. Co. of Clyde, Ohio; Dow Rim Co., New York City; Northway Motor & Mfg. Co., Detroit; Ewing Automobile Co., Geneva, Ohio; Michigan Auto Parts Co.; and the Saeger Engine Works, Flint.

In 1910 additions to the holdings of General Motors were: Rapid Motor Vehicle Co., Welch Motor Co., Ranier Motor Car Co., Heany Lamp Co., Novelty Incandescent Lamp Co. Besides these companies, varying amounts of stock were bought in McLaughlin Motor Car Co. Ltd., Michigan Motor Castings Co., Oak Power Co., and Brown-Lipe-Chapin.

Among the conglomeration of companies which Durant bought, there is difficulty in discerning his central motive. There was undoubtedly that desire of the manufacturer to have his suppliers under his own control, as about half of the acquisitions were auto parts and accessory manufacturers. Eleven were automobile manufacturers but only four were really producing companies. In other cases perhaps patents or advanced engineering designs were the attraction. Some observers thought Durant aimed to buy up his competitors and establish a monopoly. Alfred P. Sloan, who would later head the giant combination, thought Durant was groping toward the modern concept of "offering a variety of cars for a variety of tastes and economic levels." [10] If he could offer a number of different makes he would be sure to have some popular cars.

Whatever his central idea, Durant bought a number of companies making cars in the same general price field and tried to bring in more, even angling for the Ford Motor Co. and Packard.[11] As has been noted, he paid for them mostly in stock. The notable exception was Cadillac, for which he had to pay cash—cash that Buick put up in exchange for some 51,692 shares of General Motors preferred stock.[12] To cover them all the capitalization of General Motors was increased to $60,000,000. Durant was evidently an incurable optimist—but then every successful automobile manufacturer was an optimist—otherwise he could never have started out with so little capital and continued his large operation on the thinnest of equities. If General Motors was expected to bring stabilization to a very speculative industry, this purpose was nowhere evident in the procedure of its organizer.

Of the several dozen components assembled by Durant, Buick was of course the one of greatest importance. Had it not been successful, it could not have been used as a base for this ever-expanding motor-company consolidation. That Cadillac was the next most fortunate acquisition is equally plain. Buick made the whole operation possible; Cadillac insured its life until the infant company could get on its feet.

It might be asked, why was Cadillac, a sound, conservative, well-managed company willing to go into this wild-eyed scheme? Cadillac did not go in; it sold out to General Motors. The conservatism of its backers had made its growth particularly painful. Although better financed all around than some of the other automobile ventures, it had realized early the perils of synchronizing the products of many suppliers and building them into a completed car. Within two years the company had expanded to acquire all the assets of its principal supplier, the Leland & Faulconer Manufacturing Co., in an attempt to eliminate some of these risks. The stockholders had plowed most of their profits back into the business, yet the capitalization was insufficient, as demonstrated when sales had lagged during the depression and the building of a new model. When the opportunity came to get out of the business with a good profit the stockholders took it.

On the other hand, Cadillac was a wonderful buy for anyone. An investment which can earn two million a year is cheap at four-and-a-half million. The flaw in such financial reasoning was that the bankers did not believe that any motor-car company could be expected to return a dependable profit year after year. They assumed that the automobile craze would be over soon. At that time the weakness of the automobile industry was its inability to secure credit when needed and its difficulty in obtaining financial cooperation. Hence the great boon to come of Durant's flamboyant scheme, which stumbled and almost fell before it really got started, was that it demonstrated to the banking fraternity that the motor-car industry could be a new and promising field for investment.

The Lelands, father and son, went along with Cadillac into General Motors. Why, like the rest of the management of Cadillac, did they not liquidate their investment and retire into the ease and quiet of a well-earned rest? The answer is, of course, that the Lelands were primarily producers and not investors or financiers. They were not working just to make money; they were creating new machines, new devices, new improvements. They had yet more dreams to transform into mechanical realities. Wilfred Leland, it was true, had gravitated into the position of liaison between the mechanical genius, who was his father, and the board of directors, who might understand all about finance but not too much about mechanical operations. Henry Leland was now sixty-seven years old, and although he was still strong, vigorous and full of ideas, he leaned more and more upon his son in those areas in which he was not primarily interested. Both Lelands felt an intense involvement in the Cadillac car—the feeling of loving parents who have brought a frail child through its years of feeble, erratic adolescence to the brink of manhood. Their image was strong in that child and they did not yet intend to resign their tutelage.

Although busy with General Motors, Durant did recognize Henry Leland's special knowledge. In an old notebook of H.M.'s this entry remains: "Sept. 14, 1909, W.C. and I went with Mr. Wm. Durant and Wm. Little and Downey to Oakland Pontiac, Buick at Flint, and Olds at Lansing, inspection tour." And again: "Jan. 19–21, Went to Chicago, J. J. Wilson, in regard to foundry for G.M."

However, contacts between the managers of Cadillac and the head of General Motors were few and limited to occasions when Durant wanted some special service. At this period Durant was not concerned with the administration of his companies, only with the accumulation of more units, and was happy not to be bothered with problems from Cadillac. The Lelands on the other hand were self-sufficient, soliciting advice and direction from no one. Thus the Leland-Durant relationship was always cordial though never close, based as it was on this policy of little contact and non-interference. Durant was a complex personality, exceedingly polite and charming to all, but an enigma even to others much closer to him. The

Lelands appreciated his kindness and made no judgment of his operations.

Durant had created a great complex of companies, built like an inverted pyramid on an inadequate base. The structure wavered and General Motors was threatened with failure almost before it was fully born. While some of Durant's capital seems to have been evoked out of thin air, there was substantial underlying worth in the assorted companies collected in so short a time and without too much consideration of their assets and potentialities. But neither this actual solid value nor the promising future of the automobile business was recognized when credit was needed. Seltzer wrote:

> Commercial bankers, from the beginning, had viewed the automobile industry with great distrust; its rapid development soon aroused their positive hostility. Writers and lecturers in the banking fraternity cited the growing popularity of the automobile as an ominous sign of extravagance, luxury, and waste; the automobile was pictured as a siren, luring men to mortgage their homes, to liquidate their investments, to reduce their savings accounts, to divert purchasing power from all legitimate consumption and investment. Depression in the bond market, recession in various branches of trade and other ills were laid to the motor car.[13]

Confused conditions among automobile producers intensified this conservatism of the bankers as well as that of other sectors of public opinion. The constant formation of new companies, some fraudulent and the majority unsuccessful, dominated the daily news.

While this opinion was not necessarily shared by all Michigan bankers, still Michigan was not a wealthy state, nor rich in liquid resources, and when so huge a concern as General Motors began to need money for day-by-day operations, the requests met serious and nervous consideration. An emergency joint meeting of the boards of the First National and Old National Banks of Detroit in 1910 loaned Cadillac $500,000 only a few hours in advance of a payroll which otherwise could not have been met. Similar crises were not so fortunately handled in the case of the Buick payrolls.

When General Motors was first formed its prospects were rosy. Sales by all units for the year ending October 1, 1909, produced a gross income of more than $29,000,000, with a net income over $9,000,000. A stock dividend was declared. The capitalization of the company was increased to $60,000,000. Durant expanded his plants, bought more and more units, put money into his money-losing companies and extended his profitable companies. Although sales increased in 1910 to $49,000,000, profits increased to only $10,000,000. By the summer of 1910 Buick owned three million in short-term bank loans and five million for materials and supplies. It had bought faster than it could produce and sell, and there was no cash in the treasury to take care of these obligations.[14]

The Lelands were slightly uneasy about the lavish spending and spoke to Mr. Durant about the necessity of arranging bank financing for the company's operations. Durant explained that he could get any amount of money from any of the principal banks of the country and there was no cause for anxiety along that line. Thus reassured Henry Leland embarked on a trip to visit the industries of Europe with the American Society of Mechanical Engineers. Hardly had he arrived in England when the news came reverberating across the sea that General Motors was in trouble.

As the stringencies of the General Motors financial bind became more evident, banks became more and more unwilling to lend the company money for its operations. The great corporation was on the verge of receivership because it could not pay its day-to-day bills. Durant dropped everything and set out on a search for money. He arranged for Wilfred to go with him on some of his trips to different cities to visit banks with which he was carrying loans. Wilfred described these trips.

> In each instance he would introduce me to the president of the bank, or to the officer with whom he was in the habit of carrying on business relations. He would explain with evident satisfaction, that General Motors had acquired Cadillac, and that he wanted the bank official to become acquainted with me and wanted me to tell him a little about the financial condition of Cadillac. I would then give a resume of Cadillac affairs and would make needed explanations and answer questions that might be asked.
> We made trips to many different banks and in every instance, the substance of the statement made by the bank official was,

"Well, Mr. Leland, if the Cadillac stood alone, we would be glad to loan up to the limit. But the Cadillac is now a part of General Motors and is involved in all the complications and entanglements of that organization and we cannot loan a dollar." [15]

By September 1910 bankruptcy for General Motors seemed inevitable. The company needed at least 15 million dollars. All the banks which had been lending funds to G.M. joined forces and called a meeting for consultations about the matter. The meeting was held in the director's room of the Chase National Bank of New York. Mr. J. C. Van Cleaf, Vice-President of the National Park Bank, later a part of Chase National, presided.

The directors' table was lined with the representatives of the various banks. Mr. Durant and the heads of the active units of General Motors were seated a little distance to the side ready to answer the questions. Wilfred Leland represented the Cadillac Motor Car Company. The bankers maintained a very critical attitude toward Mr. Durant, their sharpest criticisms directed toward the affairs of the Buick Motor Company and its indebtedness of $8,000,000. As the discussion proceeded, the bankers voiced their disapproval one by one; a banker would say, "I cannot lend any more," or "It is impossible to extend my loan further." And the statements became more emphatic as the day wore on.

After thorough exploration of the Buick situation the debts of the other companies were taken up in turn. As the Oakland Motor Car Company could not state its debts exactly the remarks became more caustic at such evidence of casual accounting. The refrain continued, "I will not lend another dollar," "I will not extend my loan another day." General Motors was a sinking ship to which no one offered sympathy or a helping hand.

Inasmuch as Cadillac had no bank indebtedness, nothing was said of that company until after four o'clock in the afternoon. Then Wilfred Leland was asked to give a statement of the condition of the company. When his presentation was completed he was asked what was the policy of the Cadillac company with regard to the conditions which had been criticized all day. The same bankers who had been frowning for hours now began nodding their heads in approval.

Before six in the evening the meeting adjourned, to reconvene at ten the next morning. Mr. Durant and the other manufacturers left the room feeling quite depressed. The presiding officer beckoned Leland to him and requested him to wait in an adjoining room for a short time. He said the bankers would talk for a little alone and might wish to ask further questions.

After half an hour or so Leland was called back and Van Cleaf said to him, "Mr. Leland, up to the time of your testimony, we were convinced that nothing was possible except the complete dissolution of the General Motors Company. The operations you have explained to us have deeply interested us. We have appointed a committee of five bankers, who will meet tonight in Parlor B of the Belmont Hotel at eight o'clock. We will appreciate it if you will arrange to meet with them and give them all the assistance you can. You have given us some hope."

Wilfred attended the evening conference and spoke to the bankers with all the persuasiveness he could muster. He told them the automobile business had boundless possibilities; the very growth of the industry had made it difficult for the under-capitalized companies to finance their constantly increasing needs. Besides, car-makers were not always the most careful financiers. The business was a new one and everybody had had to learn as he went along. Good cars could be sold for cash as fast as they were made and it would be a mistake to dissolve General Motors; the stockholders would lose their investments and the bankers would lose the money they had on loan. All that was needed was some time and some cash to tide the company over this emergency.

I told them that if they could only re-orient their thinking in the direction of how General Motors could be saved, rather than why it should be dissolved, they would find many good portents of success. After all Cadillac alone was earning almost two million a year and General Motors had made ten millions. Surely fifteen million was not such a great sum to loan to a business earning at that rate.

Leland's eloquence started a new trend of thought. The bankers began to discuss what they *could* do instead of what they *would not do*. They found reasons for confidence and by 2:30 a.m. the members of the committee were convinced that a loan might serve the interests of all concerned.

The general conference came together next morning at 10 o'clock. Mr. Durant looked dejected; he had not known of the meeting the evening before. Through the hours of the night his ears had rung with that dismal reiteration, "I will not lend another dollar!" It was the surprise of his life when, instead of the death knell of General Motors, he heard the recommendation for a $15,000,000 additional loan.

Col. Ralph Van Vechten, Vice-President of the Continental and Commercial Savings and Trust Company of Chicago, presented the advantages of a constructive policy towards General Motors, earnestly and convincingly. The wisdom of his reasoning was plain to all.

Then the roll was called. Each banker was requested to state the amount his bank would be willing to subscribe toward the needed loan. Once around the table and the total stood at $17,500,000, an over-subscription of $2,500,000.

When the result was announced, Mr. Van Cleaf turned to Wilfred and said, "Mr. Leland, I want to congratulate you, and I want to say that you have saved the General Motors Company." [16]

Chapter IX
The Finance Committee Reigns

TOWARD THE END of the bankers' conference, which was considering whether General Motors was solvent or insolvent, one of the conferees said musingly, "Why, this loan might be made on the strength of the showing made here by the Cadillac; if the others should fail, the Cadillac could eventually pay off these loans." [1] And as it turned out there were many times during the ensuing years when Cadillac felt it was doing that very thing.

When it became clear to the large financial interests of the country that the bankers concerned considered General Motors solvent and were willing to put up the money for the continuance of the business (under certain conditions) there were several offers from banking syndicates to fund the loan.[2] The proposition of J. W. Seligman & Co. of New York and Lee, Higginson & Co. of Boston was accepted. Mr. Durant was to step down from active management of General Motors although permitted to remain temporarily on the finance committee. Control of the corporation was put into the hands of a board of five trustees, three of whom were representatives of the bankers, James J. Storrow being the most active and for all practical purposes successor to Durant.[3] The trustees were to remain in office for five years.

The bankers then underwrote an issue of $15,000,000 in six per cent five-year notes, secured by a mortgage on all the actual tangible assets of General Motors. As it turned out, confidence having been restored, the notes sold easily, and were taken up immediately by private investors before the public had a chance to buy. As is the wont of bankers, they got their discount money immediately—$2,500,000—leaving $12,500,000 cash for General Motors.

It was unfortunate, for the Lelands at least, that the bankers taking over the management of the company were not the same ones who had waded through the murky record of debt, bad judgment and inefficiency only to see underneath the strength of the growing automobile industry. Furthermore, the trustees did not see as had the bankers that the solvent, debt-free Cadillac was the rock on which the re-organized company must be built. On their first trip to Detroit the committee notified the Lelands that their compensation would be cut in half as General Motors could not afford to pay such high salaries. In view of the record which had been made by Cadillac, and the efforts which Wilfred Leland had exerted in behalf of General Motors, this seemed a most unjust reward. H.M., with the lower boiling point, reacted indignantly: they would resign. But after a few second thoughts and a good long look into the matter, the injustice was endured and the promise Wilfred had made to the bankers prevailed. What Wilfred had promised the Lelands must fulfill; he had said they would help so that all their experience and skill would be at the service of General Motors.

Consider for a moment what the Lelands were to do. They were to communicate to other units of General Motors their techniques, their methods and to an extent their policies. Yet they had no authority in the management. The new directors were appointed primarily for their conservatism—to put G.M.'s financial affairs in order; but the whole success of the reorganization hinged on the production of an income which not only would pay off the loan, but also would put component companies, where possible, into a producing condition. A schedule had been set for the re-payment of the loan, and it might almost have been set as an earnings goal for the management of Cadillac. Had not the musing banker said, "If the others fail, the Cadillac could pay off these loans"? So Cadillac felt an extra compulsion to expand and make the payments while other units were being pulled into shape. The sinking-fund provisions called for the annual cash payment to the trustees on or before October 1 of each year the following amounts: 1911, $1,500,000; 1912, $1,500,000; 1913, $2,000,000; 1914, $2,000,000; 1915, the balance, $8,000,000.[4]

The directors elected James J. Storrow as interim president and it was under his hand that the first reforms were made. Charles Nash later said of Storrow:

> He was an extraordinary man. I doubt if a man ever lived who had a warmer, bigger heart than Mr. Storrow, and who on the other hand was so unable to show it in his daily contact with men. A great many men felt that Mr. Storrow was of the "banker" type—rather cold-blooded, which was entirely contrary to his real make-up.[5]

For the Lelands he had little advice. Wilfred saw him in New York and asked him if he had any suggestions to make that would help Cadillac increase its earning power. "Oh, I am satisfied with the way things are going," he answered. "I am leaving the production know-how to you and your father since you have all those years of experience. Carry on the same as ever in whatever way is best in your judgment." Again some time later, he said, "Never mind me! My company only loaned the millions. Yours is the real job of working out the payments. I must say we are encouraged by the progress made."

In a short time Messrs. Storrow and Straus, whose union of interest controlled the board of directors, selected Thomas Neal, secretary and general manager of the Acme White Lead & Color Works of Detroit, to be president of General Motors. Standish Backus, a young lawyer, was made secretary and James T. Shaw, treasurer. These were all Detroit people and therefore somewhat more in touch with local conditions. There was plenty to be done.

> For two years expansion had been the watchword, with efficiency of operation a minor consideration. Inventories were woefully out of balance; improper storage of supplies had caused great waste. In one plant thousands of tires were found exposed to heat and sunlight; in another, valuable machinery lay rusting

out of doors. Tons of unsaleable merchandise had been built to faulty specifications or of faulty materials.[6]

For a time production figures lagged, but in that interval some of the debris inherited from the Durant regime was written off the books. Three truck companies were consolidated and Oakland reorganized. Some companies, such as the Heany Lamp Co., were simply liquidated. The patents of this company proved to be fraudulent and though its purchase price had exceeded that of Buick and Olds together, the investment was written off, entailing a loss of from $5,000,000 to $12,000,000 to General Motors. Some of the car companies, such as Ranier, Carter-car, Marquette and Welch were first consolidated and then abandoned. By 1912 G.M. was producing only four cars—Buick, Cadillac, Oldsmobile and Oakland. In 1911 the total production had fallen from 39,000 units to 35,000, though Cadillac's production rose from 8,000 to 10,000. Profits fell from $10,255,000 to $4,066,000. "But no creditors were knocking at the door, no bundles of stock were being issued for doubtful assets, and there were no deadhead motor cars in the General Motors line."[7] In 1912 production rose to 49,538 units—Cadillac accounting for 14,000 of them—but profits remained coy, reaching only $4,746,000. In 1912 Charles W. Nash, who had done such a fine job at Buick in those two years, was made president of General Motors and from then on earnings increased rapidly.

Neither Storrow, Nash nor Neal had any background of mechanical training or automobile experience. A research laboratory to serve all the units had been established but Mr. Storrow also hoped there would be an exchange of methods:[8]

> We are sure that any manager, head of any purchasing department, factory superintendent, and any other man holding an important position in any one of the companies, will be anxious to give the benefit of his knowledge and experience whenever asked in the right way by any other one of our companies.[9]

Lloyd Blunden, who had been an apprentice at L&F, then later had obtained an engineering degree and returned to Cadillac remembered:

> Thomas Neal, a Detroit banker . . . acted as interim president of GM. Buick and Oakland were in serious trouble. Mr.

THE FINANCE COMMITTEE REIGNS 113

Neal appealed to H.M. and Wilfred to help on those problems. H.M. sent Joe Wilson, L&F foundry superintendent to straighten Buick's foundry trouble, and Walter Phipps (formerly superintendent at L&F), who was already in business for himself spent much time ironing out production problems for Oakland and Buick.[10]

This was a delicate task—to go in and tell men they were doing things the wrong way. Managers and department heads would be loath to admit they did not know their jobs and have to ask for counsel and help. Few standards of performance and method had been set in the infant industry. The furious pace of automotive development had attracted to the business aggressive men, ambitious to make their mark. Craftsmen would be slow to change their techniques. It was indeed a difficult assignment and one that took infinite tact and forbearance—this effort to show men how to do things a better way. Wilfred wrote of the manner in which his father gave them help.

A large part of the educational work that we carried on took the form of conferences which had produced excellent results in both L&F and in the Cadillac organization. Father's strategy at these conferences was to teach methods, principles, practices and lines of procedure which he had found desirable in his long career. Also he took Mr. Sweet, our chief consulting engineer and other leaders on frequent trips through each of the other units and noted things that should be changed and corrected and improved. These problems were taken up and ironed out at the conferences and steps taken to have the improved procedures put into effect.

At other times one of the Cadillac leaders would call together a few interested persons and demonstrate a better method. On many occasions a few key men holding positions of responsibility in the other units were called over to Cadillac and taught discoveries that we had made and installed. There were also instances where other units were having difficulty in machining certain parts and securing the close limits of accuracy which were specified. In those cases we would have the department foreman select a capable man and send him to us. We gave the man special training until he was capable of machining those difficult parts and keeping them to their limits.

Henry Leland taught all the machinists to use the Johansson gauges. These now universally used gauges had come to Cadillac in

1907 or 1908.[11] The exact date is uncertain but H.M., "never seen without a micrometer in his hand," was quick to appreciate such standards and acquired the blocks as soon as he heard about them. The employment of limit gauges was recommended and their use multiplied throughout the other units of General Motors, thus eliminating at the source the many defective unusable parts that had to be thrown away. Further, the old machinist from Brown & Sharpe stressed everywhere that art of establishing proper limits for different types of work—where it should be accurate to the thousandth of an inch, and where such fine grinding was tossing profit out the window. This personal contact with engineers, department heads and even machinists created a fellowship that lasted through the years. The Cadillac slogan became a G.M. motto, "Craftsmanship a creed, accuracy a law."

The late Fred M. Zeder, the future head of Chrysler engineering but in 1912 of the laboratories of Everitt-Metzger-Flanders, praised the work of Henry Leland in that period of reconstruction of General Motors. "He was a prince. We called him the Grand Old Man of Detroit. He was indefatigable and so patient in his directing and guiding wherever needed." [12] One suspects that in spite of the pressure and work Henry Leland enjoyed this opportunity to spread the art of the machine.

Wilfred Leland felt that Mr. Nash had been very appreciative of the Leland services rendered to all the other units. He spent occasional week-ends at the Leland country home, Wilchester, discussed manufacturing problems with Henry Leland and played with Wilfred's little son. However, Walter Chrysler, who succeeded Nash at Buick, thanks to his prior training along technical lines, absorbed mechanical ideas more quickly.

Human nature being what it was and is, a little friction was to be expected among the various members of the G.M. family. But as the corporation's life depended on concerted action, great attempts were made to smooth over the difficulties and harmonize the group effort. Charles Oostdyke, who had been brought up from the ranks to become purchasing agent at Cadillac, was recommended to take over the job of purchasing chief for all of the General Motors divisions. His duty as director of purchases was to co-ordinate the buying for the whole company. When Mr. Neal learned that the buyer at Buick persisted in buying from his old sources in spite of the fact that Mr. Oostdyke was able to make better arrangements, Mr. Neal promptly took his young purchasing director to Flint where, in the presence of Mr. Nash and the reluctant buyer, the necessity of centralized controlled buying was made plain.

Another story of this period is told by Wilfred Leland and concerns the closed-car bodies that were becoming popular. Wooden bodies had persisted because they made less noise than metal ones on the rough roads. Builders of bodies, transferred from the carriage trade, were skilled in handling wood, but awkward with metal, a fact that Walter Chrysler remarked upon.[13]

> When we began to use closed bodies for automobiles, there was another disagreement. Our very first closed bodies before 1910 were made of wood by Seavers & Erdman on Jefferson Avenue. Mr. Nash of Buick wanted to continue making them of poplar panels. Father could see the advantage of metal bodies, and he had the first batch of them made at Fisher Brothers. However they turned out to be unsatisfactory in many respects. Father and I went over to the Fisher plant where the brothers had just started to make aluminum and steel bodies. Mr. Mendelsohn, financial backer of the Fishers, was there too. In the argument that ensued Fred Fisher could nor would not see where the bodies fell short. But Mr. Mendelsohn saw and advised Fred to take the bodies back and finish them as Mr. Leland wanted. Thereafter the Fishers finished high-grade bodies not only for Cadillac but for the other General Motors' cars as well.

Though the Lelands carried this extra responsibility of helping other units of G.M. they did not neglect Cadillac business. It was in these years under the bankers' control that the Cadillac led so spectacularly in new developments. In the annual report of General Motors July 31, 1912, capital expenditures are listed as $2,124,184, half of this allocated to expenditures for additions to the plant and equipment of the Cadillac. The other half was devoted to the acquisition of the last half of Weston-Mott Co. and otherwise divided equally to improvements of other G.M. plants.

Men worked very hard in those days of General Motors reconstruction. The more responsible, the longer the hours they spent on the job. Henry Leland kept up with the rest although nearly seventy years of age. Billie Guy told how H.M. would wander into his motor-assembly department at two or three o'clock in the morning and ask, "Billie, how do you sleep days when you have to work nights? I can't even sleep nights!" Later the night watchman would discover him asleep in the drafting room with his white head on a drawing table. The watchman was worried. "I hope the old gentleman doesn't have a nervous breakdown." As it turned out the old gentleman was the more durable of the Lelands. It was the son, who in that period twice worked past his breaking point. True, H.M. did fracture a hip by hastily stepping out of a car before it had come to a stop, but that immobilized him a very short time. After all, his head full of ideas went right on functioning.

In the General Motors Company, Durant had brought together a loose combination of companies, all with some product concerned with the automobile industry. The five years of sweat and toil under the bankers' management made General Motors an entity and established it on a sound financial basis. By 1915 the company had earned over 58 million dollars. When the final installment on the note issue had been paid, a cash dividend of $50 could be declared on the common stock, one of the most substantial dividends ever to be paid by a large American corporation.[14] This dividend was paid, however, by a new management—Durant had again seized control—but the money had been earned under the conservative bankers' administration.

Historians differ as to the wisdom of putting General Motors in the custody of the bankers. One said, "The substantial achievements of the voting trust, particularly as respects industrial managements, are generally conceded."[15] Another thought that financially "General Motors needed the prestige which the banking group gave it."[16] Some argue that the company would have gone faster and farther if the temporary financial bind of 1910 had simply been eased by a slight relaxation of credit. Certainly the stockholders regarded the banker management as "narrow-minded, shortsighted and nickel-nursing."[17] In 1910 General Motors produced about the same number of cars as did the Ford Motor Company, but in the next five years Ford went on to dominate the industry with a production in 1915 of over three times that of G.M. The period was one of tremendous growth in the automobile industry; the total American output rose from 187,000 in 1910 to 969,930 in 1915. "The General Motors enterprise had contributed about 21% of the total physical output or about 22% of the wholesale value in 1910; but by 1915 their combined share had fallen to about 7.8% of the physical output and to about 13.3% of the total wholesale value." [18] Whatever of progress and expansion may have been lost, the stockholder who kept his stock probably did not in the end lose anything. A 1910 shareholder who kept his stock would have found each share worth $18,935 in 1952.

Durant had never lost his faith in General Motors and, after his departure from the finance committee, began to plan to bring the company back under his control. On November 3, 1911, he organized Chevrolet on the usual shoestring, made it a strong producer and continuously bought General Motors stock at the low price to which the trusteeship arrangement had brought it in public esteem.[19] Later he exchanged five shares of Chevrolet stock for one share of General Motors and, as at that time there was a small price advantage in such an exchange, he acquired a great deal of General Motors stock. As the years advanced so did the price of G.M. stock, not only on account of the great demand for cars, but also because the company's reconstruction had increased the stock's worth.

Three days before the annual meeting of 1915 Wilfred Leland, on his monthly visit to New York, went to see Mr. Durant. "He took me into the back office and opened the door of a large safe and showed me a huge stack of stock certificates which he told me would control the outstanding stock of G.M."

Durant made good on this announcement at the annual meeting on September 15, 1915. The coup had been made possible by the backing of the Dupont interests, whose General Motors stock holdings were already considerable at that time.

A few days after the 1915 meeting when Durant had regained control of General Motors he came to Detroit and conferred with the Lelands. Mr. Durant did not forget his friends, and he wished to express his gratitude to Wilfred Leland. He could never forget that refrain, "I will not lend another dollar." Nor would he forget how willingly the Lelands had extended their experience to all the other companies during the interval of reorganization. Now that he was in charge again he would recognize that service substantially.

"How much did you lose through the reduction in salary made by the Finance Committee?" he asked Henry Leland.

"In excess of $500,000," answered H.M.

The great promotor declared emphatically that the action of the finance committee had been entirely unjustified. He would take steps to reimburse the Lelands: in doing it he would only be giving them what had been unfairly withheld. "You are entitled to another block of stock to reward you for all you have done."

Durant was talking straight from his heart that day, but alas, he never got around to making the recompense. Remembering it from time to time, he regretted his oversight; asserted that the stock belonged to the Lelands and he would see that they got it. He never did get around to it. Before another five years had passed the Lelands were gone from General Motors and so was William Durant.

Chapter X
Making Mechanics

HENRY LELAND ALWAYS wanted to share with others some of the good things he had found in life. One of these was his religious experience; the other his technical skill and the rewards it had brought.

The spirit of his faith he extended to others through work in his church, frequent talks at the YMCA and other assemblages and the noon-tide sessions of prayer and *Bible* reading at the plant. Likewise, he neglected no opportunity to give others the benefit of his long experience in mechanics and manufacturing. When with Brown & Sharpe he was never satisfied to sell a man a machine, he must also show him how to use it. When he went into business for himself, he never stopped instructing his men in the better way to do things. He labored to teach his workmen, his suppliers, his stockholders and even his customers. Anybody could apply to him for advice and many did. Henry Ford in the early days came over to ask him how to grind his pistons so they would not stick when they got hot. Another time, Ford sent Oliver Barthel over with a drawing of a two-cylinder motor to get H.M.'s approval. The elderly mechanic looked over the drawing and stated that a motor made from that drawing would never work. This was, of course, before either Ford or Leland had gone very far in the manufacture of automobiles.

When Henry Leland became a manufacturer he exerted himself to teach his suppliers to make a better product. The Timken Axle Company made most of the early Cadillac axles. Its salesman, frequently at Cadillac, once heard from the ante-room a lesson given to a grease-cup manufacturer by Henry Leland. In those days, many grease cups were used in car construction, particularly in axles and other parts where grease had to be forced into the bearings and moving parts.

The grease-cup manufacturer was asking why he, with all his experience and large facilities, could not get any business from Cadillac. One order had been given him but no more followed. Why?

Mr. Leland took two sheets of writing paper, laid them on his desk and marked the word "Go" on one and "Out" on the other. He then called in a messenger boy and asked him to put his two hands together and cup them. "Go to the small parts room," he said, "and tell Joe to fill your hands from the row of bins marked D with the o and oo grease cups."

The boy came back shortly carrying the grease cups. The old gentleman laid them down, took a thread gauge out of the drawer in his desk, and said, "Now we will try this gauge on all these cups which you made. The cups that take the gauge easily we will put on the Go sheet. Those that don't we will put on the Out sheet."

When he had finished testing all the cups there were very few on the Go sheet; the Out sheet held most of them. Then Leland took some of those which did not meet the thread requirements and ran his finger around the top edge, revealing a collection of raw brass splinters. "Here's another thing," he commented. "We don't like to have owners of Cadillac cars getting brass splinters in their fingers when they fill their grease cups."

The grease-cup manufacturer got up saying, "This trip has been worth a thousand dollars to me and my company. I am going back home and tear that place apart and we are going to make grease cups that Cadillac can use. Then I will be back."

When the Timken Axle salesmen bought a car after that he

bought a Cadillac, for he reasoned that if Mr. Leland was that particular about insignificant grease cups, it followed that he must be very particular about motors, transmissions and all the rest of Cadillac fittings.[1]

But above and beyond upholding a high standard of workmanship Uncle Henry wanted to attract young men to the mechanical field where he felt that a great opportunity existed. In his frequent talks to them he tried to dramatize the role of the mechanic in what he called the art of production.

"In order to be successful in business in any line," Leland told a group at the Westminster Presbyterian Church on October 30, 1910, "especially anything pertaining to manufacturing, the chief objective must be the art of production in the most advantageous manner possible. This means study—thought—work. It is marvelous what has been accomplished in this line, and yet this particular feature has in no case been exhausted; in fact, we have only touched the high points."

Then he continued with the miracle of manufacturing.

> If you take a ton of iron ore from the ground, remote from a railroad, it is worth very little. Take this ore any place where it is accessible to a railroad or a boat, and it is still worth very little. If you take it to a smelter and put it into pig iron, it is worth from fifteen to twenty dollars per ton. Put that same ton of ore into steel bars, and it is worth fifty dollars a ton. But if you then put it through fine automatic screw machines and develop little screws, so small that it is necessary to use a microscope to see them, for use in holding jewels in watches, the same ton is worth thirty thousand dollars.[2]

As the automobile industry grew, one of its gravest problems was the recruitment of skilled machinists. These essential workmen had to fashion the tools, dies, jigs, which would make possible the division of the final manufacturing process into the small, routine, repeated mass operations performed by unskilled workers.

In this field as in so many others, Henry Leland was the first to take steps to alleviate the shortage and provide an opportunity for ambitious workmen to make their services more valuable and worthy of higher wages. As soon as the Cadillac balance sheet began showing a little weight on the profit side he organized the Cadillac

School of Applied Mechanics, which first opened its doors in May, 1907.

In the foreword of the catalog of this school Henry Leland wrote:

> Ours has now become pre-eminently a manufacturing country, and with the unprecedented development of our great industrial life the supply of broad-minded, well-equipped men, who are capable of taking leading positions has fallen so far short of the demand that manufacturing progress frequently halts.
>
> First-class and important positions await those who have the right character and training. Never before has the call for well-trained men been so insistent, and never before has the response been so meager.[3]

Opposed as he was to unions, Leland attributed the diminished supply of mechanical experts to the hostility of labor unions to the apprenticeship system. There was another reason.

> The present manufacturing system—in which employees specialize upon one certain operation or process—has produced operators who become adept within a narrow field, but this practice has at the same time limited the ability and vision of men who with broader training would develop into master mechanics and thoroughly informed executives. Very few men are now being given all-around training which is imperative in those who hold commanding positions.[4]

So a school was devised to train master mechanics. There was no precedent for such a school. No educator was consulted. The whole thing was the brain child of Henry Leland.

> The contribution of the Cadillac Motor Car Company to this social and industrial need of the future is the Cadillac School of Applied Mechanics. . . . Its graduates are at least first-class mechanics, drilled in the practice and theory of mechanical construction as applied to the automobile industry, and among them will be many, if our hopes are realized, who will forge ahead to distinguished positions of leadership and responsibility. For this purpose the Cadillac School of Applied Mechanics was founded and maintained. It is no more an institution for personal profit or advantage than is the public school. It is provided by the Cadillac Motor Car Company for the benefit of the community, the industry and the country as a whole.[5]

Applications were invited from those who could comply with the following definite admission requirements. As was to be expected, character standards were set.

1. Students must be of good moral character. Smoking cigarettes, chewing tobacco or using intoxicating liquor in any form during the two year course is positively prohibited.
2. Applicants must be at least 18 years of age. [The age was later reduced to 16.]
3. We require that all applicants understand and are able satisfactorily to add, subtract, multiply and divide both decimals and common fractions.
4. We much prefer applicants who have had at least two or three months of shop experience.

The course required 6000 hours, or approximately two years, during which time the students were given thorough experience in bench work, drilling, milling, lathe work, chassis assembling, motor assembling and toolroom. Some, depending on their proficiency and also on their ambition, received experience in the gear-cutting, drafting and screw-machine departments. An additional course of 3000 hours was available for enrollees who expressed "an honest desire" to remain with the Cadillac Motor Car Company at least two years. Elementary students were not required to remain at Cadillac.

Some class work was included on one day each week. After preliminary instruction the students worked in the regular departments under the foremen, but they had to be excused for their classes. This arrangement often irked the foremen who had a lot of work to get out, but the rule was rigid and not to be broken. If the foreman did not come around and excuse the student, it was the boy's duty to ask.

Thus did the Lelands set up their Cadillac school for applied mechanics. It was the first school of its kind in the automotive industry. There was a great deal of emphasis on mathematics, particularly on trigonometry. Samuel F. Wilson, who was taken out of the job of toolroom inspector to become an instructor, had to study his mathematics when he first went into the school, as his educational background was meager.[6] He had been an apprentice at Great Lakes Engineering before he became a master machinist and he had supplemented this experience with night-school courses in mathematics. Subjects stressed, inclusive of shop practice, were mechanical drawing, blueprints and some general physics; other points emphasized were character building and rules for success. One wonders not at all that the last-named subjects were considered worthy of mention in the catalog along with machine design and cost calculations. In his talks to young men, these rules were a common theme for Henry Leland. His theory was that the one essential ingredient of success was mastery of one's self as well as of one's job.

The methods taught in the school took priority over those sometimes used by older master workmen in the shop. Even in its few years of history, automobile manufacturing had changed a great deal. For one example, irons and steels had changed. The method of tool grinding on hard steels was quite different from what it had been with wrought iron in earlier days. More strength was needed behind the cutting edge. The students were taught the latest and best techniques.

The school attracted applicants from all over the United States as well as from Detroit. One such student, Lot A. Merrill, highly appreciative of the opportunity, told of his experience.[7] One of several sons of a widowed mother, he had worked in the lumber camps of upper Wisconsin and had little formal schooling. He had taken several courses from a correspondence school. Having read in a magazine about the Cadillac school, he came to Detroit at the age of twenty-one and made application to enter. Up to that time he had seen but one automobile, a Pierce Arrow, which some tourists had brought to the lake resort kept by his mother. The young man had always been interested in machines and this course seemed to him a great chance to learn more, without any expense on his part. His application was accepted; he found room and board for $4.50 per week within a few blocks of the Cadillac plant; and his future was settled. He married the sister of a fellow student and remained in the various shops of the Detroit automobile plants all his life.

Merrill's roommate, Paul P. Vlasek, came from North Dakota and turned out to be one of the more ambitious students. He took supplementary courses at night and eventually succeeded Mark B. Hughes when that first supervisor of the school was obliged to retire on account of ill health.

The students were paid for the hours spent in classroom work as well as for their time working in the shop. In the first years the rate was 11 cents an hour. Since the hours were from 6:30 to 11:30 a.m. and from 12:30 to 5:30 p.m., five days a week and from 6:30 to 12:30 on Saturday, the weekly total was fifty-six hours and the weekly wage $6.16. Wages were increased one cent an hour every six months.[8]

Some years later the wages of the students were advanced to fifteen cents and the daily hours decreased to nine per day with five on Saturday. While the wages may seem small, they should be considered in relation to the general wage level of that time when the average worker received about 30 cents an hour. Mr. Wilson, as toolroom inspector, remembered that he was paid as much as 45 cents an hour.

The student might increase his income by winning one of a number of prizes offered. Every six months nine prizes ranging from $10 to $50 were given for top marks. Marks were based on the student's shop efficiency and his grade on the six-month examination. His shop efficiency rating depended not only on his mechanical ability but also on his perseverance, tactfulness and character. Prizes were also given for attendance, $15 for not losing any time or being late for six months; $100 for not being absent or tardy throughout the entire 6000-hour course. This prize was not won until 1914, when Joseph F. Briske managed the feat. Theodore Stec won it in 1915. As is evident from all these provisions, the Lelands wished to encourage the virtues of promptness and reliability as well as good clean habits.

This matter of no smoking was not only a matter of qualifying for entrance to the school; it was also the rule of the factory.* One of the students was seen by a supervisor smoking on Woodward Avenue. He was called in and asked if he smoked. When he denied it he was asked to show his hands, and the tell-tale yellow stains gave him away. After a stern lecture he promised to give up his "coffin-nails."

* This was the rule of not only the Cadillac factory but also the Ford Motor Company. Henry Ford never relaxed this rule. However, the Lelands provided a smoking room for employees when they built the Lincoln factory in 1917–18.

The 1915 catalog of the Cadillac school of applied mechanics gives a tabulation of the wages received by its graduates, setting down the statistical proof of the superior earning ability of such skilled craftsmen.

Highest wages per week being received by one graduate	$100.00
Average wage per week of five highest	44.93
Average wage per week of ten highest	35.85
Average wage per week of all graduates reporting	
1st year after graduation	15.85
2nd " " "	20.77
3rd " " "	21.50
4th " " "	21.05
5th " " "	23.19
6th " " "	27.71

During his last week at the school each student was instructed two hours each morning in the art of driving a car. Sydney Handyside, a graduate of 1915, remembered learning to drive on a dual-control, V-8 Cadillac, the new model of that year.[9]

The boys, particularly the younger ones, were encouraged to work at Cadillac after completing their course and many of them did. However, the alumni list of 1915 shows a number employed at Dodge Bros., Hudson Motors and Studebaker Corporation as well as one or two at each of the many other tool shops of Detroit. One was working at the Ford Motor Company. In this respect at least Cadillac contributed its methods and techniques to the motor-car industry quite generally.

There is no doubt that this was the first school of the kind in Detroit as Samuel Wilson, who was an instructor at Cadillac, was also later an instructor in the preliminary phases of the Ford trade school, a larger and better-known institution. The whole experience of Wilson is interesting, demonstrating as it does the need for machinists for the burgeoning automobile industry and the ease with which a master machinist could find employment.

After he had finished his apprenticeship, he went to work at the Ford Motor Company but left when the company moved to Highland Park from the plant at Piquette and Brush in Detroit (January 1910).[10] He had lived within walking distance of the Piquette plant and disliked the crowded streetcars he must take to reach Highland

MAKING MECHANICS 127

Park. He also disliked the location of the Ford toolroom so near the fumes of the motor-testing room. So he quit and went over to apply for a job at Packard. He was offered a job on the night shift but he had never worked that shift and before accepting decided to try at Cadillac. There Wilson stood in a long line of men waiting at the door of the employment office. When the official in charge came out Wilson called, "Need a toolmaker?" and was motioned up to the door.

When Ernest G. Liebold, a friend of Wilson's, told him of an experimental job on an electric car at Fords, the machinist went back to the Ford Motor Company. This work went on in an old barn on the Highland Park plant grounds and Henry Ford often came and talked with the four or five men working there. When the project was discontinued Wilson was transferred into the toolroom in the plant, apparently in the spring of 1915, because he remembered that in the special work he had been doing he was not classified as a Ford Motor Company employee and therefore did not have the necessary six months' service to qualify for the five dollars a day, when that policy was announced.

When it was learned that Wilson had been an instructor at Cadillac, there was talk of starting such a school at Ford. Pete Martin, factory superintendent at the Highland Park plant, consulted Wilson and set aside a room for a school. Here the idea was to give some instruction to the machinist's helpers, who were just hanging around in the toolroom, not learning much from observation. Worse, sometimes this observation taught them obsolete methods. So Wilson went through the factory choosing various types of machines which were set up in a room on the balcony, and the school began. Some time later, in the fall of 1916, Henry Ford brought in some younger boys from the state vocational school, and the Henry Ford trade school was formally organized.[11]

Wilson was then sent to the Ford Rouge plant to pick out machines and set them up for an apprentice school there. Charles Sorenson, who resented any ideas originating from the men at Highland Park, scorned the idea and began needling and ridiculing Wilson. As the harassment persisted Wilson quit in disgust. But from that time down to the present the big motor-car manufacturers have maintained in-service schools of one kind or another.

Chapter XI
The Self-Starter

FIFTY YEARS AGO the ritualistic routine of starting the engine of an automobile required finesse, strength and agility. First a check must be made to see if the engine was out of gear, for if it shouldn't be the car might well run over anyone in front of it when the motor started. Second, the spark must be retarded and the throttle advanced to an extent known only after long experience with that particular motor. Finally, the motor must be turned over with the hand crank—one or two turns if the luck was very good but usually many turns until, with the operator's patience and strength almost spent, the spark caught and the motor fired. Then the cranker must spring quickly to the controls at the steering wheel to advance the spark and retard the throttle, before the engine died and the whole maneuver had to be repeated.

Even though this routine might be carefully followed there remained a further hazard and one widely recognized. That was the danger of a backfire in the motor and a consequent backward kick of the crank. To the problem section of an early automobile magazine came this query: "Dear Editor: I am the owner of a new car and although it may sound foolish I am what the old Indian chief would call Young-Man-Afraid-of-His-Car. Every time I start to crank it, visions of a cracked wrist flash through my brain and I flinch. Can you reassure me as to the chances of danger while cranking a car?"

This query was taken seriously and answered in detail with two pictures showing how the crank should be held in starting a car. "The chances of danger are practically nil if you take hold of the starting crank in the manner shown at B. Fig. 1 (fingers folded about handle with thumb overlapping first fingers) instead of the way shown at A. Fig. 2 (thumb hooked around the shank attached to the crank handle): Always pull up on the crank, never push down. It is even better to always use the left hand. In this way should a backfire result you will be unhurt; the crank simply unbending your fingers as it flies back. If you are so nervous as to still be afraid, buy a self-starter or a safety starting crank." [1]

Under such circumstances it was not surprising that few women drove cars without an attendant strong arm somewhere among the passengers. But one who did started a chain reaction that solved this whole finicky, difficult, dangerous operation.

On a December day of 1910 this intrepid woman drove alone through Belle Isle Park in Detroit. Approaching one of the numerous bridges on the island, she took the incline too slowly and stalled her motor. A kindly passing motorist, seeing her difficulty, stopped to help by cranking the motor for her. Not realizing the spark had not been retarded, the good Samaritan turned the crank and the motor back-fired. Lashing back, the crank broke his arm and smashed his face and jaw.

Within a few minutes came another car containing two Cadillac engineers, Ernest Sweet and Bill Foltz who, with their wives, were also driving about the island. Seeing the injured man, they stopped to assist. They started the woman's car, sent her home and took the man, Byron T. Carter of the Carter-car Co., to the hospital. Although Mr. Carter's broken jaw and arm did not seem to be serious injuries, he never recovered, dying within a few weeks of pneumonia.

When the engineers reported the accident to the Lelands, H.M. was disturbed. "I'm sorry I ever built an automobile," he burst out.

"Those vicious cranks! I won't have Cadillacs hurting people that way!" The more he thought about it the more it bothered him. He had been improving his car steadily but now no other improvement was so urgent as some kind of mechanical starter.

This was not to say that starters had not been built and were not in use. There had been a number of them offered for sale and some used here and there. The Winton automobile had had a compressed air starter for several years.[2] Some of the foreign-car manufacturers had pioneered starters as early as 1905.[3] Yet none of these devices had proved very practical or dependable, and they had drawn little attention from the buying public.

The engineers of the Cadillac organization were called together to a conference that was something more than the usual daily morning session. Not only were Frank Johnson and Ernest Sweet there, but also Lyle Snell, Fred Hawes, Herman Schwarze, D. T. Randall, Herman Zannoth and R. T. Wingo. Henry Leland, with eyes glittering and voice husky, told them they had a big job to do. "The Cadillac car will kill no more men if we can help it. Lay all the other projects aside. We are going to develop a fool-proof device for starting Cadillac motors."

The engineers went to work with a will. Many attempts had already been made, so there were plenty of half-successes and total failures to work on. There had been many patents taken out on starters, one by Thomas Alva Edison more than a dozen years before.[4] Ralph Lewis and his father, who owned the first Cadillac show room in Boston and retailed and serviced foreign cars as well, became familiar with a self-starter on the French car, De Dion-Buton. It did not work well and at times would not start the motor at all. They tinkered around with it trying to improve it. At the same time Lewis corresponded with another would-be inventor who was working on a self-starter. This fellow, Charles E. Wilson, was destined to become the president of General Motors.[5]

On the basis of these trials and half-achievers the engineers went to work. They soon concluded that an electrical device was the only one that could be relied on to give dependable results. They had learned a good deal about using electricity for power on Wilfred

Leland's country estate on Lake Angelus, Oakland County, Michigan. Wilfred explained this:

In early 1910, I had purchased a large tract of land on the shores of Lake Angelus. At that time no electric power had reached that area, and we were compelled to create our own electric current. A power house was erected close to the lake and a large battery house nearby. The main line shaft was driven by a four-cylinder Cadillac motor. The generator, driven by that line shaft, kept a large room full of electric batteries properly charged. Those batteries supplied current for the electric lights in the residence, the large garage, the superintendent's bungalow, and five other buildings on the property. They also supplied the lights for nearly a mile of roadways. The power house equipment supplied spring water to all the buildings and lake water to the lawns and to vegetable and flower gardens.

Having had the experience which was involved in keeping all those batteries functioning properly, the engineers realized that suitable batteries would do all that was required of them in operating the starting device and that the generator would keep the batteries properly charged. The work of developing and perfecting the starter went forward with dispatch.

The engineers pooled their ideas, argued out their premises and tested their theories. Ralph Lewis, curious about the development of the starter, asked Frank Johnson, "How did you fellows happen to cut teeth in the periphery of the fly wheel?" It had seemed no great idea to Frank. He answered, "It was just the natural thing to do."

The day came when Mr. Sweet brought to the front office the good news that all the principles had been worked out, difficulties had been overcome, and tests proved that before long Cadillac cars could be equipped with a good self-starter. The day after Wilfred Leland told Earl C. Howard, assistant sales-manager at Cadillac, that he was soon going to need a new sales pitch, for the engineering department had designed an electric-starting device which would start the motor of the Cadillac car and do away with hand cranking. He added that the only problem was that the experimental motor used to work out the idea was too large to install under the hood of a car and a smaller motor would have to be built.

Mr. Howard then recalled that when he had worked at the National Cash Register Company of Dayton, Ohio, Charles Kettering, an engineer there, had invented a very small electric motor for operating cash registers. Perhaps Mr. Kettering's experience with small motors might be helpful to Cadillac. Pleased with the suggestion Wilfred went straight to the telephone, called Kettering in Dayton and explained the problem. Kettering came to Detroit the next day, went over the starting device with the Cadillac engineers, and agreed to work out the smaller motor.

As Kettering himself said, "We didn't make the automobile self-starter as a piece of electrical apparatus first. We made it as a piece of automobile first and as an electrical device second." [6] It was a happy combination: the starter worked out by the Cadillac engineers and the motor that Kettering had worked out for the cash register. As it turned out Kettering was able to use the motor he had devised for the cash register.

> Kettering developed a different kind of motor, one with extra high turning power for its size and a clutch for engaging the mechanism of the cash register and then releasing it at just the right time. . . . His new clutch was called an over-running clutch, and some years later he used it again and also the principle of a small motor with high torque effect, in the electric starter.[7]

Came the day when the engineers had the starter ready for installation and Kettering arrived in Detroit with the motor. The apparatus was complete and the whole group stood waiting rather breathlessly to witness the turning of the motor when the switch was pressed. All the engineers who had had a hand in the creation were present on that momentous day, February 27, 1911. The switch was thrown; the motor throbbed instantly into life. It was a great satisfaction. The Lelands, father and son, shook hands with and congratulated everyone present, Kettering included. Mr. K. said on that occasion, "I am very glad to have had an opportunity to be of some help in this important development, but the Cadillac engineers deserve the chief credit." Many times Henry Leland gave Kettering credit. "We had previously discovered a young and generally unknown electrical genius living in Dayton, Ohio, named Charles F. Kettering and to Mr. Kettering is largely due the credit for success of the electrical application of the device." [8] It was a happy co-operation for everybody.*

The earlier discovery of the young electrical genius had resulted in the use of his ignition system on the Cadillac, beginning in 1910. But now with the electrical application of the starter, which he had devised, why not go farther? The ignition was powered by a battery, why not take the acetylene tank off the running board and give the Cadillac electric lights too? All these things could be incorporated into one electrical system. Now there was an even bigger job for the electrical engineer, and Kettering went at it eagerly in his laboratories. The Cadillac engineers, particularly Mr. Sweet and Mr. Owen, made many trips to Dayton before the plans for the 1912 Cadillac were complete.

At this time, the Lelands, deeply involved in the rehabilitation of General Motors, were straining every nerve to increase their production. Already in 1909 they had been running a night shift and the capacity of the plant had now been about reached.[9] Expansion was imperative, but that was a step which could be authorized only by General Motors which, in this first year under the bankers' rule, was cutting down rather than expanding. Hence the contract for

* Wilfred Leland in his older days felt that historians and writers generally continued to give Mr. Kettering more honor in regard to the self-starter than was his due. When some of the statements in *The Turning Wheel* by Arthur Pound (p. 272) were brought to his attention, he wrote a letter to Mr. Kettering in which he set down his knowledge and understanding of the events leading to the presentation of an electric starter on the 1912 Cadillac. Mr. Kettering replied on May 24, 1946.

"I have your letter of May 21 enclosing your write-up of the conception, development and installation of the starting device on Cadillac cars. This looks O.K. to me and I am returning it herewith."

In reality the Cadillac electric self-starter was a rather simple mechanism and probably none of the engineers who worked on it felt that it incorporated any startling invention or radical innovation. The introduction of an electric starter on the 1912 Cadillac proved to be a great commercial coup. It was only later that advertising geniuses began billing it as the brilliant conception of a master inventor.

5,000 of the combined starting, lighting and ignition systems was given to the Dayton Engineering Laboratories Co. Said Wilfred Leland:

> We stipulated that they could not sell the starters, which we had created, to any other manufacturer. Cadillac must have the exclusive right to the electric starting device for one year. This was a perfectly justifiable stipulation, since we had conceived and developed the starter. After that first year we would give our consent that other automobile manufacturers might use the starter. This for the good of the industry.

Wilfred Leland was at that time Chairman of the patents committee of the National Automobile Chamber of Commerce. The committee was working out the cross-licensing agreement which was later adopted between the chamber and each individual member. This was in effect a reciprocal exchange of patents and designs within the industry without payment of fees and royalties. The National Automobile Chamber of Commerce patent pool finally went into effect in January 1915 with ten years to run. Some ninety concerns were in it, each contributing ten or twelve patents, making about 1,000 patents in the pool. All were available to the use of any or everyone in the Pool.[10] This arrangement made possible the unprecedented growth of the automobile industry unhampered by lawsuits and restrictions. It facilitated continuous improvement, each advance being built on past developments available to all.

The perfecting of the starting, lighting and ignition system took much experimentation and testing. Rumors of the revolutionary changes to be made in the 1912 Cadillac ran wild throughout Detroit and the automobile industry. When finally the new equipment fulfilled the rigid standards of Cadillac and Henry Leland the announcement was made.

> Detroit, August 20, 1911. Formal announcement of the 1912 Cadillac, awaited with interest by the entire trade for some time, has been made at last, and reports of radical innovations, current for some time, as a matter of gossip, were confirmed in part. According to the announcement, the new Cadillacs will be equipped with an electric device capable of automatically starting the motor. The device is on the storage battery principle, a dynamo generating electricity being attached to the motor.

THE SELF-STARTER

The starting device is operated by retarding the spark lever and pushing down gently on the clutch. It is said that the battery when charged, is capable of turning the motor 20 minutes. When the motor starts its explosions, the electric device stores up current until fully charged, when it automatically cuts off from the motor. As an ignition device, the Cadillac's equipment will furnish a spark at slow speeds for the storage battery at 300 r.p.m. The apparatus shifts automatically and furnishes the spark through the high-tension system.[11]

This announcement set off a burst of activity among the automobile manufacturers. Velie, Everitt, Pullman and Chalmers all announced the introduction of a compressed air self-starter on their cars. Everybody had suddenly decided that the public was weary of standing in the mud and turning over a heavy motor. The Cole Motor Car Co. announced that its 1912 cars would be equipped with an acetylene starter. The Hupp Motor Car Co. came out with a splashing ad proclaiming that it would be the first to offer a self-starter with a touring car under the $1000 price.

While all this activity seemed to denote that this was the self-starter year, there was no agreement on which was the most desirable kind. One shrewd journalist wrote:

> Despite the sudden and pronounced "arrival" of the self-starter in the form of compressed air starters, gasoline starters, acetylene starters and spring starters, to say nothing of others more or less worthy, it has been a matter of comment that there has appeared in commercial shape but one starter in which an electric motor is used to rotate the crank shaft, notwithstanding the theoretical beauties of such an arrangement.[12]

This last reference was, of course, to the Cadillac. Even the astute engineer, Howard Coffin, guessed wrong. Speaking before an assemblage of English engineers in London on November 15, 1911, he stated that few American cars of any power or price would go into the next season without self-starting motors. He added that, although six months before the electric generating outfit had looked like a walk-away for lighting, this threat of competition had brought gas-lamp improvements. These, he predicted, with the use of the acetylene self-starter augured well for the retention of the gas light in combination.[13] Mr. Coffin was wrong in his prediction but it was a year or so before that could be demonstrated.

As it was so late in the season when Cadillac upset the whole industry with the starter announcement, some manufacturers were unable to supply starters and attempted to meet this competitive thrust by spreading rumors that the Cadillac device was unseasoned and would cause endless trouble. Ran the gossip, probably every car would have to be sent back to the factory as such a "half-baked invention" could not possibly be reliable. Worse yet were the reports that people had been electrocuted in such electrically equipped cars and that lightning was apt to strike them.[14]

The finance committee of General Motors, with a nervous ear out for any flighty adventures into unknown and untried waters, heard the rumors. Cadillac might be their best, most reliable component, but this was no time for any company to get itself out on a limb which might have to be cut off, at great expense. The committee went to the General Electric Company and requested that three capable and experienced engineers be selected to make a thorough test of this electrical system. The three engineers were chosen, one from General Electric, one from Westinghouse and one from Haltske Co.[15]

As his father was away Wilfred Leland received the deputation of engineers when they called at the Cadillac plant. They announced their mission and outlined the task that had been assigned to them.

They listed ten features of the system which they feared might make trouble. Of this episode, Wilfred wrote:

> I called the Cadillac engineers together and the visitors explained the tests they wished to make. It was evident that in order to convince them of the worthiness of the device and dispel their fears of its workability, a great amount of equipment would be necessary and at least two days of time. The materials were brought in promptly that afternoon and the testing started the next morning. I telephoned Mr. Kettering to let him know what was going on and to give him an opportunity to be present since he was at that time filling the order for the starters, etc. as given him previously.[16]

By the end of the first day, seven of the tests had been run and these, with the lucid explanations of the Cadillac engineers, had convinced the examiners that so far their fears were groundless. Mr. Kettering arrived on the second day and witnessed the performing of the last three tests, which also turned out to the complete satisfaction of the investigating group. The electrical system was approved.

One wishes the date of this test had survived so it could be known whether it was after this that General Motors decided to allot over a million dollars to purchase land, buildings and equipment to extend the Cadillac plant. At any rate this capital expenditure was listed in the annual report of General Motors issued in November 1911.[17]

Cadillac was desperately squeezed for space. In 1909 when it was running to capacity, 5902 cars were built; in 1910, 8006 cars; and in 1911, 10,019. When the demand increased for the 1912 car, with its self-starter, Cadillac found itself in a very difficult situation. The winter was snowy and the weather bad. Railroad cars were not readily available. President Neal of General Motors complained and threatened, "If freight service does not improve, the Cadillac Motor Car Co., one of the largest and most important of the General Motors group of plants, will choose some other city as a location for the large additional plant the company is about to build." [18] In April new Cadillac cars were standing along the streets everywhere in the vicinity of the plant. Although the freight service did improve with spring and several loading stations were built along the railroad, as late as July building operations were only "about" to begin and Cadillac was using an immense tent near the plant to shelter part of its operations.[19] By such makeshift means, Cadillac built 13,994 cars in 1912. The price of the touring car with all of its new equipment was still $1975.

Besides the immediate public demand for this "self-starting, self-lighting, self-igniting" car, a second recognition of the superiority of the Cadillac electrical system was the adoption of it under the name of Delco by other companies.[20] The 1913 models of Hudson, Packard, Cole, Oldsmobile, Oakland and Jackson all used the system. By 1914 cars using generators and batteries rather than magnetos included, besides the General Motors cars, Chalmers, Peerless, Regal, Reo, Studebaker, etc., altogether 33 makes.[21] For the simple, logical, workable starter had definitely nudged the whole industry into a new direction. Wrote one perceptive reporter as early as December 1911:

> Every car manufacturer who already has not adopted a self-starter is on the hunt for one. But the available starters made at prices that permit their use on low-priced cars are of types calling for the use of a spark to ignite gas in the motor cylinders and as everyone knows, a magneto in a state of quiescence is of no use whatever as a spark producer. In order to retain the magneto, the car-maker must either add a battery and its accessories to his ignition system or use a more expensive type of starting device. Either course will entail an added outlay that will be serious, and so there is but one course open apparently—to do away with the magneto and substitute a battery system for the ignition and starter. It looks just now as if this very thing would happen, and that before long. In fact, one manufacturer has already made the move, and I know of several others who are considering it with wrinkled brows. It is one of the most unlooked for situations that has developed in a long time and that was apparently unthought of until the self-starter really arrived.[22]

Some manufacturers hung on to their magnetos for some years—Henry Ford until after World War I—but generally the change came rapidly. The importance of the pioneering Cadillac system was recognized. On November 10, 1936, Wilfred Leland, with 250 leaders of the automobile industry, attended a banquet at the Waldorf Astoria in New York. At that anniversary celebration the center of attraction was a 1912 Cadillac car equipped with one of the first electric-starting devices. The car stood on a large platform covered with royal purple plush and illuminated by floodlights. On another pedestal also floodlighted stood a complete Cadillac electric starter. The message on the placard read, "This simple mechanism became the cornerstone of the modern motor-car industry."

Fred Bennett in England dramatized the Cadillac starter by building a tiny 4-foot wheel base car, powered entirely by the Cadillac starter. This midget would travel 12 miles an hour and would operate 15 miles on one battery charge. At the various auto shows in Europe the car ran round and round the exhibition floor and then when the shows were over the Bennett children drove it in the public park near the royal palace.

One day a member of the royal family saw the car and made inquiries about it. The result was that Queen Alexandra bought it for her grandson, Prince Olaf of Norway. When Wilfred Leland heard this story he asked to have a similar car made for his small son's birthday. By the time Bennett got around to build it Prince Olaf had outgrown the car and a larger one was ordered for him. So the original car was sent over for Wilfred Jr., on his fifth birthday.

The Royal Automobile Club was also interested in the new features of the Cadillac and tested them separately in 1912. Complete tests in 1913 on a 1914 Cadillac brought the accolade of the Club and the award of the Dewar trophy for the second time, the only time the trophy had been won twice by the same make of car. In this trial, "Observation was not directed to the behavior of the car as a whole but to its special features as embodied in all 1914 Cadillacs, viz., electric lighting, engine starting, electric ignition, two-speed back axle with electric change mechanism." [23] This last feature, which had been added in 1913, did not prove popular and was soon discarded.

Chapter XII
New Lines, More Power

BY 1913 TWENTY YEARS had passed since Frank Duryea had driven the first American-made automobile in Springfield, Massachusetts. Through the next ten years he and other persistent experimenters brought their hand-wrought vehicles to the point where industrial production was possible. In the second decade the factories had poured out such an increasing stream of automobiles that this manufacture had developed into the sixth largest industry of the nation. Already there were one million-and-a-quarter registered automobiles in the country and the production of 1913 would add to that figure half a million more.[1]

The swift crescendo of demand and the production to meet it was to have an enormous impact on America and its social patterns. From the very beginning the automobile demanded more adequate roadways so it might get away from the pavements of the cities to the country in all kinds of weather. Motorists and their automobile clubs waged a constant campaign for better highways. Narrow strips of pavement crept out beyond the city limits and construction engineers argued the merits of macadam and cement, the depth of the road bed and the width of the pavement. In 1913 the Lincoln Highway Association was formed with the idea of establishing a trans-country road, ocean to ocean, properly built, following easy grades and fitted with bridges and road signs and free to all travelers. The long campaign for this highway proved a great educational project and, though the road was never finished under its original name, the result was a national awareness of the necessity for a comprehensive road system and the gradual assumption of government responsibility for and supervision over the construction of highways.[2] The consequent ease of travel made the United States not only a more mobile but also a more homogeneous nation.

In the early years of motor-car manufacture the chief attention of the fabricators had centered on finding efficient methods and systems for the manufacture of a reliable vehicle. By 1910 this had been accomplished and the following years were to see the industry take other directions. Henry Ford would extend the automobile market enormously by building the Model T to serve the less well-to-do. The rest of the manufacturers would follow a more traditional course; they would perfect and refine their product. Competing fiercely with one another, they would make their cars more convenient, more powerful and more beautiful.

Ford dominated the low-priced market, with a car selling for as little as $590 in 1911. The medium-priced field, $635 to $1500, was occupied, in the order of the size of their production, by Willys-Overland, Buick, Hupmobile and Reo. Higher-priced cars, $1500 to $2500, were produced by Cadillac, Chalmers, Hudson and Oakland. In luxury cars, priced above $2500, the market was divided among Packard, Pierce Arrow, White, Franklin, Winton and Locomobile.[3]

The more expensive car makers were naturally the leaders in the adaptation and evolution of the motor car. Each manufacturer tried to outdo the other and set the pace or the fashion, which would trickle quickly down to the less-expensive models. Annual auto shows were awaited with anticipation, and lucky indeed was the car that gained the favor of the buying public. The 1912 Cadillac with its self-starter was one of the rousing successes. Sometimes the improvement that seemed most inconsequential was received with enthusiasm; other promising innovations were ignored. Hence any study of the evolution of motor cars is also a study in social patterns and the twists and turns of public opinion.

For some years the argument between the right-hand and the left-hand drive had been going on. The driver on the right was admittedly in the best position to draw up alongside the curb and park. But was he in the best position to get around a slow-moving cart or street-car on a city street? On a country road which side of the car was the more dangerous one? Was it more important to keep an eye on the ditch at the right or on the passing traveler on the left? Certainly in the beginning the ditch was the great hazard, as there were few other cars to be passed, and the horse and buggy were already in the ditch. But as the roads in the country got better and wider, the ditch was not so close. On the other hand, motor traffic had increased and other cars were met often. It was probably better to go into the ditch than to be side-swiped.

In cities the discussion moved on to the matter of getting the passengers, or more particularly the passenger in the front seat, out of the car when it stopped at the curb. The driver on the right got out handily but the passenger, lady or not, must disembark on the left in the face of traffic; and the gallant driver must go around into the traffic and hand out the lady in this exposed, unprotected position. One writer-in to a newspaper argued seriously that the motor car with a left-hand drive put a premium on rudeness, as it was an invitation to the driver to get in first and let his passenger scramble in later unaided. But the actual reason that the steering wheel remained on the right was the necessity for the driver to get out again and again to crank the motor. This necessity eliminated, the change-over to the left-hand drive took place rapidly.

This change made other problems since the gear shift and hand brake must come up through the floor at either the right or left of the driver. Should they be put in the center of the car or must the operator manipulate the levers with his left hand? Different makers tried various positions; but as the motor age advanced and traffic thickened the steering wheel became fixed on the left with the manual controls in the center of the car.

The Cadillac, in the forefront with mechanical inventions, was a little slow on these matters of style. The right-hand drive was retained until 1915, although a hinged steering wheel, used for several years previously, made it easier for a passenger to get into the car from curb-side by sliding under the wheel.

Electric lighting, while eliminating the need for the driver to get out and light the lamps when the sun went down, also brought complications. The lighting of lamps was a great chore and not many drove at night unless it was unavoidable. As an advertisement put it, "Perhaps you yourself have driven down town, along about five o'clock at night on a fall day, been detained and come out at six o'clock in gusty winds and tried to light your gas and oil lamps. One day I used twenty-six matches in getting my lamps alight." [4] The new electric lights were most convenient but they were so bright they dazzled the oncoming motorist. In country driving this hazard was pretty well ignored, but cities began passing restrictive ordinances. Drivers coming into the city would get out and tie handkerchiefs over the lamps or even paste paper over the glass. Cadillac took care of the glare by equipping its cars with tilt-beam headlights in 1915.

Thus while the first cycle of motor-car development concerned itself with these mechanical matters which made the motor car a reliable form of transportation, this second phase was dedicated to making it safer, more comfortable and better looking as well as more economical. Though many conveniences and attractions would be added to automobiles, improved methods of manufacture would decrease the cost of making them. The Ford Motor Co. was undoubtedly the bell-wether in this regard. The pressure there was steady for economy in production, floorspace and man-power. The product was standardized and changed little from year to year, the demand seemed endless and price reductions were made almost annually. Hence the attention of the management centered on factory systems and processes which would reduce costs. Time studies were instituted; conveyors, belts, overhead trolleys and all kinds of devices for handling materials were invented and installed. The culmination was the moving assembly line which, in one huge, flowing, concentrated effort, put the thousands of parts together and turned out a completed car every two minutes. Thus it was that what had before been merely quantity production became mass production.[5]

Undoubtedly other manufacturers followed where Ford led in this regard; but in other plants there had not been this overwhelming push toward economy of operation. Outside of Ford and his competitors in price, rivalry between car makers who put out a variety of models concentrated increasingly on power, speed, comfort, beauty and style. Nowhere do we find evidence that Cadillac pioneered any advance in factory management, nor do we find either that methods or system were neglected or became obsolete. Undoubtedly when new buildings were built in 1913 the best of the new methods were planned for and used. It was ever H.M.'s habit to use the best of everything. But the Cadillac car now appealed primarily to the discriminating, and the attention of Henry Leland ran to mechanical innovation and quality rather than to price.

Besides the move towards efficiency in the organization of factory processes at this time there was cost-saving action towards the standardization of car parts common to the cars of all manufacturers. All cars used screws, bolts and washers, for instance, but the sizes all varied from car to car and had to be separately fabricated by the parts supplier. One supplier made 600 different sizes of lock washers; another 1600 sizes of steel tubing. Such practice not only made cars more expensive but also must have caused a great deal of bother and irritation to the motor-car owner when his car needed some simple repair.

The pressure for standardization of parts common to all makes of cars started under the old Association of Licensed Automobile Manufacturers and continued under the aegis of the Society of Automotive Engineers and the National Automobile Chamber of Commerce. A standards committee was set up in 1910 to formulate the standard sizes which were to be adopted gradually by all manufacturers. These formulas concerned such parts as nuts and bolts, cotter pins, lock washers, threads on spark-plug sockets, grease cups, wheel diameters, gasoline and water connections and light-bulb sockets. For instance, the committee found sixteen sizes of lock washers to be sufficient where 600 had been in use.[6] While the utility of such cooperation seems easily demonstrable, it took years to effect this standardization throughout the industry. The Lelands were whole-heartedly in favor of the idea, but the change to standardized parts had to be gradual so it would not render obsolete parts of older Cadillac models. Those well-built early Cadillacs lasted a long time.

Bodies too began to receive attention. The evolution of the automobile body is a most interesting study. The motor car was born a spidery "horseless carriage" contraption perched high on buggy wheels. No wonder the wits called it a "benzine buggy," "joy wagon" or "gasoline bug." Very shortly the motor came out from under the seat and was stuck under a bonnet in front—the designers were still working within the horse-and-buggy concept and put the motive power in front. The riders perched high on the seats, giving the whole rig a top-heavy appearance. Springs and axle stood out in angular, knob-kneed nakedness. It is said that the first bumpers were designed to cover up this bare look rather than for any utilitarian purpose.

Doors appeared on the sides by the back seats. Then they appeared in front, surmounting the objection that the front-seat occupants would suffer from the heat of the motor if air could not circulate freely. Strangely enough, the windshield, which would seem to have been the most obvious of conveniences, was slow to come into use. Perhaps this delay was due to the fact that buggies and wagons had no such equipment and because auto speeds were not great in the beginning. Yet goggles were soon universally worn by motorists and eye troubles were mentioned as one of the health hazards of motoring.

In 1910, when the so-called torpedo body was introduced, the windshield was still considered to be an extra accessory rather than an integral part of the car. The torpedo body was described as one "which had a full height front door and a torpedo or stream line design from the cowl backwards." [7] This new line, as displayed at the annual show by Winton, Franklin, Marmon, White and Cadillac, was hailed as the hit of the year. Although the design was hailed as revolutionary, modern eyes find it hard to see that "torpedoes" were such a sharp break from the past. Undoubtedly the body looked more streamlined with front and back doors, but the incorporation of the hood into the general design was not successful and still stood a section apart. Looking back from the present, it seems the great advance of the year 1910 was the offer, by the Owen manufacturer, of a completely equipped car-top, windshield, electric horn and lights. Heretofore the exclusion of accessories from the list price tended to imply that those things were not necessary equipment. But no one manufacturer up to that time was accepting the idea that comfort and convenience should be offered as an integral element of motoring.

The evolution of the body continued, the door got higher and the seat backs lower, stressing the unbroken horizontal line. The wheels were smaller, the center of gravity lower, and the body covered the naked underpinnings. Radiator hoods, losing the distinction of early makes, came into line with the bodies. In keeping with the boat concept, passengers now sat in cars rather than perched up on them.

The Cadillac changed rather radically in 1912. Its typical car was a four-cylinder "1912" with 116-inch wheel base (compared to a 76-inch wheel base in 1903) and a price of $1975 for the standard five-passenger touring car. This price included the top, windshield, demountable rims, electric lighting and self-starter. The advertising of the Cadillac had changed too. Where before performance and workmanship—"There are 112 parts of the Cadillac which are accurate to one-thousandth of an inch"—had been given the main emphasis, now the appeal changed. "The handsome lines, the deep soft upholstery, the yielding springs, the riding qualities of almost velvety smoothness," were given top billing.

Cadillac had had a smash hit in the self-starter in 1912. The new idea for 1913 was not so well received. On July 12, 1913, an advertisement proclaimed another new and decidedly progressive development in motor-car construction which would distinguish the 1914 Cadillac—a two-speed back axle with an electric-change mechanism. This improvement seems to have attracted little attention and no emulation. All eyes were focused instead on the new six-cylinder motors.

Six cylinders, it was claimed, gave more power, speed and smoother action in the motor. Wilfred Leland said:

> If they had made that longer six-cylinder crankshaft strong enough, and had supported it well enough, they would have obtained the smoother action they talked about in their advertisements. But they did not do that, and those early sixes had a very undesirable periodic vibration at certain speeds. That

NEW LINES, MORE POWER

vibration more than offset the gain that they would have realized, if they had treated the crankshaft properly.

Henry Leland and his engineers went to work to eliminate these deficiencies. Cadillac had first made its reputation on engines, and it did not intend to be surpassed in that field. Attention centered on the matter of supporting the crankshaft so it would be free from those periodic vibrations. Good progress was being made when Wilfred Leland left on one of his monthly trips to New York to preside at a meeting of the National Automobile Chamber of Commerce. The trip was remembered thereafter because of an idea that came to the Cadillac general manager when for a short time he had a chance to ponder the matter uninterrupted.

> On the train I was going over the problem of Sixes versus Fours and the disturbing periodic vibrations with which the six-cylinder manufacturers were contending. I realized the emphasis our competitors were placing on the fact that six smaller cylinders, producing the same maximum power as four larger ones, would result in smaller individual impulses, and consequent smoother action.
>
> I knew that we were having good results with well-balanced four-cylinder motors. I first reasoned that if six light cylinders gave the same maximum power and lighter impulses than the four, then eight still smaller cylinders would give still lighter impulses than the six cylinders. I also reasoned that, because of the lighter weight, those smaller eight cylinder pistons could be run at higher speeds than either sixes or fours. Furthermore I did not like the six crankshaft. If made small enough to be in proportion with those light pistons, the extra length might introduce those undesirable vibrations; if made heavy enough to avoid those periodic vibrations there was the weight problem to contend with.
>
> As I lay awake pondering these factors, the idea came to me that we were having good success with four-cylinder motors; we would surely have equally good results with blocks of lighter four cylinders and pistons. Why not make up those smaller blocks of lighter four cylinders and pistons, and put two of the blocks together at an angle and avoid that troublesome long crankshaft. The more I thought of this idea on that trip, the more convinced I became that it could be worked out.[8]

When Wilfred returned to Detroit the Cadillac completed the more powerful six-cylinder motor in which the objectionable vibrations had been overcome. That was fine. Still Wilfred was intrigued by the idea which had come to him on the train and he told his father about it. H.M. was favorably impressed. He called in the top Cadillac engineers and laid before them what the Lelands believed to be the merits and advantages of the V-eight.

The matter was considered from every angle. The discussion progressed until all present were convinced that it would be wiser to develop an eight-cylinder V-type motor instead of producing the six-cylinder which the engineers had just finished. It would be in the Cadillac tradition to bring out something entirely new rather than just an improvement of another's concept.

As it developed later the V-type eight-cylinder motor was not a new or revolutionary idea, but had been used in France earlier although it had not come to the attention of many American manufacturers. As far as the Lelands were concerned, they had not known of an earlier application of the idea, but that knowledge would have made no difference to them. In his long life in shop and factory Henry Leland knew that an idea meant little unless a practical application could be made of it. Leonardo da Vinci had envisioned many of the principles behind modern machines even to the airplane, but it was hundreds of years before materials and processes could be developed to implement such ideas. It was the constant uninterrupted flow of ideas, processes and improved materials that had built up finally to modern industrial civilization. Any patent or secret process that impeded this was in Henry Leland's mind a roadblock to progress. Hence the Leland ideas were not patented, and the Lelands were enthusiastic supporters of the cross-licensing agreement among automobile manufacturers which was to come into effect in 1915.

Nevertheless, competition being what it was, it was agreed that the development of the V-eight motor would be kept secret until it could be completed and tested. Perhaps the building would not be easy, no matter how bright and promising the idea appeared. Every person at the engineers' conference was pledged to do everything in his power to respect the agreement and keep the proceedings quiet. The Lelands took special measures which Wilfred detailed.

As a first step toward assuring secrecy, H.M. decided that we would not design the motor in the Cadillac Engineering Division. Instead we rented a row of several offices on the 22nd floor of the newly constructed Dime Building, across from the Detroit City Hall and adjoining the corner suite of private offices occupied by my father and myself. The offices were properly equipped for the work to be done, and selected Cadillac engineers were transferred from the plant to do the experimental work. They were instructed to spare no effort, leave no stone unturned, make every possible investigation and maintain the customary exacting standard of Cadillac productions.

The work got off to a satisfactory start, and when it was well under way the Lelands learned that a European manufacturer had made a V-8 type motor and that one had been shipped to this country. Inquiries were set afoot and the motor, presumably a De Dion-Bouton, was located and purchased. The Cadillac engineers found it poorly built by Cadillac standards but found suggestions in it. D. McCall White, an English engineer who came to Cadillac about that time, also worked on the design. He had a drawing of an 8-cylinder motor but was not entirely familiar with all its parts. Having brought all possible knowledge to their aid the engineers labored together and in the end had a fine, workable motor.

Then followed the next step—getting the individual parts of the motor manufactured without giving away the fact that Cadillac was producing an entirely new and revolutionary engine. The Lelands realized that if those parts were made in the Cadillac plant it would be next to impossible to maintain the desired secrecy.

Father well knew the character and ability of many of the New England manufacturing establishments, and many of the heads of those establishments professed deep gratitude for invaluable help he had given them in the past. He wrote six of these gentlemen, explaining that he would be very grateful if each would make for him a certain number of parts which he needed urgently. Each was glad to help. When all parts were designed and the blue prints made, Robert Pike, a young college graduate in our employ, was selected to take a set to each of those manufacturers. These prints were so selected that none disclosed that a V-type was in the making. Mr. Pike kept in close touch with each company until all parts were completed and boxed for shipment to Detroit.

To continue this highly confidential secret operation, the parts were not delivered to the Cadillac factory but to an abandoned box factory on the corner of Pelham and Drydock streets in Detroit. So carefully was the project guarded that George Clement, a top Cadillac tool man, said that not even his wife knew where he was working the whole summer of 1914.

There, under the name of the Ideal Manufacturing Company, the new motors were put together. Wilfred remembered:

> While the motor was being assembled, the members of the National Chamber of Commerce were invited to hold their summer meeting on the estate of Sam Miles in Christmas Cove, Maine on July 21, 1914 instead of in the New York office. On that occasion I was plied with many questions by my colleagues in an effort to find out what Cadillac was going to bring out next. Needless to say they received no satisfaction from me and I took a lot of joshing and sly digs as to how Cadillac was wavering and losing its initiative. But I had the last laugh when the V-eight was put on the market and immediately took its place at the forefront of the industry. The six-cylinder boys stopped talking about lighter impulses, more frequent impulses and smoother action.

Interest in Cadillac's preparation for the new model was not confined to rival manufacturers but extended to the general public as well. In answer to many rumors and queries, a Rochester, N.Y., distributor ran an ad in the local newspaper stating, "From rumors one hears these days the Cadillac Motor Car Company is liable to have among its 1915 production anything from a submarine to an airship." [9] When the Advertising Manager of Cadillac was asked whether the company was about to put an 8-cylinder car on the market, he quoted the Rochester dealer's statement.

When the announcement of the new motor was made in September 1914 there was immediately much discussion in the automobile journals and in the engineering societies. It was noted that the V-8 motor was 60 pounds lighter than the 4-cylinder motor previously used. It was also shorter. One reporter wrote that he was "inclined to be in the skeptical division and questioned the appreciable advantage of taking on two extra cylinders." But a 60-mile run over rolling prairie country resulted in his complete conversion to the eight. "Considering the Cadillac motor in detail, one is struck with the high speed, high efficiency machine which has been produced almost without precedent or previous experience with this type." [10]

Although the secret-service operation, by which the V-8 type motor became a stunning reality, makes an entertaining tale of mystery and surprise in the competitive arena of the motor car, it should not obscure the tremendous labor and planning that such a revolutionary change in the model of a car entailed. The new car departed from the former design in a number of ways besides the increase in the number of cylinders. The crankshaft had only three bearings; the cylinder arrangement necessitated a change in the lubricating system; a multiple-disc dry clutch replaced the cone type; and the transmission was mounted on the engine, making a unit-power plant.

An interesting story remains in regard to the work with this new motor. The engineers disagreed on some of the tolerances. D. McCall White insisted on nine-thousandths of an inch of clearance. In the testing a noise developed in the motor. Mr. Sweet and Mr. Johnson thought that this was due to too great clearance and Charlie Martens, who tested all Cadillac engines and had an infallible ear for locating noises, thought it was in the connecting rods; Mr. White was sure it was in the cam shaft. H.M. was called in for consultation and he asked Martens' opinion.

Charlie replied, "The noise is caused by too great clearance in the connecting rods."

"How much is the clearance?" asked the big boss.

"Nine-thousandths of an inch."

"That's too much," reacted H.M. sharply and immediately. "I'll leave it to you, Charlie, to determine just how much the clearance should be reduced, no matter how long it takes."

The motor was carried to a quiet spot in the building and placed up high so that Charlie could get under it handily. He started with 2½ thousandths, reducing next to two-thousandths of an inch. The noise stopped at a clearance of 1½ thousandths.[11]

In his later years (after 1930) on a trip east H.M. rented a new

Cadillac. He found the motor defective and noisy and it saddened him. On his return home he phoned Kettering and complained about the new Cadillac. Ket's answer was that it was impossible to tell when some piece was cracked or broken in the motor. H.M. answered, "We did not have a million-dollar laboratory, but we could tell about such things by the sound."

The actual cost of producing the first three experimental V-8 engines, not including overhead, was more than $46,000, or $15,000 each; while the cost of the first three automobiles was more than $63,000, or $21,000 each. As will be remembered, Cadillac was at this time still under the sharp eye of the bankers' committee which was supervising General Motors. The Lelands were criticized for such wild extravagance until they learned a V-8 motor was being produced, then the daring of the idea quite jolted them out of their pinch-penny attitude.

It is likely that the Leland penchant of going their own way without thinking of asking the advice of their General Motors superiors was trying. A story of Lloyd Blunden's indicates this:

> Some years ago going from New York to Detroit I saw Sloan, Kettering and Knudsen in the diner. Early next morning Kettering came into the club car, and to my complete surprise recognized me and sat with me for an hour. Naturally our talk was of Cadillac, Lelands and many things. He told me how Nash on becoming president of G.M. complained of being unable to make any progress in learning of Cadillac affairs.[12]

The production of a new model of any kind of an automobile is an expensive thing, and not to be entered into lightly. Some suggestion of the great labor and expense involved in preparing an already well-equipped factory for the manufacture of this new model may be gathered from the following list of items, which included but a part of the thousands of tools which had to be purchased or made: 1700 counterbores and countersinks; more than 9000 cutters of various kinds, some costing as high as $75 each; more than 4200 dies for cutting threads; more than 26,000 drills; more than 2000 end and hollow mills; more than 3300 reamers of various sizes; more than 17,000 taps of various kinds. In addition it was necessary to add to the already well-equipped shop some 269 machines, which alone cost more than $180,000.

There were about 10,000 parts in such a car, including the axle and the electrical system. The task of the drafting room on such a job was immense, requiring 1922 experimental drawings. There were 10,869 tool drawings and 1958 patterns for tools. Blueprints used 67,970 yards or 38½ miles of blueprint paper—sufficient to reach from Ann Arbor to Detroit. Ninety-one engineers and draftsmen gave it their attention, and the time involved in making the drawings alone would have kept one man busy for 64 years.[13]

Though it is now widely agreed that when in 1914 Cadillac gave America its first V-type automotive engine it created a whole new standard of motor performance, this fact was not immediately recognized. The Smithsonian Institution at Washington heralded the V-8 as a noteworthy achievement and placed one of the first models in its museum. But competitors and more conservative engineers had plenty to say along the line of "the more cylinders the more trouble." They doubted that the eight would win out over the fours and sixes. After all, when ordinarily not more than 30 horsepower was used, why provide 50 or more? Already engines would outwear other vital parts of a car. Why then make the engine more vibrationless and durable? With such a radical departure from the customary, it would be impossible to find mechanics who could understand and repair such motors.

So pronounced was this sniping that Cadillac replied with a most impressive advertisement in the January 2nd, 1915, *Saturday Evening Post,* entitled "The Penalty of Leadership." This classic page, without picture or any mention of the product, began, "In every field of endeavor, he that is first must perpetually live in the white light of publicity. Whether the leadership be vested in a man or in a manufactured product, emulation and envy are ever at work." The text ends with, "That which is good or great makes itself known, no matter how loud the clamor of denial. That which deserves to live—lives."

The V-type eight-cylinder motor deserved to live and it did. Every Cadillac built from 1914 to 1927 was powered by this same type of engine. Even the bore and stroke, piston displacement and SAE horsepower rating remained the same.[14]

Henry Leland never ceased to give the major credit for the V-8 motor to his son Wilfred. For the rather astonishing perfection of such a revolutionary motor within no more than a year's time he gave credit to his engineers, not more to one than another. The V-8, like the long list of other Cadillac developments, was a group effort.

On January 6, 1916, the Cadillac Old Guard presented him a large platinum plaque designed with a solid-gold replica of the V-type motor at its top center, with the inscription below. "To Wilfred Leland, in recognition of his conception of the high speed, high efficiency V-Type Engine, and its application to the motor car."[15]

Chapter XIII
His Civic Duty

ALTHOUGH HENRY LELAND's greatest contribution to the world was in the mechanical and manufacturing fields, his life was by no means restricted to business. He was intensely interested in his church, politics and civic matters. Whenever he heard or read in his newspaper of abuses, inequities or hardships, he was powerless to hold back his indignation. He would arrive at the plant in the morning with a newspaper in his hand and fire in his eye and the whole office force knew that it would shortly be called upon to help "save the country" as they designated H.M.'s public activities. The trigger that aroused his ire might be the tariff, the mayor, a distant famine, or a flood. If something seemed to him to be wrong he wanted a hand in correcting it; if something seemed right and effective he wanted to support it.[1]

When Leland realized fully the corruption in his city government he organized a crusade to eradicate it. The Detroit to which he had come in 1890 was not a well-governed city, and as it grew with the automobile industry the deficiencies of its controlling board of aldermen became every day more evident.

The city was divided into 18 districts, later increased to 21, each of which elected two aldermen. Each of these districts was a little principality in itself and its aldermen were chiefly concerned that they get enough jobs and improvements in their district to assure their continuance in office. Enough wards or precincts in some districts were controlled by the bosses or combination of bosses so that a vote could be delivered on any issue. Out of 300 precincts, it was said, control of 60 key precincts enabled certain politicians to rule the city year in and year out. As one observer was to express it, the real powers behind the ward organizations, some Democratic, some Republican, were the "men usually found on both sides of mahogany bars." In other words it was the liquor interests which controlled the board of aldermen.[2]

This situation of long standing had not gone unheeded. The old municipal league, whose secretary was Anthony Pratt and whose most aggressive and courageous supporter was Joseph L. Hudson, had raised a voice of protest but without much effect. It seemed likely that any crusade against the saloon would fail. Detroit had too many citizens of Old World background where a drink of beer or wine was deemed no sin but a daily necessity. An attack on the saloon left these citizens cold and unsympathetic toward all reformers.

Convinced that some way must be found to clean up the city, Henry Leland and his secretary, John Bourne, conferred with Pliny Marsh, a practical politician, who had been for a number of years legal representative and lobbyist with the Michigan Anti-Saloon League. It was decided that for any effective campaign for civic reform an organization would be necessary and it was agreed that this organization would be initiated by Mr. Leland and his friends and fellow workers in the Westminster Presbyterian Church.

A set of resolutions, dated May 16, 1912, and signed by 37 men, members of the brotherhood of the church, invited the men's clubs of the other Protestant churches in Detroit to join in an organization "for moral and civic betterment in general, including politics when necessary."[3] Among the signers were John C. Lodge, a Detroit alderman, and Harold Emmons, a prominent attorney. In due course response came from other like groups that included such men as Divie Duffield, Tracy McGregor, Sebastian S. Kresge and Charles Van Dusen.

Two mistakes were made in that initial period. An unfortunate name was chosen for the organization—the Civic Uplift League—which was soon translated by editorial cynics and shrewd politicians into the Goo-goo League.[4] The second mistake was the exclusive use of the Protestant churches as a base for the movement. The name of the organization was quickly changed to the Citizens League, but years were necessary to erase the Protestent label and persuade the city that the league was not only non-partisan but also non-sectarian and welcomed the participation of all churches and creeds.

It was the good luck of the infant organization that in the very beginning of its career the Detroit aldermen put on a shocking demonstration of personal corruption, underlining the need of reform in municipal government. The Detroit *News,* in the evening edition of July 27, 1912, broke the story of the venality of at least thirteen aldermen.[5]

As the newspapers had announced some time previously the Wabash Railroad had petitioned the city to close Seventh and Congress streets where they intersected, as it wanted to build there a terminal freight house to facilitate its handling of freight and package shipments. The petition was supported by the board of commerce and prominent merchants of the city as a needed improvement. But the board of aldermen could not seem to come to a vote on the matter but kept postponing the decision for various petty reasons. Certain aldermen were stalling the vote until the proper graft or "take" would be offered for their support of the ordinance. It was finally arranged and certain of them were paid off and then arrested. The pay-off man was found to be a Burns detective operating under the office name of the New England Historical Society and the whole project was a trap set up to expose the corrupt aldermen. Some nine of them actually received the marked money. One, Thomas E. Glinnan, was arrested just outside the pay-off room and the marked money found on his person. He was so unnerved by the shock of his arrest that he confessed. The plot to catch the aldermen was financed by Andrew Green, manager of the Semet-Solvay Company, who lived in the 18th district, from which Glinnan was elected.

This incident caused a tremendous scandal at the time, and its aftermath was even more scandalous to citizens who believed in honest government. None of the aldermen but Glinnan was prosecuted and when, after a long delay, he was brought to trial, he was not convicted. Furthermore, while under indictment he continued to be elected by his district. The whole affair was a demonstration of the impregnability of the politicians in power as well as proof of the need for a higher public ethic.

When Henry Leland was elected president of the Citizens League he went again to Pliny Marsh and asked him to become the legal counsel and director of the group. Marsh resigned his post with the Anti-Saloon League and accepted the position on September 10, 1912.[6] Financial support was encouraging. By October 10 thirty well-known Detroit citizens had subscribed $50 each to the cause of honest government and several thousand memberships had been secured at one dollar each. The goal was 5000 members and sizable contributions from business firms and financially able sponsors. It would be years before the league became self-supporting but in the meantime Henry Leland would make up the deficits.[7]

Now the league had the leadership and the muscle for active measures. Reformers, uplifters, conscientious and dedicated citizens on down to the "excited chap with a half-baked scheme" had ideas of the direction the league should take. Henry Leland became the autocrat of the board table. Backed by the long experience of Marsh in reform movements, he would not let the league go out gunning for the saloon, big business or even the Detroit United Railway, long the whipping boy of reform movements. Confident that if good citizens could be informed and persuaded to vote, and if their votes could be fairly counted, good government would result; the first objective seemed plain. The league would inform the electorate and expose crooked election practices.

> Mr. Leland in a series of conference meetings laid down with characteristic insistence the financial and organization needs of the movement, beginning with election reform. He wanted hundreds of workers to serve as election officials, challengers, and circulators of popular petitions. . . . Then followed organization of factory workers, clerks in stores and offices, and the larger circle of interested clubs. . . .
>
> Having secured attention and moral support, Secretary Marsh

proceeded with organization for members . . . workers at the polls on election days, and distribution of pre-election information, with definite recommendations. . . . All lines of class, creed, race and nationality were ignored. Employers and workers ranked on an equality in the army of civic allies. When the issue was joined at the polls, the bulletins of fact and opinion were widely circulated in the factories, clubs, churches and among thousands of individuals whose names were on the mailing lists. . . . One trench at a time and a job for every man—such was the procedure. In the long program Marsh insisted on doing one thing at a time, and doing it with relentless thoroughness.[8]

At the polls the watchers found all the old tricks in use by those who wished to rig the election results as the bosses dictated. The inspectors *helped* the voters with their ballots and the help was given with such dispatch that the voter was not sure exactly how the ballot had been marked. Men were voted in blocks, a specialty of Billy Boushaw's precinct, the "first of the first." This maneuver was almost impossible of detection and could be effective even when officials were honest. The first man in received his ballot and pretended to mark it in the booth but instead of casting it he slipped out with the blank ballot. This ballot was marked by the boss outside the door and handed to the next man who, when he went in to vote, cast this ballot and brought another blank one out for the boss to mark. This routine could be repeated endlessly and was in some precincts the controlling factor in an election. Other tricks included

> the surreptitious insertion of the voting cross-mark on ballots, during the day or during the count, with a pencil stub concealed between the fingers, juggling the tabulations on the tally-sheet, usually by two men in co-operation; and deliberate "errors" in addition which could never be checked because the ballots of tally-sheet became "lost." [9]

For some years nothing could be done about these things except that the league could publicize them through its releases and through the newspapers. The officials who ran the elections were elected in the precincts in which they presided as officials and no action could be obtained against them by the city council or the courts, which were also controlled by the bosses. But in the end the publicity built up in the public mind a vivid image of deliberate and insolent frustration of the will of the people. Through the city newspapers this image spread gradually out into Michigan until the whole state shuddered a little at the wickedness of Detroit. When Charles Flowers, a state legislator from Detroit, presented the Scott-Flowers honest election law to the State Legislature the bill passed quickly into law, much to the consternation of the Detroit political bosses. This was in 1915 and for a year Detroit officials claiming the law was illegal held off its application to Detroit. The Citizens League went out and got petitions signed for a referendum on the law and on August 29, 1916, the people approved it two to one.[10]

Beginning in October 1913 the league published a bulletin, *The Civic Searchlight* in which it informed the members of its projects, promotions, triumphs and failures. Members were urged not only to vote but to vote intelligently. The *Searchlight* would endeavor to inform them to this end. The first campaign supported by the league concerned the revisions of the city charter as worked out by a charter commission and presented to the voters on February 10, 1914. A great effort was made to get the voters out. Some 422 representatives of the league made 8915 personal calls on registered voters; 75,000 copies of a bulletin explaining the charter revision were distributed in churches, factories and theaters; 150 men acted as watchers at the polls. The charter was defeated, as the *Searchlight* bitterly commented, because out of ten eligible voters only four voted.[11]

The *Searchlight* published its first information on candidates before the primary election on August 25, 1914, explaining that as there were so many candidates, 210, a voter could not possibly know much about all the men he had to consider. The league had gathered this information by sending questionaires to all the candidates. Not all deigned to reply. Two examples from among the candidates for aldermen in the 18th ward show the information presented.

JOHN COWAN, 40 Leverenz. Bricklaying contractor. Born in Detroit. Taxpayer. At present estimator (city official) with excellent record. Favors municipal ownership and operation of street railway, reduction of the number of saloons in accordance with the Warner-Cramton law (one saloon to 500 residents), separation of local from national and state elections, non-partisan preferential system of voting, making the term of all heads of departments co-terminous with that of mayor, establishment of a recreation commission, abolition of the board of estimates. References, M. J. Maloney, George Bohuka, Charles Kurth, Dr. A. B. Wickham.

THOMAS E. GLINNAN, 71 Blackstone. Under indictment for taking bribe. Elected by constituents following indictment. No reply to questions submitted. Attended 20 of 52 sessions of council during 1913.[12]

Of these two, Glinnan was elected. But despite disappointments the league could cite some victories. Since it was at this time working intensively to eradicate the crooked election boards, it had asked its members to become candidates for registrars and inspectors on these boards throughout the city. In response, 120 men had become candidates, 82 were nominated and 58 elected.

The practice of asking candidates for information on their qualifications continued although it altered in form somewhat as time went on. References were requested and consulted but their names were not published. Later the candidates were not asked for their stand on a variety of issues as at first. The league did not rate candidates as "qualified," "preferred" or "recommended" until 1918. The practice was in the early days a source of considerable controversy and the league was sometimes sued for defamation of character or libel, though little came of such attempts.[13] However, the compiling of information on candidates was so helpful to the conscientious voter when confronted with so many names that today, more than fifty years later, the *Searchlight* continues to send out its information on candidates before Detroit elections.

As was well known both Henry Leland and Pliny Marsh hated the saloon and were unalterably opposed to municipal ownership of public utilities. Therefore the attitude of the league was interesting. The league did not crusade directly against saloons but it backed every movement to restrict them. When in 1912 James Vernor, alderman, introduced to the Council an ordinance abolishing the sale of liquor in dance halls the league rallied strongly behind him. The ordinance was based on a survey of dance halls taken by the Girls' Protective League, which found more drinking than dancing in the halls, commonly located over saloons and frequented by girls as young as twelve. All the newspapers also supported the ordinance and the public hue and cry was such that the council, despite its strong orientation toward the liquor interests, passed the ordinance and, when the mayor vetoed it, re-passed it over his veto.[14] In like manner the league supported a measure introduced by John Lodge, designed to cut down the number of saloons that clustered around factory entrances and planted themselves in residential districts.[15] When it is remembered that this was the period of the crusade for national prohibition and that Michigan approved a prohibitory amendment to the state constitution in 1916, it is surprising that the league devoted so little attention to the matter.

As to municipal ownership, which in this case was focused on the streetcar system in Detroit, the league was in a rather anomalous position. The "reform element" including the influential newspaper the Detroit *News* was strongly in favor of the city's taking over and operating the streetcar system. Undoubtedly a great many members of the league supported such action and, in deference to that group, the league asked candidates how they stood on the issue and put their stand in the *Searchlight*. Finally, the October 1915 number of the *Searchlight* was devoted to a discussion of the matter with this explanation:

> Many members of the League have importuned us to give expression to our views on the proposed contract for the purchase of the street railway lines. We have consistently declined, believing it to be outside our function. That our readers may have the benefit of opposing views from fair-minded, temperate advocates of both sides, we present herewith statements from men whose sincerity of purpose and fairness of judgment is above reproach.

Rev. S. S. Marquis, Dean of St. Paul's Cathedral, spoke for municipal ownership, stating first that it was an economic issue, not a moral one; the city seemed to be for it and for fifteen years the best thought of the city had been centered on the streetcar question. He wanted it to be settled and then "The attention of our citizens can be turned to problems that to me are even more vital to our city's development."

Clarence M. Burton, who took the other side, said he was against it because municipalities under the American system of government never seemed to be able to manage financial affairs as well as the same enterprises when they were privately managed. He also mentioned that the fares in Detroit were at that time lower than those of any other city.

Thus with some tact and forbearance the league managed to avoid two questions which might have torn it apart and destroyed its effectiveness with many people who were not members. Someone said of Henry Leland, "He was a zealot but not a bigot." He was also a practical man and would not allow controversy to deflect him from his pursuit of honest government.

After the election of November 7, 1916, "the first honest election in years," according to the *Searchlight*, the league concentrated on bringing various issues before the people such as an election commission, non-partisan elections, a smaller council elected at large, local elections at different times from state and national elections, and finally the appointment of another charter commission to revise the city charter in conformation with some of these ideas. When 10,000 signatures were needed on the petitions, 10,450 were obtained to put the proposals on the ballots. In 1917 the petitions to force general charter revision carried 18,764 signatures. By this time the people seemed ready to approve the suggestions that the league put before them. When the charter revision came to a vote twice as many marked the ballot for it as against it. It passed in every ward in the city. In Billy Boushaw's precinct, the vote was 43 to 1 for the new charter. It was a magnificent victory.[16]

In 1916 Divie Duffield ran for mayor and no doubt the league hoped for his election, as he was one of its own. However, the incumbent mayor, Oscar B. Marx, having practically adopted the league's program, was re-elected. After the charter revision had been approved on June 25, 1918, the next step was the primary election for the new mayor and nine councilmen to be elected at large under the new charter. Again Divie Duffield's name was put forward as a candidate for the mayoralty. However, at this moment James Couzens stepped forth and asked that his name be considered. Said he, "I want it to be understood that I am not being forced into this race by the overwhelming request of my friends or anything of that sort. I believe I can serve the people of Detroit faithfully and well as mayor. That is the reason I am running." [17]

Perhaps the league or its directors were not entirely pleased, but it was their policy not to promote candidates of their own, and they placed Couzens' name first in the *Searchlight* list of candidates and wrote up his qualifications at some length. After mentioning his background and his work with the Ford Motor Company and as Police Commissioner, the item concluded:

> Reputed to be very wealthy. As police commissioner he sincerely labored to enforce the law. Advocates drastic policy with transit question. Supported campaign for charter revision, small council, etc., in fall of 1917 but did not publicly favor or oppose new charter. Energetic, aggressive, self-confident, but handicapped by lack of tact and insufficient knowledge of underlying principles of city government, and lacks ability to co-operate with numbers of people.[18]

Undoubtedly the league and Henry Leland felt that Couzens, while unwilling to give public support to the reforms the league sponsored, was rather too quick to take advantage of the climate and opportunity the league had created. But as the item said he was not a cooperator. Nevertheless, he was an honest and stubborn man determined that the city should obey its laws and ordinances. He would take over the streetcars but he would also require strict law enforcement.

Supported by the Detroit *News,* Couzens ran first in the primary as well as in the election. The league congratulated itself that five of the seven candidates for the council, who had been rated exceptionally well qualified, were elected. Alderman Thomas Glinnan was still in the race, placed 13th in the primary, but was defeated in the election. The league had softened somewhat towards him and the *Searchlight* refrained from mentioning the old story of the bribe. In fact it stated that although he had not served his district badly as alderman his talents were not suitable for the smaller council which must represent the whole city.

All in all the league had made an amazing record. In six years it had entirely reorganized the city government as well as clearing out the corrupt politicians who had dominated the city. The transfer to the new system was smoothly made and the new government functioned well from the start. Today Detroit, operating under the 1918 charter, is still considered one of the best governed of the large cities of America.

Though the league could rightly claim much of the credit for the transformation there were contributing factors. These were years of great interest in governmental methods, and new instruments of government such as the initiative, referendum, recall, etc., were being tried. The Detroit *News* supported the reforms throughout. In the end all the newspapers helped until some thought and said that the city was exchanging saloon domination for newspaper domination. In 1917 America went to war and patriotism was aflame. An observer said, "The new public conscience created by the war has expressed itself locally in the irresistible enthusiasm for the new charter." [19] Perhaps so. Even the league was astonished at the great majority given the new charter.

One task done the Citizens League concentrated on other areas of the government. The board of education was re-organized. In 1919 the league obtained 31,000 signatures on petitions for the submission of a municipal-court law to the voters. This reform measure was adopted in 1920 and provided Detroit with a municipal-court system known as the Recorders Court, which was later referred to by the American Judicature Society as "The best criminal court in the United States." [20]

In 1920 Pliny Marsh resigned as director of the league and was succeeded by William P. Lovett. In 1924 after twelve years in the league's presidency Henry Leland resigned because he believed his part of the work was done.[21] Good government and an organization to watch and support it had been brought to Detroit. Others could now man the bastion and keep watch at the guard post. He had followed the civic mal-function like a problem in manufacturing and little-by-little some of his ideals had been stamped on the city government. The league has continued under the guidance of other men. It still distributes information on candidates and issues; it still remains a vigilant supporter of good government.

Automobiles, government and religion, next to his family, were the matters of chief interest to Henry Leland. His was a religious family; it was accepted by all that the Lord and his Son were near and dear friends, to be called upon at any hour and consulted on every action of the Lelands' lives. The family letters show that when H.M. was away from home he might devote the first page to his health and the success of his business visits but inevitably the next three pages or so would be a resumé of the sermon he had heard that Sunday. He would quote the text, discuss the point of the sermon he had heard that Sunday and detail his agreement or disagreement with it. Letters of the other members of the family show this same devotion, for this was a family singularly attuned to the same lifebeat.[22]

Nor did their letters ever fail to show their affection for one another. Wrote Henry to his son, "You have the love and pride of your mother, sister and a fond father." Answered Wilfred, "Your kind, helpful, encouraging letter was most joyfully received." And Gertrude on the receipt of her brother's picture acknowledged it fondly, "It doesn't do you justice, love." Just as Wilfred had given up his own career so as to work with his father at L&F so Gertrude consistently contributed her bit to the family funds in the early Detroit days when money was scarce and the family income stretched only to the most modest of rental homes. She taught many years in Detroit elementary schools.*

It was perhaps chiefly the harmonious relationship that kept the son and daughter in that home until 1907, when Wilfred married Blanche Molyneaux Dewey and Gertrude married Angus Woodbridge.** Wilfred took his bride to live in a flat at 135 N. Grand Boulevard (later 2980 West Gd. Blvd.). The Woodbridges established their new home in the up-stairs flat at the same number. In 1910 Henry Leland bought the house next door and soon built a covered passageway to the home of his children. So here were the Lelands, in separate households but still together. Henry's wife

---

* According to the city directories Gertrude Leland from 1892 to 1903 taught in Cass, Williams, Estabrook and Columbian schools.

** Gertrude Leland married Angus Woodbridge June 8, 1907. They had two daughters, Gertrude and Miriam. Wilfred C. Leland married Blanche Dewey June 27, 1907. They had one son, Wilfred Chester, Jr.

Ellen died in 1914 and thereafter he lived alone but took his meals with his daughter, who looked after him lovingly.

In Detroit Henry Leland was a member of the Westminster Presbyterian Church though he had been previously a Baptist, a Congregationalist, a Second Adventist and a Quaker. The denomination did not matter as long as he served the Lord. He wrote, "I find I need the church and its services to keep me headed right." [23] His part in the promotion and establishment of a joint Thanksgiving Day sermon by all faiths, Protestant, Catholic and Jewish was one of his proudest accomplishments. He gave support to Sherwood Eddy's Chinese YMCA as well as Father McCarthy's Chinese Catholic Mission Society. The old family account books tell an astonishing tale. From an annual income of $38,941 a total of $20,627 went out under the head of benevolences. When the income was $69,377 the benevolences rose to $49,190. The recipients of this bounty ranged widely: the Salvation Army, Tuskegee Institute, Florence Crittenton Home, Anti-Saloon League, Wellesley College, Boy Scouts, Detroit Tuberculosis Sanitarium, etc., etc. The largest of the Leland gifts were the funds for an annex to Grace Hospital in memory of the daughter Miriam.* Personal gifts were many: a scholarship for a girl training to be an anesthetist, $100 to an arthritic for treatment at Hot Springs, a check to a widow to pay her taxes, bail for an 82-year-old derelict so he would not have to spend the night in jail.

Henry Leland was an employer of many men. When they were not so many he called them by name and they spoke of him as Uncle Henry. But as his enterprises grew the inevitable misunderstandings crept in. When L&F moved into its new foundry there was a brief strike. This Mr. Leland would not tolerate—he would not let labor tell him how to run his business. After this experience H.M. took an active part in the organization of the Detroit Employer's Association. Yet he believed that workers needed unions. He said in 1911,

> If tonight it was a question if every trade union in Detroit should be abolished, then I would stand with my rifle if necessary

* This youngest Leland daughter, born 1882 in Providence, R.I., died in Detroit in 1894.

and say No! you don't do it. Because that is the only weapon they have against the unscrupulous employers. Because there are many employers so unscrupulous that if it were not for the organization they would have been crushed, perhaps just as the agitators picture it. Therefore we must have organized labor, but we also must have organized employers." [24]

Detroit was known in this period as an open-shop town. Some historians have argued that Detroit became the automobile manufacturing center of the world because the struggling entrepreneurs were free from the strictures of organized labor and therefore had the flexibility to experiment, meet and surmount their early difficulties.[25] Without any great backlog of skilled labor, they were able to take, train and use in their method of operation the totally unskilled men who flocked in to take the jobs which the growing industry demanded.

In a speech before the Round Table Club on January 30, 1917, Henry Leland stated his feeling toward his workers.

During my years as an employer I have always and constantly striven to increase wages. I have gone through several panics in which I have sweat blood to keep the men employed. . . . I do not believe any man can say that during all that time I have treated my employees with anything but justice and consideration. Some of you know that the most humble employee who has a grievance is welcomed at the president's office.

There are many stories of the attitude with which H.M. regarded his employees. When Joe Yagley cheated the time clock and was caught at it he was scolded severely by the big boss. "You lowered yourself with such a trick. But I won't dismiss you. Go back to your department and use that ingenuity of yours the right way."

When in 1918 the Lelands built their own automobile plant, the Lincoln, they provided many special conveniences for the employees, comforts far beyond anything offered by other plants at that time. There were two restaurants, one for women and one for men, as well as rest rooms and recreation rooms. Even a smoking room was provided, though the Lelands did not approve of smoking. An employee magazine chronicled the doings of bowling teams, chess clubs and musical choruses.[26] Probably the women at the Lincoln plant were the first employees in a Detroit factory to be given what would grow into the universal "coffee break." Ada Grimm, an inspector in the factory, told how it came about.

> The head of personnel tried to stop the girls from nibbling on the job, but one of the inspectors told her we wanted happy people on the job and nobody could be happy and hungry at the same time. So we gave the girls a ten minute recess in which to eat an apple or candy.

The girl's club had a dance and invited H.M. He came, made a little speech adjuring them to save their money and then danced with the homeliest girl in the room.

Henry Leland's activity in the Anti-Saloon League was triggered by his experience with a valued engineer employed by Cadillac. This man drank too often and too much. The Lelands did everything they could to help this man, even going to the saloon and persuading him to go home. They sent him and his family to a far western state, hoping the removal from boon drinking companions would make sobriety easier. When this failed the man and his family were brought back to Detroit and the battle continued until all hope was gone and the man had to be released.

The elder Leland often spoke publicly in opposition to the liquor traffic. In the agitation against the prohibition amendment to the U.S. Constitution, post World War I, he was called a "fanatic" by Henry B. Joy, a fellow manufacturer who took the other side. Leland's reply to this accusation was featured in the *Manufacturer's Record,* February 18, 1926. H.M. was not disturbed by the appellation and welcomed the buffets of the opposition since it made possible this public reply.

However, not all of Henry Leland's efforts outside the factory were devoted to crusades. He belonged to many groups related to his manufacturing profession. Some of these he organized himself, such as the National Foundries Association and the American Institute of Weights and Measures.[27] He was president of the Society of Automotive Engineers from 1909 to 1914. With this and other groups he went to Europe several times, visiting the factories of Germany, France and England. On one of these trips in 1910 his wife went along and they traveled in Italy where both the Lelands became interested in the Waldensians.* Ellen Leland brought back a sprig of ivy from the grave of Elizabeth Barrett Browning, slips from which still thrive in the Leland family.

After the death of Mrs. Leland in 1914, Henry turned more and more to his church, community engagements and travels to the meetings of the various groups in which he was interested. On these jaunts he was often accompanied by John Trix, another Detroit manufacturer and associate in the Detroit Employers' Association. Sometimes his son-in-law, Angus Woodbridge, went along. Another close friend was William Mullins of Salem, Ohio, who was an active promoter of Leland's Lincoln collection.** Mullins presented H.M. with the statue of Lincoln, which was unveiled in front of the Lincoln plant February 13, 1919. The statue now stands on the grounds of the downtown public library in the heart of Detroit.

All in all, his later years brought not only many satisfactions and recognitions, but also some leisure to Henry Leland. The crowning honor of all came to him on August 11, 1920, when the man who had enjoyed so little formal education in his youth was given an honorary degree as doctor of engineering by the University of Michigan. The citation accompanying it was especially gratifying because it recognized not only his professional success, but also his civic endeavors, which had been as often a subject of public derision as of admiration.

> A son of New England and for thirty years a resident of the commonwealth, Mr. Leland brought with him the sterling virtues characteristic of early New England life and has been a dynamic influence in the industrial development of his adopted State and a distinguished leader in movements for civic betterment.

It seems evident that it is because of that dynamic influence and distinguished leadership and that adherence to the highest ideals that Henry Leland has, for a long period of years, been frequently referred to as the Grand Old Man of Detroit.

* The Waldensians were a sect that claimed descent from the very earliest Christians—believers who had neither been absorbed by the established church nor obliterated by pogroms against them.

** William Mullins manufactured fenders and other automobile equipment.

Chapter XIV
A New Dedication

To THE CADILLAC MOTOR CAR COMPANY and the American automobile world 1914 was the year that the V-8 was introduced to an admiring and eventually captivated audience. In Europe 1914 marked the outbreak of the first world war.

The Cadillac company entered on its most active and profitable period. General Motors was looking toward its deliverance from the bankers. Cadillac was expanding, looking for new quarters to contain its almost frenetic activity. It was at this time that Henry Leland broke his hip and was talked into going down to Florida where the sunshine would accelerate his recovery and factory problems would not stimulate him to too much movement. As a further diversion he was persuaded—although still on crutches—to take his first airplane ride. He likened the plane's motor to a coffee grinder, and promised himself some day to build a real engine for aerial transportation.

Airplanes were then in their infancy, but their utility in war became more evident day-by-day and battle-by-battle. Britain was beset with the troubles of supplying the planes for its armies. Bennett, the Cadillac man in London, was obsessed with the idea that airplane motors should be put on a production basis in the factories, but there was no experience, tradition or even belief in this American method. Britain continued to produce planes one-by-one.

Bennett, in Detroit on business, determined to talk to Henry Leland about the matter, only to find that his friend was in Florida, waiting out the healing of his fractured hip. Disappointed, the Englishman completed his business and was in New York ready to sail, when some impulse made him cancel his passage home. Instead, he went down to Florida to see Henry Leland. They talked for several days about the possibility of the Cadillac company's making airplane engines. But after all the discussion it still seemed a rather wild-cat idea. Cadillac could scarcely take care of its normal production; it had no room for other experiments. Furthermore, the official American policy was that the European war was none of America's business. Discouraged, Bennett went on home.[1]

But for all his reluctance Henry Leland had long had a presentiment of this war, and his mind and emotions were more concerned with it than he had made evident to the worried Bennett. The old engineer had gone to Europe twice with groups of other engineers, first in 1910 and again in 1913. As president of his group—the Society of Automotive Engineers—on the latter trip he had visited many plants and talked with many prominent men. Shortly after his return home in 1913 he sat with others in a little dinner group. Someone asked what he thought of the political, industrial and economic situation in Europe. After a moment's pause he said slowly, "It will not be many years before Germany and Great Britain will be locked in the bloodiest war of history, and unless we intervene our present civilization may be destroyed."

There was astonished protest. "What about the Peace Palace at The Hague which Mr. Carnegie has endowed?" What indeed! The discussion proceeded and all except Mr. Leland agreed that our civilization had so far developed that any future war was impossible. Yet the war had come and the sad old man still believed that America must eventually intervene.[2]

Only a few weeks after his arrival home Bennett received a cable from Henry Leland advising that he was coming to England to go more deeply into this matter of airplane engines. Happy at this evidence of interest and yet curious as to the Leland change of mind after he had agreed that the whole matter was impractical, Bennett was not long in asking why the old gentleman, awkward on his crutches, had made the perilous trip to England. The answer was prompt and positive, "If God has put me in a position in any way to shorten the War—if only by a few minutes—then I shall not have lived in vain but have fulfilled a great purpose." [3]

Leland was immediately caught up in the English frenzy of war activity. He was admitted to the weightiest business councils of the empire, made the rounds of the immense munitions works, and offered such advice as he could give.[4] He was particularly engrossed in that most essential part of the airplane, the engine, and spent some time studying the building and testing as it was done in England. He advised munitions boards of the capacities of American production and counseled them concerning possible sources of supplies. He modestly offered the Cadillac motor as a reliable source of transportation power.*

When Henry Leland returned home from England he thought only in terms of war. He proclaimed his belief that the war was also America's war and that the United States should and must prepare to enter. He called on President Wilson and presented his argument with all the force of his burning belief that this country must prepare for the inevitable struggle. But Wilson was already deep in his campaign for re-election and curtly repudiated all such suggestions. He would keep America out of war.

In 1915 Cadillac had produced 13,000 cars. In 1916 the pace quickened and 18,000 units rolled off the line. Durant, the eternal optimist, was again in charge. General Motors would expand and so would Cadillac. The British Air Board, moving ponderously, eventually sent a Rolls-Royce engine over to Cadillac to be examined. Would the Lelands give an opinion as to whether it could be made a production job rather than the hand-made operation it was in England? It did not seem likely. Cadillac built a large new building and acquired real estate on Clark Avenue at the railroad, where a new plant might be built. Then world events became critical: war,

---

* Cadillac eventually supplied 2,350 cars and 1,157 V-8 artillery tractor engines to the U.S. Army.

so long evaded, ignored and brushed aside, was at the door and could no longer be avoided. Wilson acknowledged its necessity, and Congress declared war on April 6, 1917.

On April 7 Wilfred Leland went to New York to see William Durant and put a proposition before him. Cadillac had just finished a large new building in which it proposed to build bodies for closed cars. Could not that building be used to build airplane engines? Cadillac could continue to buy its closed bodies from outside manufacturers.

For once Durant closed his mind to a new idea. He was in the midst of one of his pyramiding schemes and unwilling to be interrupted for any reason. "No," he said flatly and finally. It was a stunning refusal; never before had the head of General Motors failed to give Mr. Leland a free hand in directing Cadillac.

"It is nonsense," fumed Durant, "this war should stop tomorrow."

Wilfred was disposed to argue. "We have to help win this war. If it isn't won, our children will have to fight it out later. This is our war now."

"No! I don't care for your platitudes. This is not our war and I will not permit any General Motors unit to do work for the government."

When his son returned with his uncompromising answer, Henry Leland blew off his many months of anxiety in a mighty explosion of wrath. For once Wilfred agreed and could find no words to justify Durant or mollify his father. He too felt the overriding need to do something for his country. They decided to send in their resignations to Durant and General Motors and find a way to help the war effort independently. It was a heart-rending decision to choose between the solid well-built Cadillac organization, culmination of their life's work, and a nebulous, half-formed plan—more hope than plan—to build motors for the government and help win the war. More cautious, more calculating men would have waited until the future was more plain and the plans of the government more clearly defined before taking such a decisive step. But the Lelands had a way of following their ideals, and in this case they delayed not one moment to count the cost. Even could they by some clairvoyance

A NEW DEDICATION 175

have seen the denouement five years ahead, they would still have taken the step. It was not in them to deny what was to them the call of duty.

After resigning, the Lelands went to Washington and announced to Col. George Squier and his associates of the Signal Corps, under whose supervision aviation was at that time, that if the government would assign them to it they would willingly build a plant and produce as many airplane motors, and of at least as good quality, as any manufacturer who was already organized for that work. They confessed they had no factory, but declared they had the know-how and the wherewithal. Though impressed by the Leland offer, the War Department was not ready to give out contracts. Without receiving any official assurance that they would be asked to make motors the Lelands returned to Detroit and, knowing that time was the important element, they immediately organized to manufacture the motors they knew the government must have within the near future. In 1917 the United States had only a few small airplane factories. The automobile industry naturally assumed that, if plane motors were to be turned out in quantity, it could not fail to be chosen for the task on account of its experience and equipment for manufacturing motors.

The Lelands purchased a group of residences and small factory buildings on Holden Avenue at the viaduct for $300,000 and began remodelling them. About 109,500 square feet of factory space was made available.

The need of the French and English for armament and particularly motors was desperate. They had their own designs and methods of manufacture and long experience in them. But their ways were not American ways and their designs, like that of the Rolls Royce engine, would not lend themselves to American quantity-production methods which now seemed the best hope for quick and steady supply. But the development of a complicated motor or even an adaptation of one was not a matter of weeks and months but often years. However, in this crisis Jesse G. Vincent of Packard Motor Co. came forth with an aircraft engine upon which he had experimented for several years. He had developed the motor as a racing-car motor which was more nearly comparable in requirements to an airplane engine than the standard automobile motor. This powerful engine had been testing for months at the race tracks where it had produced speeds above any attained by the British.

Vincent offered the design to the government and offered to manufacture it in quantity and allow others to do so.[5]

As initially presented the motor weighed about five pounds per horsepower, but it was agreed that it must be re-designed and built so that it would weigh less than two pounds per h.p. Other engineers were called in, notably E. J. Hall of the Scott-Hall Motor Car Co. of San Francisco,[6] who with Vincent "laid down the general features and got out the first assembly drawings personally between mid-day of May 29 and the afternoon of May 31, working in Col. E. A. Deeds' apartment in a Washington hotel in response to a request for a report on the aircraft-engine situation."[7] By June 4 the plan was completed and was

> ... submitted to a joint meeting of the Aircraft Board and the Army and Navy Technical Board. It was for an 8-cylinder engine that was to develop somewhere around 300 horse power. It looked good on paper and everybody was jubilant. The whole affair was dramatically stated and chronicled.[8]

From this plan the first engine was built in one month, the different parts being produced by ten different manufacturers. The Cadillac Motor Car Co. of Detroit made the connecting rods, connecting-rod upper-end bushings, connecting-rod bolts and rocker-arm assemblies.[9] On July 4 occurred the miracle that upset all conservatism for, as Mr. Vincent put it, "We primed the engine in the usual manner and it started promptly the first time Mr. Hall pulled it over compression center by the propeller."[10] The miracle motor was christened the Liberty motor and the public, reading of the great success it had achieved in such a short time, visualized American planes flying over the battlefront within a few weeks. The Air Production Board proposed to build 22,000 planes using the Liberty motor.

The Lelands had announced their resignation from Cadillac on June 18 and actually left their post there on July 3. By this time Durant had perceived his error and had come to Detroit and spent one whole day trying to persuade the Lelands to reconsider. He was

A NEW DEDICATION   177

now willing to let certain of the General Motors plants take war contracts to a limited extent. But the Lelands had already gone too far with their own plans and had made too many commitments otherwise. Besides, they did not want to be limited; they wanted to go all out with the job.

When Henry Leland left Cadillac a farewell banquet was given in his honor. It was then he said, "The Cadillac has been dearer to me than any other one thing in the world except my home, but there has arisen now a claim on my loyalty that is nearer and dearer still. I do not believe the people of this country realize the monumental nature of their task. The time is coming though when this realization will be forced upon us. The world's greatest need at this moment is America; and America's paramount need now is to provide means for mastery in the air." [11]

The Leland motor project was initially organized to build a maximum of 20 eight-cylinder motors or 14 twelve-cylinder motors a day. It was to be organized and financed by the Lelands themselves, a volunteer contribution to their country for the purpose of ending the war. They were ready to stake their all on the venture, for they felt that no sacrifice was too great when civilization itself was in jeopardy. However, very soon certain long-time friends came asking to be taken into the enterprise. One was William H. Murphy, who had been a pioneer with the Cadillac; another was Joseph Boyer of the Burroughs Adding Machine Company, for whom Henry Leland had repaired machines when Boyer had no money to buy new ones from Brown & Sharpe. There was also John Trix, president of the American Injector Company, fellow fighter with Henry Leland on many local and national industrial issues.* Charles Kettering too came in under the name of the Dayton Metal Products Co. These proffers of help were not to be denied, as the added strength and stability they could bring to the new project would be considerable. Hence the capitalization was set at $1,500,000 with additional borrowing credit to the extent of $2,000,000. Many Cadillac employees also followed the Lelands, among them George

* John Trix (1848–1932) was one of sixteen men who started the Detroit Employers Association and was president in 1909. He manufactured grease and oil cups.

Layng, W. R. Johnson, Frank Johnson, A. W. Widman, Ernest E. Sweet, D. T. Randall, J. Wilbur Brown, M. W. H. Wilson, William T. Nash, C. C. Martens and William Guy.

The name chosen for the new organization was the Lincoln Motor Company. Associates had urged the Lelands to use their own name but H.M. in retrospect was back in the days of his youth when he, a young apprentice, had worked his heart out making guns for Lincoln. If the new organization honored anyone it should be Lincoln, and so it was named. Father and son Leland became president and vice-president respectively, while William T. Nash became secretary-treasurer.

In August the government summoned representatives of the six companies selected to produce airplane motors to discuss terms and conditions of the contracts. It was at this time too that word came back from General Pershing in Europe that the 8-cylinder motor developing between two and three hundred horsepower was inadequate, that 12-cylinder motors developing four hundred horsepower would be needed.

Before Wilfred Leland went down to Washington he had understood from Alvan Macauley, president of the Packard Motor Car Company, that the Packard company estimated it could produce the 12-cylinder motor in quantities for $5000 each. However, this estimate was based on production of the original motor weighing five pounds to the horsepower. Because of the uncertainty which would be involved in building a new complex, light, untried, high-powered motor under war conditions, it was thought the price should be high enough so that the manufacturers would not lose money. In comparing the cost of high-powered foreign airplane engines, it was found that the cost of such motors ran from $20 to $50 per horsepower, and that the Rolls Royce, which most nearly approximated the Liberty motor, was costing about $23 per horsepower. In the course of the discussion, government officials suggested that the price of the Liberty motors should be placed at $7000. Assuming that this price included a 15% profit, the estimated cost would amount to about $6087.[12] With the Liberty producing 330 h.p. this would be at the rate of $21.25 per h.p. If, however, the Liberty motor could be made to develop 440 horsepower, as it was estimated it might, this price would make the cost $17.50 per h.p.

To protect the government in the event that the cost of production went far below the estimated figures, it was proposed that instead of paying a fixed price for the motor the government should have the motor produced on a cost-plus basis. To guard against the abuse to which a cost-plus contract is subject, a modification was worked out. The government was to pay all items of actual cost of production and, if the contractors were able to produce the motors for less than $6187, the government was to pay the contractor 25% of the saving in addition to the fixed profit of $913.05 per motor. In such an arrangement there would be an incentive for the contractor to increase his efficiency and earnings by reducing the cost to the government.

In these first few months after the entry of the United States into the war all was confusion in Washington. The government had to find out quickly what must be done, how to do it and where to find the men who could and would do it. The Aircraft Production Board as finally constituted in the late summer of 1917 was composed of Gen. George O. Squier, chief signal officer of the Army; Col. Edward A. Deeds, chief of the equipment division; Col. Sidney D. Waldon, assistant chief; Lieutenant Harold H. Emmons, U.S. Navy. Howard E. Coffin was chairman of the board and Major J. G. Heaslet was in charge of the Detroit district. Detroit knew many of these men. Emmons and Coffin were Detroiters, Deeds was a partner of Kettering in Ohio, Heaslet had been with Studebaker and Waldon of Packard.

Now the Lelands, getting ready to build 14 motors a day in their little plant on Holden Avenue, were suddenly asked to prepare to build 70 motors a day. Before the contracts had been signed or even the final design of the motor fixed, their plant had been outgrown. The Lelands had been willing to drop all their own work, invest all their own resources to assist the government, but within three months they were asked to go far beyond their own resources and mortgage their own future in a project so vast it would have appalled lesser men. Caught up in the surge of their great commitment, they hesitated not but set out on the great adventure with perhaps too little thought of the cost, mindful only that they could and would do what was asked of them. Others would in the end build quantities of motors too, but only the Lelands would erect a mammoth plant, build motors and be left at the war's end with problems that could not be solved and no normalcy to which they could return.

The contracts had been discussed but not issued. When they were finally sent out, it quickly became apparent that they varied in a number of points from the understandings which had been reached in the preliminary conference. In Detroit one executive after another telephoned his fellow in another plant complaining of the impossible conditions in the projected contract. The Lincoln Motor Company had not yet been formally incorporated and registered at Lansing when the telegram came ordering the companies to get their representatives down to Washington at once to sign the contracts. Wilfred dashed to Lansing to file the incorporation papers. Henry sat down with his executives to sort out from the innumerable pages of those contracts the specifications which were impossible of performance and must be corrected. Just before the train left for Washington the record was completed, listing eight vitally important conditions that must be corrected in the contract as well as twenty less important items that in all fairness ought to be changed.

The story of Washington red tape is an involved one. Some of the manufacturers were disgruntled and doubtful of the reliability of the officials in charge of the program, men who could agree one week and the next send out specifications which differed from the agreement. Wilfred Leland was a believer. He believed that the chaotic confusion in Washington bred mistakes and that the errors which crept in were not so much from intent as from ignorance and misunderstanding. On this basis he set about exploring with tact and steady persistence one-by-one the items in which the contract varied from the agreed specifications. All day on August 30 he talked with one official and another, who agreed after discussion to revise the offending items. With Julian Harris, government representative; William T. Nash, the Lincoln treasurer; LeRoi J. Williams, Leland attorney; and a stenographer, Wilfred Leland spent most of the night re-typing the contract, incorporating the changes.

A NEW DEDICATION

In the morning another impediment confronted them. The House of Representatives had appointed a committee of three to investigate the cause of delay in the program and no contracts could be delivered until each member of that committee had submitted his findings. Two members had done so; one had not. Again the day was spent in offices, finding out who was the tardy Representative, locating him by long distance and then unearthing his report from the mails after a determined search. The findings of the report did not preclude any of the clauses of the contract. Finally, only the signature of General Squier was wanting. But the general had gone home.

Col. Robert Montgomery, former New York banker in charge of contracts, agreed to send his secretary along with Wilfred to the home of the general. When they arrived the general was taking a bath, so they waited in the parlor. They waited afterward while he read every word of the document and affixed his signature. It was late but not too late. It was still August 31 and the Lincoln Motor Company had signed the first United States Liberty motor contract on Wilfred Leland's wife's birthday. A sentimental man was this Leland, but a practical one too. The contract called for 6000 Liberty motors.

As the fall of 1917 wore on the U.S. government signed contracts with several producers specifying amounts, as follows: [18]

September 4	Packard Motor Company	6000
September 7	Nordyke & Marmon	3000
September 11	Trego Motor (later cancelled)	500
November 22	Ford Motor Company	5000
December 11	General Motors (Buick & Cadillac)	2000

Chapter XV

Engines of War

WHEN THE WAR enveloped America, there was, for all practical consideration, no airplane industry in the United States. During the eight years preceding 1916 the country had produced fifty-four airplanes of all types. By the time the U.S. entered the war it was estimated that there was a total of 5000 effective planes in the services of all combatants in Europe.[1]

One of the serious mistakes made by the Allies had been the development of a multiplicity of types of aircraft. The British were said to have had as many as 37 different kinds of planes and the French twelve while the Germans had but five. As a consequence, the trained personnel necessary at the front to maintain and repair these machines had grown to such proportions that it was estimated that from thirty to fifty men were required on the ground to keep each plane in the air on the fighting line.[2]

Contracts had been let in the United States early in 1917 by the British for their Gnome plane and by the French for their Hispano-Suiza, but great difficulty was experienced in getting these planes into production although both were in a perfected and standardized state, according to foreign practice and condition.[3] While the production of U.S. Haviland motors providing up to 22 horsepower was continued so as to provide training planes, the United States threw every effort into the manufacture of only one motor—the Liberty motor—with the idea that in the end it would power every kind of plane to be used in the war effort.

When Wilfred Leland returned to Detroit with the contract for 6000 Liberty motors, signed on his wife's birthday, he had had only a week's notice of the enlarged quota of motors expected of the Lelands. To fulfill this contract a new large factory would be needed. The work of remodeling and equipping the Holden Avenue plant was pushed forward while efforts were directed toward finding a site and drafting building plans for the new factory.

A fifty-acre piece of land was located beyond the terminus of the streetcar line on Warren Avenue. It was little more than a prairie although it had been subdivided and a hundred lots had been sold. Streets had been laid through it but none of the utilities had been put in. In a whirlwind of negotiation with the hundred owners, deeds were transferred and contracts signed so that in three weeks' time the ground was broken for the building of a factory aggregating 615,959 square feet. The main building was to be 1275 feet long, 68 feet wide, and four stories high. There were eight buildings in all. The Walbridge-Aldinger Company, which had built Selfridge field, was to build the Lincoln plant.

By this time the whole United States was in a fury of war preparation and very soon George Walbridge came into the Leland office to inform Wilfred that every manufacturer of building steel was overwhelmed with orders and the best promise of delivery he could get on any order was nine months. He had left the blueprints covering the needed steel with the American Bridge Company. Wilfred got the general manager of American Bridge on the phone and made his earnest plea for help. They hoped to be making motors in six months—they must have the buildings at once. This plane building was fundamental; these motors could stop the slaughter abroad more quickly than any other weapon. Patriotism was aflame at American Bridge too. The manager said, "Hold the phone, I am going down into the factory."

When he returned he reported, "Mr. Leland, the sizes you need are being run through the factory right now. We will continue running them until your order is filled."

The order was filled as promised, and in ten days all the steel needed for the Lincoln plant was landed on the site. By October 22 some 1900 laborers and five steam shovels were at work on the grounds.[4] By Christmas the main building was practically completed. The first machinery was set up in that building January 1, 1918, and the steam turned on in it on February 12. Meanwhile the tooling-up went ahead. Eighty-five designers and draftsmen worked through the months designing 6522 different special tools. Altogether 89 separate concerns located in different parts of the country extending from Maine to Illinois built for the campany 91,807 special tools. They cost around two million dollars.[5]

It was no easy task to persuade manufacturers to build these tools for Lincoln. It was a new firm and had no suppliers who owed it service. Ernest E. Sweet, chief consulting engineer for Lincoln, later told a story illustrating how Henry Leland got at least some of these tools in record time in spite of the hectic pressures on the tool industry.

When the new building was approaching completion, Mr. Leland called Sweet to his home and gave him a letter with instructions to deliver it personally to the president of a New England company which made a certain type of machine he needed. It was an order for a large number of machines to be delivered in thirty days. Sweet protested that the plant probably had advance orders for a year or more.

H.M. replied, "I know, I know, but just do as I tell you and then come home."

When the messenger delivered the letter the toolmaker said, "Doesn't Mr. Leland know our plant is booked to capacity with orders for at least a year?"

Sweet answered, "He does, because I told him that would be the case."

Pondering a moment the manufacturer said, "Go back and tell Mr. Leland he will have the machines in thirty days."

Sweet, astonished, asked for an explanation. The tool maker told him this story:

Twenty odd years ago I had invented this machine and then used all my available capital in making up a number of models. These were shipped to manufacturers in different parts of the country with the request that they be given a trial. If satisfactory I would manufacture as many as the company could use. If not satisfactory I asked that they be shipped back at my expense with a report. I soon began to get my machines back with such comments as, "No good," "Not practical," "Too many defects." Then a letter came from the Cadillac Motor Car Company over the signature of Henry M. Leland, President.

He wrote he believed I had a machine that would prove of great value to the industry if certain defects were corrected. He enclosed a check to cover the expense of my sending one of my expert mechanics to work with him in perfecting my machine. "If successful," he concluded, "we will place a substantial order."

The defects were corrected and our mechanic returned with a good order and a check in full payment. That was our beginning. What you see here now is the result. You may tell Mr. Leland his order will be filled and delivery made as requested.[6]

So the miracle of tooling up the new Lincoln plant was accomplished. The good will earned by Henry M. Leland through all the days of association, of encouragement, of holding out the helping hand, brought him now a return so heartening that the Lelands gained a new lease of energy and courage to struggle on with this project which had become so frustrating. Other plants were going through the same experience getting into production except, of course, that most of them did not have to build a plant from the ground up.

Although the Leland contract required them to build engines "in accordance with the drawings and specifications attached to the contract," the fact was that at the time of the execution of the contract the final design of the motor had not been completed. In truth, for a year after the first contracts were issued the Liberty motor was actually in the process of development. From September 1917 to July 18, 1918, 1398 changes were made in the varous designs and specifications. Crankshafts, connecting rods and bearings were found to be too light and had to be re-designed. Lubrication systems were troublesome, as were radiators for motors of that size.[7] The tools and equipment, which had been so hard to come by in the first place, had to be altered or replaced as these changes were made. It was almost impossible to get into production under such fluctuating, extraordinary conditions.

That nerve-wracking period is reflected in one of Charlie Martens' stories. Mr. Leland told him he would have the job of testing the government airplane motors just as he had tested the Cadillac motors.

> Major Heaslet came over from Washington and ordered us to run the new motor for 50-hour periods. But they always burned out before that time. Packard had a pile of burned-out ones. H.M. was there all the time. He decided to buy a motor himself to experiment with, but the government wouldn't sell him even one. So H.M. said, "Charlie, we'll experiment anyway." After running ten hours the motor began to show signs of burning up. Packard's highest hours was 35, before they broke up.
>
> I decided to disassemble it alone. I stayed up day and night. After I reassembled it, it ran for $37\frac{1}{2}$ hours, then it suddenly gave out. In the early morning I called H.M. "I wrecked an engine."
>
> He asked, "Anybody hurt? We can always build an engine." And when he came in, he said, "I know you are tired Charlie. Go home to sleep and later I will help you with it."

The next time the engine was tested Charlie noticed a weakness in the connecting rod and Major Heaslet was summoned to discuss the matter. He refused to believe anything was wrong with the design. He went away. Charlie was indignant. He wanted to build an engine and run it for 20 hours and examine it every five hours. Major Heaslet would not agree, so H.M. went to Washington and got permission.

> We ran it 20 hours and tore it down to see what part was beginning to wear out. We examined the parts every five hours until we reached 30 hours, when a crack appeared in the babbitt on the connecting rod. Again we called Major Heaslet and told him about the weakness. He insisted that the motor would be good for another 25 hours.
> "You're crazy," I said.
> The major answered, "You're bold!"
> Mr. Leland intervened, "No, he's only frank."
> I said, "I'm quitting."

H.M. phoned Captain Hall the designer and he came into the testing department the next morning and asked Charlie what he thought was causing the trouble. Charlie was sure he knew. "I think the connecting rod is too weak. The forging is too small and we need a large bearing to back up the babbitt."

Captain Hall saw what I meant. "You are perfectly right, Charlie. It's the first time we've seen one not broken up so we could see the cause. We'll re-design the connecting rod, and get ready for larger bearings." All the factories had to rebuild tools and get new supplies of forgings. That change delayed production of engines, but the new engine ran 50 hours without difficulty.[8]

There was also the matter of personnel, the problem of hiring labor and keeping it under war-time conditions. The Lincoln Motor Company started in September 1917 with 142 men on the payroll; by July 1918 they had close to 6000 employees—skilled and unskilled, men and women. The labor turnover was terrific, and the problem of getting the work done with such a mass of green hands can be imagined. Some of the figures are revealing.

Labor Turn-over of Lincoln Motor Co.[9]
Monthly Turnover percentage

1918	Quit	On Payroll	% Turnover
January	186	755	.246
February	171	977	.175
March	237	1667	.142
April	714	2331	.306
May	838	3391	.247
June	728	3844	.185
July	694	5600	.122

There was a scarcity of trained mechanics. The shops were manned largely by unskilled men and women—many of whom would find it difficult to secure any employment in normal times, yet who now demanded two and three times the wages of the men they replaced, and for a few cents more would throw down their tools and take another job.[10] To meet this situation the manufacturers agreed to discontinue advertising for help. The Employers'

Association Employment Service conducted a campaign and distributed a large number of workers. Also the Bureau of Aircraft Production set up employment agencies for industries engaged in the aircraft program.[11] Still the time lost in training new operators and the waste resulting from their indifferent efforts was discouraging.

Mishaps—whether caused by sabotage or carelessness—occurred constantly. Machines would be thrown out of adjustment overnight, so that the operation next morning might go on for hours turning out scrap before inspection could catch it. Screws were loosened, bolts were removed which would allow parts to fall and be damaged. Loose nuts were found in the crankcases of engines, feed pipes were plugged. On one occasion, cans full of powder were found in the coal supply, and fire extinguishers were plugged with cotton. Emery dust was found in machines.[12]

The pressure from Washington for production was intense. Officers and privates swarmed around the plant—accountants, inspectors, checkers, clerks. They stopped production whenever one of the change orders came from Washington and tried to reconcile the change with machineshop practice with which they themselves were not too familiar. The delicate steels prescribed at first required almost laboratory methods to fabricate. It was almost impossible to make threaded parts out of these steels without having them tear, and the threads that came through were consistently poor. While manufacturers tried day and night to get the steel specifications changed, inspectors consistently reported poor results and lack of improvement until special inquiries were set up and the harassed executives spent hours explaining to government representatives a condition which could only be remedied in Washington. Eventually commercial steels were allowed, the screw threads improved and production accelerated.[13]

It was not only the specifications of the motor that changed, as time went on, but also the form of the contracts. Through its banking connections the Lincoln company had made arrangements to finance the enlarged program. Col. Robert Montgomery, who was then in charge of financial arrangements for the signal corps, had made a special study of the monetary conditions in the country at large and concluded that, in view of the financial program contemplated by the government, local banks might be placed in a situation where they could not promptly handle big operations. He took the position that further financing of Lincoln Motor Company should be done through the government and indicated that the government desired this method. However, he advised that he would not recommend such assistance unless the fixed profit per motor was reduced to 12½% from 15% and the estimated cost reduced from $6087 to $5000.

Since no manufacturer had yet gotten into production, the actual cost of making the engine was still not known. Furthermore, the Lincoln undertaking involved building, at highly inflated wartime labor and materials prices, a plant much more elaborate than good business judgment would dictate. Also, for commercial operation such a plant would require complete rearrangement. The company therefore insisted that a substantial amortization or depreciation be allowed. It was agreed that this depreciation should be 40 per cent. So the loan was made, secured by a mortgage on the plant. Payments on the loan were to be satisfied by witholdings from amounts due the company from the government. The modified contract was signed on December 10, 1917.

Again unfavorable criticism of cost-plus contracts made the government anxious to set fixed prices for the Liberty engine. This placed Lincoln in a peculiar position. Adequacy of return depended on whether it would be allowed to produce enough motors to take care of the extraordinary expense and the hazard of termination at war's end. If the project was to break even, then a certain production should be guaranteed. A new non-cancellable fixed-price contract was made on July 31, 1918, calling for the delivery of 9000 engines altogether at $4000 each and providing for an additional order of 8000 more at $4000 if the government should need them.

It was also provided that if the company was not allowed to produce 17,000 motors, additional amortization was to be granted.

The first Lincoln motor was produced in the Holden Avenue plant Feb. 4, 1918, and the total production in that month was five motors. The process gradually accelerated until by the end of the war's first year 200 motors had been completed and production was in full swing. In May 127 motors were shipped and in June the tally rose to 344.[14]

By now materials, processes and parts had been standardized and quantity production would go up steadily, yet the whole matter of airplane motors was in disrepute with the public and the greater part of the government. The initial rosy prospects had been too widely publicized. Two men went into a hotel room and designed a motor in three days, the first model of which, when tested a month later, ran where it sat on its testing table. The uninformed, unmechanical public mind expected production would be immediate. Certain officials, just as anxious for results, gave out premature and anticipatory news reports. When planes did not flood quickly to the armies the investigations began. As early as 1917 a disgruntled would-be contractor made the first charge that triggered an inquiry. Then a Senate committee investigated. The War Department looked into the whole matter in March 1918, and the Department of Justice, headed by Charles Evans Hughes, also began an exhaustive survey of the situation.

The so-called Liberty-motor scandal broke with a news report in the New York *World* of March 21, 1918, and remained on the front page for months.[15] Colonel Deeds was removed as head of the production effort until the facts of the matter could be assembled. "Quantity production on a large scale was due to begin in December. We were to have three thousand motors in March. In April the motors began to come out at the rate of 15 to 20 a day." The Senate report was savage, stating the picture presented was "a composite of wild incompetency, waste of time and money, conflict of selfish interests, lack of energy, and lack of ordinary horse sense." [16]

The investigations put a further tax on the laboring executives who were trying to get production going. They had known, as apparently had no others, that it takes almost a year to put a motor or complicated mechanism of any kind into quantity production. Through almost unimaginable difficulties they had gotten the Liberty motor, an admirable motor, ready for manufacture in less than a year, and their only reward was abuse.

But while the fury raged over and around and about them, the

Lelands and other men making motors had the satisfaction of having solved their problems, and the motors now came out in an ever-increasing stream. By the time the Lincoln Motor Co. was a year old it had produced 2000 motors. In contrast the leading English manufacturer, Rolls Royce, with three years of aircraft-engine experience and 10,000 employees, was producing at the rate of 50 motors a week, about the amount the Lincoln was capable of in one day when full production was established. Only Packard got into production more quickly than Lincoln and only Ford put out motors in a comparable quantity. Ford's late start after some of the kinks had been worked out made production come there more quickly. Neither Ford nor Packard had built an entirely new plant and tooled it under war conditions as had Lincoln.

So stimulated was Fred H. Colvin, editor of the *American Machinist,* after visiting the Lincoln plant, that he wrote the following lines while traveling homeward on his train.

THE LINCOLN MOTOR COMPANY

Out of the virgin prairie, which never before had known
Aught but the sod and sweeping wind, the Lincoln plant has grown,
Born in the brain of its planner, reared by the brawn of his men.
We close our eyes, and like magic, 'tis done when we look again.

Filled with its thousands of workers, toiling by night and by day,
Each with the earnest endeavor of doing his bit in this way
Crankshaft and camshaft and timer, cylinder, valves and the rest,
Each part of the Liberty motor must everywhere be of the best.

Out of this spot on the prairie—the dream of the Lelands came true—
Have come thousands of Liberty motors, to fly for the red, white and blue,
And when the great honor roll's written, two names are sure to be there,
The names of both Leland and Lincoln with honor enough and to spare.[17]

However, the end of the war was already within sight, and the Liberty scarcely had time to demonstrate its superiority on the war-torn fields of Europe. It was the height of irony that Henry M. Leland in his desire "to do one more big thing before I die," sacrificed so much and in the end accomplished so little to end the war.

The Hughes report came out just before the end of the war (Oct. 25, 1918) and straightened out some rumors, quieted some criticism and revealed some interesting facts. It concluded,

> There is slight ground for criticism by reason of loss of time in perfecting the Liberty motor; the difficulties were inherent in the task and the task itself was worth while. It would have taken about as long to put any other high power motor into successful quantity production in this country according to our methods of manufacture, as it has taken to develop the Liberty Motor.

Going further into the matter the report went on,

> What has been called the *immaturity* of the Liberty motor placed a time limitation upon the program for the planes made to take this motor, but it may be observed that by May 4, 1918, 778 motors had been made, a time when only four DeHaviland planes had been delivered and no other army planes to take this motor were available.[18]

Hence the final delay in getting the planes to France was due to the plane manufacturers, not the motor manufacturers.

The comparative cost of the Liberty motors was also of great interest. Packard, which got into production first, and therefore felt most keenly the heavy expense of the experimental period, found the first 600 motors to have cost about $3800 each, the first 1200 to have an average cost of $3500, and expected at the end of the 6000-motor contract to have brought the cost down to $3200. The Lincoln project was considered in great detail and its costs on the first 600 motors was $3500. For the entire 6000 it was estimated that the cost would not run over $3000. As a matter of fact in the end the average cost came out $2900, the lowest in the industry.

Further, the Hughes report considered in detail the financial arrangement that had obtained in the motor-production effort of the Lelands, since it had been subject to some criticism in the industrial world as well as by the general public. The sore point with the critics was that some established firms which wanted war contracts did not get them; yet the government had given a large contract to the Lelands, when they had no plant in which to manufacture motors, and then had lent them the money to build the factory. Mr. Hughes gave the matter a thorough airing in his investigation, and it was only in this area that he gave anything less than praise to the Lelands. There was a detailed discussion of the great amount, $10,677,000, which had been advanced by the government and notation of the fact that initially the Lincoln Motor Co. had put but $850,000 real cash into the enterprise and had borrowed on its own account but $2,000,000. The Lelands argued that what they had to offer the government was special and superior experience in motor production. They had established a plant with their own resources and had not solicited help from the government but had only accepted it when urged by government representatives. They had paid interest to the government on all loans extended and had asked extra depreciation only on testing and inspection facilities that were of use solely for the Liberty motor production. Other depreciation covered only an allowance for the increased costs due to the haste and excessive competition of war conditions. They further pointed out that although under the contracts they would be able to pay for their plant, they would have nothing left but the plant, an installation of such size as they never would have built for themselves.

The Hughes report summed it up.

> It is pointed out very clearly that the company has provided an excellent plant for the manufacture of Liberty engines, and that ultimately its profit, after paying taxes, will represent only an equity in its plant, without any assured business as it has been devoted exclusively to Government work. On the other hand, it may be said that there is a very liberal flat depreciation allowance on machinery, tools and equipment; that the plant is a permanent one, admirably designed for commercial work, and not merely for a temporary exigency, and that there is every prospect that it can be successfully utilized. It should also be said that from the standpoint of the Government it was free to make arrangements with existing plants, and the amount of the profits it should allow should be determined accordingly.[19]

The Hughes report was scarcely out when the war ended. Fortified with an uncancellable contract to build 9000 engines, the Lincoln Motor Co. as well as others continued to manufacture motors for a time, but when notified that the government wished to abrogate the contract the Lelands cheerfully acceded. If they had formed the Lincoln Motor Co. to help the government in war, they could scarcely now refuse to help it return to peace. It could be truthfully said that they rejoiced in the peace although it left their financial affairs in a precarious position. After 6500 motors were delivered in January 1919, the activity ceased and the humming plant fell silent.

Chapter XVI
Another Fine Car

THE WAR WAS over and the Lincoln Motor Company had a plant but no business. Nobody wanted airplane motors; the air industry's future was twenty-five years and yet another war away. Although the aircraft's military development had been sound enough, the everyday, peacetime world needed more time to accustom itself to the speed and novelty of air transportation.

Henry Leland was now seventy-six years of age and might well have sought retirement. He did not consider it for a moment. As a matter of fact he had come through the trying war days in better shape than his son, who had to be shipped off again to New Jersey for a milk cure. But then Wilfred had had to bear the brunt of the investigations while H.M. operated almost exclusively in the factory itself.* There he had had a problem that followed his bent exactly. The Liberty motor was a magnificent challenge to a machinist, and H.M.'s soul must have delighted in its mastery. He was untiring in

---

* For the Hughes investigation Wilfred went to Washington and was questioned beginning June 12, 1918. His testimony ran to 158 typed pages. The T. P. Myers inquiry was held at the Lincoln plant beginning Sept. 1, 1918 and continued into October. Transcripts are in the Leland Papers.

his efforts. At one of the hearings the investigators voiced a doubt that the old gentleman was fit to handle such a demanding job. When witnesses were called up from the plant—workmen, inspectors, and supervisors—a last question was put, "It has been mentioned that Mr. Leland owing to his age might not be competent to run this institution. Have you ever seen any evidence that led you to believe that or suspect that?" [1] No one had.

The factory supintendent, William H. Ebelhare, who had been on loan to Lincoln for a year from the manufacturing engineering company of R. T. Pollock of Boston, explained why he felt Mr. Leland was entirely adequate.

> The conferences that he has are more frequent than I have ever seen in any institution larger or smaller. These conferences cover the vital points of manufacturing problems and also engineering problems in the motor. There is not a single piece of machinery purchased but what he does not know its use. He signs the requisition for every piece of machinery purchased; there is no new process put in but what I do not take up with him personally, and sometimes my judgment is reversed. I don't know of any other man in so big an institution as this that covers the factory as broadly as Mr. Leland.[2]

Mr. Leland was not only able to still do his work in the factory, but he could also look a long way into the future and he enjoyed playing with mechanical conceptions that might be developed and some day put into an automobile. Clarence T. Wilson, a prominent Detroit attorney, cited in a recent letter some of these advanced ideas:

> Mr. Leland took an interest in me and we discussed his plans pertaining to a car he intended to manufacture. I now recall very vividly, in answer to my inquiry as to what improvements would be involved in the future automobile, that he told me his plan was to bring out an automobile which would have all four separately sprung wheels, and would not have a transmission, differential or brakes in the conventional sense as the braking would be accomplished through the driving mechanism on each wheel. The car would be powered similarly to the manner in which steam cars had been, in that there would be a pressure chamber, with the pressure constantly retained automatically by the engine and the power transmitted to the wheels either through a liquid

or by air. The braking operation would consist of obstructing or controlling the return of the oil or air to the tank and/or reservoir. In this car of the future as indicated to me, the engine would have automatic controls to maintain a constant pressure in the reservoir at driving pressure and would be independent of human operation.

The engine would be in the rear of the car, making it possible for the front seat to be much nearer to the front and the rear seat ahead of the rear wheels. This would greatly improve riding comfort and driver control.

There was another item discussed which is not too clear to me at this time, but it would seem that, in addition to all four wheels' being separately sprung, the rear wheels would be on a knuckle joint, similar to that on the front wheels, to facilitate parking.

I do not recall seeing a specific drawing of an assembled unit containing the items herein mentioned, but I know Mr. Leland was very handy with pencil and paper and that he outlined the items mentioned that he expected his future car to contain.

Another stimulus contributing to Henry Leland's desire to go onward in the mechanical world was the challenge of new ideas which the war had brought. The new, spacious plant was crying to be used. As Judge Hughes had pointedly stated in his report, it had been "admirably designed for commercial use and not merely for a temporary exigency." The construction had been a reflection of H.M.'s life experience; he believed things should be built *right* and true to purpose. The Lincoln Motor Company had spent $2,000,000 in special tooling for the Liberty motor, compared to about $1,000,000 spent by its nearest competitor and as a result its manufacturing cost was ultimately found to be lower than that of any other company.[3] In the end the plant and its equipment had been an economy.

At the time the final settlement had been made with the government, there seemed to be little disagreement over any of the details.[4] In January 1919 the Lincoln Motor Co. complied willingly with the desire of the government and

> Entered into a supplemental contract for settlement based on curtailment of its production to 6500 engines. By this contract the different rates of depreciation previously provided for in different items were merged into a flat depreciation of 55% on the entire plant and equipment provided for the purpose of the con-

> tract. This method it was agreed would work out to practically the same result as the previous contract and would obviate the necessity of drawing lines of distinction between various items of plant cost . . . Although it was agreed between the government and the Lincoln Motor Company that the profits that would have resulted from the completion of the contract (non-cancellable) for 9000 motors would have amounted to an additional sum of not less than $2,700,000, it was agreed that the Lincoln Motor Company should accept $1,000,000 and profits on certain inventory items in consideration of cancellation of all engines over 6500.[5]

This settlement contract was signed by no less than Newton Baker, the Secretary of War himself. After the contract was signed the Lincoln Motor Co. paid $4,126,000 tax on its 1918 income.

When the war ended some consideration was given to the project of making motors for other manufacturers, but it was decided that since the Lelands had built their reputation through the motor car they could best profit by the great good will of the public if they were to put out another Leland-built motor car.[6] Therefore, the cavernous spaces of the great factory were cleared for a new project. Little of the previous equipment could be used and most had to be scrapped. Again the Lelands were faced with a scrambling period of industrial reorganization. The industry of the whole country was reconverting from the war effort to the business of domestic supply, so machinery was costly and hard to find. Yet Henry Leland persisted in getting ready to produce "a better, a finer and a more enduring motor car than had been previously built." This activity was begun in the face of conditions which were most unfavorable to the manufacture of a quality-built product.

> The war had just ended and the inevitable reaction was present. Everywhere was indifference to quality and craftsmanship. The unit of productivity per man had reached the lowest point in the country's industrial history. On top of all this the automobile industry was just coming back into its own on an unprecedented scale in 1920, accompanied by the most vigorous competition for labor and materials.[7]

The motor developed for the new car incorporated an idea new to automobile motors, which was undoubtedly suggested by the Liberty motor. In the 8-cylinder engine the two rows of cylinders were set at an unconventional angle. For some years engineers had agreed that the V-type motor must have the cylinders set at right angles, and they had ordinarily been set at 90 degrees. But in the Liberty the sides of the V had been brought closer together, to 45 degrees, to lessen wind resistance. As a result it was found that not only had the wind resistance been decreased, but also the internal periodic vibrations of the motor were lessened to a degree that had never before been attained. In the Lincoln motor the V was set at 60 degrees. To accommodate this arrangement it was necessary also to depart from the conventional equal interval between explosions in the engine, but the result was an almost vibrationless motor. This arrangement also made possible a general lowering of the center of gravity in the chassis, which made the car "hug the road" more securely while making a sharp turn at high speed. There were other superiorities in the new car as well as more precise machining and fitting.[8]

Henry Leland explained this greater precision.

> Something of the task of building such a product, in quantities, will be better appreciated by a reference to the limits of accuracy worked to. A thousandth of an inch is one-third the thickness of a human hair and ordinarily is regarded as a fine degree of accuracy. But dimensions of certain Lincoln parts are defined by measurements as fine as three-tenths of a thousandth, or about one tenth the diameter of a human hair. By actual count there are more than 5000 operations in which the deviation from a mean standard is not permitted to exceed one-thousandth, and more than 300 in which one-half of one-thousandth deviation from a mean standard is the extreme limit of tolerance.[9]

The machinery and equipment for the new undertaking cost $4,249,000 and the special tooling or adapting of this machinery to the manufacture of the cars cost $1,750,000.

While the development of the design went on, the company was reorganized. The old Lincoln Motor Company, devoted to Liberty-motor manufacture and registered under Michigan laws, was succeeded by one of the same name incorporated in Delaware. The book value of the assets, $5,500,000 in January 1920, was turned over to the new corporation in exchange for 160,000 shares of Class B stock and 24,200 shares of $50 Class A stock. The class B or voting stock was held by the insiders, the stockholders of the earlier company; more than 100,000 shares of it belonged to the Lelands themselves. The value of this B stock was placed at $3,770,000 on January 14, 1920. The class A or 10% preferred stock was offered to the public at $50 per share and so potent was the Leland name that the offering was over-subscribed in three hours. The company reserved 35,000 shares of the preferred stock for employees to be purchased by them on an arrangement to pay $5 down and $1 a month.[10]

Although many thought the fine automobile might have been most appropriately named Leland, H.M. would not have it so. He thought Abraham Lincoln the finest man who ever walked this earth; the factory had been dedicated to the Emancipator and so the car should be named. The original plan was to manufacture 6000 cars during the first year and increase production to 14,000 the next year. These projections were made in the latter part of 1919 when the automobile industry was running on a capacity basis and when most manufacturers were months behind in deliveries.

There was a great clamor among distributors to obtain the Lincoln franchise. One enterprising applicant mailed a check for one million dollars along with his application, only to be refused. Milton J. Budlong signed a dealer's contract with Lincoln on November 14, 1919, having been selected from a list of 43 applicants from the New York territory. Forty-one applications were on file for the Boston territory and 36 for Kansas City.[11] In the end 16 carefully selected distributors were chosen, all in the larger cities of the country since the production was to be limited in the beginning. This car was to be no mass model; it was an exclusive luxury item. The least expensive body style was the roadster and touring car at $4600, the most expensive the limousine and town car at $6600. There were eleven body models from which to choose. In the interval after the car was announced and before it was exhibited, 1500 orders with deposits had been received. No car ever had a more enthusiastic welcome.

The financial reorganization was completed by January 1920 according to plan, and it was expected that cars would be available for sale by April. But materials up to Leland standard were not so easy to procure, and the cars were not ready on time. Right in the middle of this wracking period, when every nerve was strained to the utmost, there came a notice from the United States Treasury Department on March 9. An additional income tax of $5,725,673 was due on the Lincoln Motor Company's war profits.

The accountants were re-assembled, the tax experts recalled, and the accounts again gathered together and taken down to Washington. It was politically popular then, as now, to accuse big business of making excessive profits on government contracts. Newspapers enjoyed the big black headlines. The investigators who had filed the claim were arrogantly sure that their figures were correct, and it was with the greatest difficulty that they could be persuaded to go over the figures again. But in the end they waded through, striking off item after item until finally they capitulated and agreed to withdraw the claim.[12]

The new Lincoln car was not ready to be unveiled to the public until September 16, 1920. The whole spring and summer—the active car-selling season—had gone by. In the annual report of that year Henry Leland stated the delay was occasioned by "disappointments and delays in obtaining materials of the desired quality and in necessary quantities." Lloyd Blunden, who worked at Lincoln from 1917 to 1922, gives one specific instance.

> Things were progressing nicely when a strike occurred at the Mullins plant in Salem, Ohio, where Lincoln fenders and certain body parts were made. We had no stock of such parts on hand; the production of cars had to cease for lack of fenders. The production assembly line stood loaded, with no bodies and no fenders available.
> H.M. and W. H. Mullins were about the same age and friends of long standing. In fact H.M. had put Mullins into big business by giving him Cadillac body and fender work for years. H.M. sent me to Salem to help in any way I could, and he came down to Salem almost every week. The situation at Lincoln became critical, and finally H.M. told me that I must get fenders if we had to move the equipment from Salem to Detroit. . . . All the stamped material, jigs and tools were loaded onto railroad cars, moved to Detroit where we set up a fender shop on the top floor of the main building. In my opinion that Mullins strike was the direct cause of all Lincoln's troubles.[13]

At any rate the advent of the new Lincoln car had been delayed almost to the very day when the economic depression of the early '20s made itself felt. Five days after the long-heralded beauties made their debut, other manufacturers, disturbed by the slackening of demand, announced price cuts. It was a most unpropitious time to launch an expensive car no matter how great its virtues.

Instead of going immediately into profitable production, cancellations of orders came pouring in, and the company with a large and expensively obtained inventory of material on hand was forced not only to curtail its production quickly below a profitable level, but also to pay out large sums in refunding deposits to dealers.

In September only 23 Lincolns were sold, in October 125 and in November 367. In December the tally was 159, making the total for the year slightly over 700 instead of the hoped-for 6000. The cancellations were heavy and some of the distributors were in trouble.

One particularly worrisome dealer in California was Walter Murphy, a nephew of William H. Murphy. He was a young man of little experience in the business and not one that the Lelands would have chosen had not his uncle urged his acceptance and affirmed repeatedly that he would stand behind Walter, provide him with good advisers and see that he did not make any bad mistakes. The young dealer was most optimistic about the number of cars he could sell and prior to the actual test ordered lavishly. Suddenly in November he began cancelling orders. Not only was he overstocked, but he refused to take the cars that were in transit or finished for him in the factory. The banks insisted that the drafts which had been issued must be taken up. This sudden burden thrown back upon the company was almost more than it could bear. There were drafts on more than 400 cars which had been refused.

Wilfred Leland sought William H. Murphy and found him in conference with others of the Murphy family trusts. After about an hour-and-a-half Mr. Murphy came out and said that Dr. Murphy would make a statement. This was the first time that the Lelands had spoken more than casually with Dr. Fred Murphy, and his very first words were not calculated to sooth or help the situation.* It

---

* Dr. Fred Murphy, born 1872, was the son of Charles Edmond Murphy and a grandson of Simon J. Murphy. Educated at Andover, Yale and Harvard he became a physician and Professor of Medicine. During World War I he was in charge of a base hospital and received the Distinguished Service Medal. After the war he left the medical profession, came to Detroit and devoted his time to the management of the Murphy estate.

was, he said coldly, the duty of the Lincoln Motor Company to care for its distributors, not the duty of William Murphy. When he was told that the banks were demanding $350,000, he announced that $350,000 was too great an amount for William Murphy to handle anyway, and he proceeded to censure the Lincoln for being in its unhappy plight.

Earlier, when Dr. Murphy had first come to Detroit, he had been desirous of obtaining some stock in the Lincoln Motor Co. His uncle William had pleaded his cause and the Lelands had sold him $125,000 worth of their stock. But up to this time he had taken no apparent interest in the company's affairs. The original directors, Henry and Wilfred Leland, William Murphy, Joseph Boyer, William T. Nash, John Trix and John T. Emmert still composed the board.

Now in this irritable mood, no doubt because he had been confronted with a sticky problem at an inopportune time, Fred Murphy said he would join his uncle in providing half the amount the banks were demanding on account of Walter Murphy's defection, providing he could have the appointment of two additional directors on the board and could bring in a man to direct the company's finances. Furthermore, the Lelands would have to turn over to him $50,000 worth of their voting stock.[14]

The Lelands were dumfounded by his audacity. They had come merely to ask William Murphy to redeem his promises in behalf of Walter. Now Dr. Murphy was inferring that the financial affairs of the Lincoln Company were in bad order and in need of supervision. Nor could they believe that the Murphys, whose fortune was reputably one of the largest in Michigan, could be short of cash no matter how drastic the bite of the economic depression. They could see this declaration—that the Murphys did not have such a small amount of money as $350,000—only as a subterfuge, taking advantage of a minor crisis to gain a strangle-hold on the Lincoln Motor Company. Thus was the suspicion born in the minds of the Lelands that Dr. Fred Murphy coveted the Lincoln Motor Company and would use any pretext to get it.

The next day when the Lelands talked to William Murphy, they found a more understanding conferee. He would take care of the drafts himself, he said, because it was his responsibility and Fred should not have made such exorbitant demands. But now this obligation on top of the others he had assumed in behalf of the Lincoln company—well, it was just not consistent with the amount of the stock he had in the company. This reasoning the Lelands could understand. They trusted William Murphy. They were the controlling stockholders of the Lincoln; and yet, as they well knew, the banks continued to give the company unlimited credit not because of the Lelands, who had their every cent tied up in the Lincoln, but because of the signatures of William Murphy and Joseph Boyer on the company's notes. The Lincoln operation was deeply in debt; it was imperative that the Murphy and Boyer credit continue to support the loans. The Lelands sold William Murphy a sufficient amount of the B stock so that his share equalled that of each of the Lelands. What else could they do?

This transaction was the beginning of an ever-widening schism between the Lelands and their old friends and financial supporters. For one thing the guard was changing, a new generation was taking charge. Not only was H.M. older now but so were his three old' friends. William H. Murphy was 66, Joseph Boyer and John Trix were both 73. They showed a disposition to let the younger men of their families take over the business responsibilities. Fred Murphy had assumed more and more of the burden of management of the Murphy estate. John Emmert, former Murphy financial adviser, was transferred elsewhere, and Dr. Murphy took his place on the board of Lincoln Motor. Mr. Boyer's sons-in-law, Standish Backus and W. A. C. Miller, had become active in the administration of the Boyer business affairs. They soon would be added to the Lincoln board of directors and, as the Lincoln's troubles deepened, they too, particularly Miller, began taking a strong hand in the board's decisions.

The tragedy in this for the Lelands was that although they had proved themselves and their methods and capabilities with the older men, the young men "knew not Joseph." [15] Nor had these young men had experience in the automobile business, in the heady gamble of the new model, and the great profits when it succeeded. They saw only the red ink on the balance sheet from month to month.

There is a fundamental difference of viewpoint between the producing end and the financial end of any business. The economic dislocation of the time aggravated this difference within the Lincoln company. The Lelands felt that their long experience qualified them to know how to make a popular car; they had never failed before. By all the standards of their successful operations in the business, they had a winner. All that was necessary was to be able to wait out this economic paralysis which had fallen on the country. Everyone must have patience and confidence.

The financiers, however, were not altogether convinced that the lack of Lincoln sales was due entirely to hard times; they thought the fault might lie rather in a wrong conception of the possible market for such a car. The automobile industry had always swarmed with apparently good cars which had not been able to survive. Maybe the Lincoln was one such. Conservative men were not accustomed to keep on throwing away good money on lagging investments.

The new year did not open auspiciously. In January 76 cars were sold and in February 78. During these two months the factory had gone on part time, and the working force was again reduced. The financial report for the year 1920, given at the annual stockholders' meeting on March 10, 1921, was sad indeed. Opening the year with cash on hand of almost $8,000,000 the company had disbursed over $14 million and at the year's end had but $111,328 on hand. Henry Leland, president, explained this in his report.

> It is to be expected that operating under the conditions referred to, the finances provided by the flotation of the Class A stock a year ago last January would prove insufficient. To meet the situation the Company obtained loans from banks amounting to $4,250,000. Accommodation has also been taken by giving to merchandise suppliers, trade acceptances to the extent of $2,000,000.

In optimism and high hope, the quarterly dividend on the A stock had been paid on April 30 and July 30, 1920, but by October caution had come to the fore and the dividend had been deferred.[16]

Other automobile manufacturers were having their troubles too. As sales slowed everywhere in the summer of 1920, many followed Ford's example and cut prices. On November 20 Durant resigned from General Motors, losing control for the second time over that great empire, which was again heavily in debt. On November 22, Nash Motors shut down. In December many others followed suit—Willys-Overland, Packard, Dodge and Studebaker. Ford closed his factory operations on December 24 without setting an opening date. The Willys Corporation was already deep in a reorganization under Walter Chrysler.

The condition of the Lincoln treasury at the beginning of 1921 indicated that a new supply of working capital was imperative. The Lelands asked for $500,000, believing that with the opening of the spring season automobile sales would surely pick up. Dr. Murphy did not think this amount would be in any way sufficient; he believed they would need at least $2,000,000. But at this time the directorate was still hopeful that the Lincoln car would fulfill its promise, and the directors signed for the loan at the bank. However, there were protests and warnings that this deficit financing could not go on much longer. Dr. Murphy then brought forth the phrase that was to echo and re-echo down through that whole desperate year, "This is the end of the trail!"[17]

Sales did pick up in March when 205 cars were sold, and increased again in April to 351.[18] Then fate in the shape of the U.S. government dealt the struggling company another blow on May 12 in the shape of a claim for $5,400,000 additional income tax on the old Lincoln Motor Company operations. It was the same old claim, only now pushed by the new Republican administration eager to show up the laxity of the former administration in allowing excessive war profits.[19] Essentially, the claim was based on the premise that the depreciation allowed on the tools and buildings of the Lincoln Motor Company after the war was really a form of income and income tax should therefore have been paid on it. Again the old records were opened up and thoroughly explored before the claim was again withdrawn. Was there no way that this matter could be settled permanently? No, but a letter was given the company by the U.S. Treasury Department stating that the claim had been withdrawn and no tax was due.

The sales in May instead of going up went down to 273. Another money crisis impended for Lincoln Motor.

Chapter XVII
Disagreement and Desperation

THE LELANDS WERE now playing a new role, one in which they had had no experience and for which they had neither training nor heart. Between them, father and son, they had designed, created, organized, produced and managed but they had never before been the major financial sponsors of a great business venture. Previously the financial responsibility of their business operations had been borne by others. Mr. Faulconer had put up most of the money for L&F; Messrs. Murphy, Bowen, *et al.* had provided the capital for Cadillac until General Motors took over. While the Lelands had started out independently in the Liberty motor project, in the end the United States government had underwritten the operation.

Attracted by their name and reputation, a host of small investors had put their lifetime savings into Lincoln stock. Some of these people were co-workers, who had followed H.M. from L&F through the Cadillac days. Some were employees who were paying for their stock at a dollar a week. Some were friends and acquaintances gained through the years of H.M.'s activities in the religious and civic fields. When the public offering of Lincoln stock had all been sold in three hours, that accomplishment had been deemed a tribute to the Leland reputation; now that same tribute had developed into an agonizing responsibility. Many of the Lincoln stockholders were not anonymous names on stock certificates; to the Lelands they were living, breathing friends, who would be dreadfully hurt, perhaps impoverished, if their trust was betrayed and their money lost.

An example of the personal attitude of the Lelands toward their stockholders was shown in Wilfred Leland's testimony before the Hughes investigators. In enumerating the names and investments of the original stockholders of Lincoln, he mentioned Mrs. John Shaw, who owned $10,000 worth of stock.

> Perhaps I should state the reasons she is in the company. She is the widow of John T. Shaw, who was the president of the First National Bank. He was one of the directors of the Cadillac Car Company and he was killed by accident a few years ago. He was a very helpful counsellor for the Cadillac Motor Car Company, at the time. We hoped this investment would help her and her family.[1]

It was manifestly impossible for the Lelands, men of tender heart and unswerving integrity, to take a cold, dispassionate view of the financial straits of the Lincoln Company. Many automobile companies had had money troubles; some had undergone a variety of reorganizations, combinations and other stratagems to keep alive and their directors and management had not been considered dishonest or insensible of their trust even though investors may have lost a portion or all of their equity. But such a course was unthinkable for the Lelands; as long as there was breath in their bodies they would oppose it. They had themselves invested everything they owned in the company. On the other hand, they thought the Murphys and the Boyers could save the Lincoln Company without any great personal sacrifice; all that was needed was their credit, not their money. They believed that William Murphy would have extended the aid they needed had not Dr. Fred Murphy interposed and that Joseph Boyer would have continued to support the company's borrowing at the banks had not Dr. Murphy's arguments undermined his confidence. In such a situation it was not remarkable that the Lelands—and particularly Wilfred, who conducted most of the negotiations—came to believe that the real villain who was destroying the Lincoln Company was not so much the economic depression as it was one man.

Undoubtedly the Murphy and Boyer protagonists could present an entirely different view of the situation, and an historian might then make a weighed assessment of the diverse viewpoints. But there is no place for such evaluation here. This is the Lelands' story and it must be told from their viewpoint just as they lived it at the time and as they remembered later.

When sales turned downward again in May 1921 gloom descended on the Lincoln directorate. Although the federal income-tax claim had been withdrawn, there was left an uncertainty; an uneasy ghost had been laid, but might it not walk again? The management must have more money if the plant was to be kept going, and it had to keep going or the creditors would certainly descend upon it.

What could be done to stimulate sales? A price cut? Through the last of May and the beginning of June, the price of every model was reduced. The seven-passenger touring car was reduced $300 to $4300, the five-passenger sedan from $6000 to $5400, the limousine and town car to $6000.[2] It was a hard step to take when the company was already losing money on every sale. But in spite of these losses and the continuing deficit, the Lelands thought they had proved a point. They had managed almost six months on $500,000 when Dr. Murphy had predicted they would need $2,000,000 for that length of time. Surely now their estimates would be given more credence and their judgment more weight!

The conference called on June 18 to consider means of further financing exploded into an open quarrel before the afternoon was finished.[3] Dr. Murphy proposed the appointment of a supervisory executive committee consisting of Dr. Murphy, Standish Backus and the Lelands, H.M. to preside but have no vote. He also suggested that an outside firm of engineering accountants be called in to survey and report any weak spots in the conduct of the business and to find out why it seemed impossible to get onto a paying basis. It was at this meeting that Wilfred first proposed that some of the real estate, owned by the Lincoln Company but not necessary to its operation, should be sold. There were three parcels of this real estate—the old Holden Avenue plant, still in use, a tract north of Tireman in the same general area and some lots at Kirby and Woodward where the company had once proposed to build a salesroom. The two latter items were about half paid for.

Dr. Murphy was already at this time exploring a plan for securing a $2,500,000 mortgage-bond issue and had persuaded Mr. Boyer to waive his objections to it. When Murphy had first mentioned the bond issue to Wilfred he had expressed the opinion that the only difficulty would be to find a man or an institution willing to take the bonds. It might be necessary to give with the bonds some B stock and perhaps submit to certain restrictions and controls. Some days afterwards it developed that Fred Murphy himself had arranged to provide a large portion, if not all, of the funds and take a temporary mortgage, ostensibly for the reason that any bank or trust company would need time to make its investigation. The Leland suspicion that Fred Murphy, under the cloak of helping the company, was actually working to gain absolute control now flared up anew and could not be kept within bounds.

In the course of the meeting Dr. Murphy stated that Wilfred had made a despicable remark to a mutual acquaintance—an intimation that Dr. Murphy desired to get control of the Lincoln Company. Thus openly accused, Wilfred recited in detail the actions that had indicated intent to control, beginning with the difficulty over making good the drafts which Walter Murphy had refused to honor and proceeding to the present plan. In both cases Dr. Murphy had demanded special concessions before condescending to offer the assistance needed. If he did not desire control why then insist on more and more powers in the board of directors and more and more supervision over the management?

To this long heated recital of what Wilfred felt so deeply was a great injustice Dr. Murphy answered briefly and coldly, "I, myself, place very little value on my Lincoln stock, either A or B. My only interest in this whole situation is to help and protect my uncle, William Murphy." [4]

Dr. Murphy, less articulate than the Lelands, had by this time emerged as the most positive and influential director on the board. He seldom engaged in argument and made his statements briefly without much explanation or background presentation. He was unalterably opposed to the investment of more money in the Lincoln Motor Co., but he did formulate a plan to get more working capital for Lincoln by means of the bond issue, which by its nature would in any re-organization have first claim on the company's assets. This cautious, self-saving procedure gained him only further scorn from the Lelands, who could give no credit to any attempt to take care of the Murphys and leave the rest of the stockholders out in the cold.

As the summer wore on, the attitudes of the Lelands on one side and Dr. Murphy on the other became more and more painful and incomprehensible one to the other. At a meeting of the executive committee, when only the Lelands and Dr. Murphy were present, the contradictory viewpoints clashed sharply.

H.M. made the first attack:

> If this company goes on the rocks, the responsibility will certainly go where it belongs (to the Murphy influence). . . . You said that we had inveigled two of the sweetest-spirited, innocent men (Wm. Murphy and Joseph Boyer) in the world and got them into this dilemma.
>
> Dr. Murphy: I feel that way today.
> W.C.L.: We did no inveigling, no brow-beating. We laid it before the board. (The borrowing of millions from the banks.) They said, "Go ahead."
> Dr. Murphy: I think some men take endorsements as a very casual thing. I personally never have endorsed and don't propose to endorse anybody's paper. My good father lost a good part of his fortune and mine doing it and I think it is a poor way to do business . . . When you endorse you must have an appreciation of the seriousness of it and must out of your estate be able to pay.
> H.M.L.: Does the future mean nothing?
> Dr. Murphy: Mr. Leland, do you realize that your Pittsburgh Bank called your loan recently and I had to get it extended personally . . . ? Out of the last money provided, out of the $1,750,000—$1,570,000 has come out of 2248 Penobscot Building (Murphy offices), Wm. H. Murphy providing $500,000 and Fred Murphy and William H. Murphy providing together $1,075,000. Is that not fair backing?
> W.C.L.: Absolutely, but not enough.[5]

But whatever the resentments which could not always be kept dammed up and unexpressed, and whatever the individual purposes of the members of the board of directors, the Lincoln Motor Company had to have money. The Lelands were out-voted; the bond plan was accepted; Scovell, Wellington & Company of Boston was chosen to make the survey of the Lincoln organization; and the executive committee began its surveillance.

The executive committee was in fact a rather ridiculous arrangement and one that immeasurably increased the burden of the Leland management. Unfortunately, Standish Backus, who was well-known to the Lelands and their former attorney, was unavailable and W. A. C. Miller took his place as announced defender of the Boyer interests. Miller, who constantly proclaimed himself as uninformed on the automobile business but a *fighter*, alternated between peevish criticism and petty harassment. Letting the world in on the troubles of the Lincoln, he interviewed bankers, businessmen and distributors in regard to the company, asking them what was *wrong* with it. These criticisms he brought to the executive committee meetings and put them up to the Lelands. He called in Ralph C. Getsinger, the Lincoln salesmanager, and asked him his *honest* opinion of the attractiveness of the Lincoln bodies. He proposed that the phrase "Leland-built" be eliminated from the advertising.

There had been some trouble with the bodies with the result that Angus Woodbridge, husband of Gertrude Leland, had relinquished his supervision over this phase of production.[6] A new supplier had been sought and in the summer of 1921 there had been difficulty in securing bodies. However, the sales-manager defended the bodies.

> Mr. Getsinger also stated that he did not believe all the distributors' losses could be laid to body design, that much less criticism would have been received on bodies if business had been good, that we continue to hear less and less about body resistance.

As to the phrase "Leland built" as an advertising asset, Mr. Getsinger replied,

> . . . that he believed it should continue to be emphasized just as prominently as it has been in the past, that that particular

phrase stands for a great deal in the automobile industry and that he believed it to be the biggest selling asset the Company has.[7]

Miller advocated at various times the appointment of a comptroller and a production manager. He once drew up a list of thirteen criticisms that he asked the Lelands to refute. Some of these were:

The Messrs Lelands do everything themselves.
The conference method employed in the factory is of doubtful value.
The Lelands have not given the matter of finance the importance it deserved.
The Lelands are optimistic until the last minute.
Too many changes have delayed manufacturing.
The factory maintained too high a degree of accuracy in its inspections.

Dr. Murphy, who also admitted that he knew little about the automobile business and had only been through the Lincoln plant once, took a different approach. He specified that the committee would meet twice a week; on certain subjects a daily report would be given to members of the executive committee; on other subjects only a semimonthly report need be submitted. He asked that no commitments in excess of $1000 be made without the approval of the committee. He summarized his view of the situation of the company and stated that the matter of first importance was the sale of cars, second the conservation of resources, and third the reduction of expenses.

To the independent Lelands who had for so long run their own show; who had prayed, suffered and thirsted for more sales; who had long ago cut expenses to the very bone, such pronouncements were gall-bitter. It was hard to bow the head to the yoke, but they did answer. The reports were provided as requested.

The survey of Scovell, Wellington & Company of Boston concerning the Lincoln Motor Company on "Organization, Methods, Budget, Inventory and Related Matters" was an interesting one and gave an excellent picture of the company as it was in June–July 1921. The conclusions were almost wholly complimentary about everything but the financial status. "The whole organization, it appears to us, is unusually harmonious and uniformly competent." The advertising was "certainly far above average, in some cases possessing a distinction as marked as that which is claimed for the car itself." The sales plan was "highly appropriate and skillfully adapted to the marketing of a high-grade motor car." The cost schedules were "as orderly and well-arranged a piece of work as we have recently seen." The valuation carried on the inventory was too high and would need to be scaled down in accordance with the now depression-reduced prices. A possible production budget had been discussed with all executives and the reporter agreed with them that "The evidence supports the opinion that a schedule of 300 cars per month will be maintained, and will in all probability be somewhat exceeded." If such a budget could be fulfilled "we find an improvement in cash and debt position at the end of the year of about $50,000." [8]

Some time after the inventory had been taken the financial report was submitted. According to this accounting the Lincoln company had lost $1,781,000 the first six months and in the next six months would lose another million. In vain did Wilfred Leland point out that much of this loss was a bookkeeping item caused by the scaling down of the inventory. These enormous loss figures were to remain fixed in the mind of Dr. Murphy and to haunt him the rest of the year. He said:

> I think that those figures do not in any way shake one's faith in the ultimate development of this business but they do destroy —have for me at any rate—destroyed completely the idea that by driblets, by temporary means such as have been used in the past, there can be any hope of working out of such a financial situation.[9]

The "reasonable certainty" of selling 300 cars a month did not immediately materialize. The loss for July was $106,000, for August $131,000, and for September still $80,000 although 302 cars were sold.[10] The Lelands were encouraged. Prices on supplies as well as on labor were going down. A gasoline tank which cost $40 had come down to $30 and a bid had come in quoting them at $14. Labor was getting 40 cents an hour and skilled operatives were receiving 58 cents per hour as against one dollar some months before.[11] These reductions would help the business to reach the break-even point more quickly. Besides the company had now pretty well worked through its original high-priced inventory and worked off those disastrous California orders.

The confidence of the Lelands throughout this whole period of constant attack and disparagement had never broken. They never gave up and strangely enough the endurance of the prolonged tortures of the executive committee had borne a little fruit. Although Wilfred complained that Dr. Murphy had listened only to the discouraging figures of the expert's survey and had given the Lelands little credit for the excellent organization of all other phases of the company enterprise, the old minutes of the committee bear evidence that both Miller and Murphy had gained new respect for and interest in the future possibilities of the Lincoln Company. But no agreement could be reached on how to insure its continuation. The summer-sales season was past, and winter was bound to bring a period of decreased activity.

Then came real morale-boosting news. In 1920, the Lincoln, a new car with few sales, had had to take 84th place at the Automobile Show in New York—an obscure location on the third floor. In 1921, when allotments were made for the show based on the volume of business done during the year ending June 30, Lincoln was found to have passed 59 companies and was therefore entitled to the 24th choice for space—down on the first floor. In the quarter of July, August and September 1921, Lincoln sales went ahead of Chandler, Peerless, Pierce-Arrow and Velie. Lincoln shipped eleven more cars than the combined totals of Cunningham, Daniels, Lafayette, Locomobile, McFarland, Pierce-Arrow and Winton.[12] This report cheered the Lelands enormously. They were doing better than some of the others.

The Lelands also could and did say that in the same three months of time Maxwell had lost $3,000,000 compared to which their loss was small. But it was also a fact that Maxwell was in receivership with a debt of $26,000,000—a receivership allowed by the judge in court although the stockholders had pleaded not to be deprived of their equities. Other companies were in trouble although their difficulties were not so well known. Many were having a hard time. By pledging all its stock for a loan of $3,000,000 from a syndicate in Toledo, Willys was able to go on. Only Ford, who had reopened in February, seemed to be getting back into something like a regular rate of production. Prior to the war the automobile industry had never failed to increase its production and sales year-by-year. But in 1921 the figures regressed to those of 1916.

When Dr. Murphy had made the $1,250,000 available in July for the Lincoln Motor Company he had taken a temporary mortgage on all the physical assets of the company. The Lelands had protested the inclusion of the three pieces of real estate which were not necessary for the company's operation, and had been told that later they could be taken out of the mortgage. The Detroit Trust Company completed its investigation and in about six weeks stood ready to issue the full amount of the $2,500,000 worth of 7% bonds. But for one reason or another—all false in Leland eyes—this further action was delayed. Wilfred still urged the sale of the real estate and even found a buyer who would take the Holden Avenue property.

To the Lelands it seemed logical to handle this financial stringency as they had in 1907 when things had been tight. The firm had borrowed a little and made as many cars as possible and then borrowed more. In such fashion they had muddled through until times became better and buyers reappeared in the market. Of course, Cadillac had not entered the 1907 depression with a heavy debt and it was a much smaller operation. But Dr. Murphy was opposed to financing in "driblets." While the pressing merchandise creditors did not seem to bother the Lelands much—only once did Wilfred say it would be more comfortable to have more funds for them—they were very much in Dr. Murphy's mind. The discussion went like this:

> W. C. Leland: I think it would be the right thing to do to sell the Holden Avenue plant and sell the balance of these bonds and use that money in the business and then, when conditions are better, discuss some other plan.
> Fred Murphy: I want to say a word and offer a motion. I think what we are all trying to do is just exactly what Mr. Leland has outlined. We want to make this company a great success—we are trying to protect the interest of those who invested in

it. It is perhaps a question of opinion as to how that can best be done. Personally to sell the property and realize $400,000— to sell the bonds and realize $1,250,000 giving a total of $1,650,000, all in cash, and then to apply that against your outstanding indebtedness of $2,375,000 as of the first, and perhaps more today, leaves you $725,000 due on open accounts with no cash in the bank and no credit in the bank and $4,250,000 being carried by the banks. I simply cannot see how it will carry you through.[13]

In this long struggle between the Lelands and their opposition, many of the words used in arguing their differences had come to have a strange double meaning. When Dr. Murphy spoke of protecting the interest of the investors this meant to the Lelands only the investors who were also endorsers, not the great mass of stockholders. By this time they were convinced that Dr. Murphy, now persuaded of the value of the company, wanted to throw it into receivership, thus shucking off the majority of the stockholders. Then in the process of reorganization, as so often happened, the Lelands would be replaced, a new management would be called in and the Lincoln could go on to the success which they all expected. On the other hand, when the Lelands appealed for constructive action and suggestions the opposition translated it simply as "Give us more money."

The executive committee discussed a complete refinancing plan. Dr. Murphy stated that to make possible such a plan Mr. William Murphy and Mr. Boyer would have to subordinate their claims as guarantors for the short-term loans at the banks. This concession they were willing to make, but there was also the distasteful possibility that any banking group who would be willing to refinance the company might also impose a financial controller on the management of the plant. Were the Lelands willing to accept such a restriction?

> H. M. Leland: I have been on this job sixty-five years. I never before had people I couldn't work with. If we have to lose everything then let us go and do it.
> W. A. C. Miller: We don't want anyone to lose anything.
> H.M.L.: We have done a great deal to save you since last January. We will do everything that two human beings can do to

> save this property. . . . I believe it is a bad time to begin going to banks and brokers to discuss a refinancing plan.
> Miller: How can we finance it?
> H.M.L.: I believe the suggestion made by my son and repeated over and over again—to get along from hand-to-mouth until conditions improve—they are improving every day—is the right method to pursue. . . . All the directors have to do is to go and see these bankers, say "Whatever is past is past; we have reached agreement and we will stand together—we are going to see this thing through." It can be cured in that way. It cannot be cured and we cannot go on by destructive means used by our board of directors.[14]

But this plea fell on unresponsive ears. The directors, who could have saved the company by going to the bankers and saying they would see the thing through, would not go. They would not risk anything further; the company might go out and find financing for itself if it could; they would not press their own claims upon it, but neither would they again lend their credit.

On October 17th, Fred Murphy, Wilfred Leland and W. A. C. Miller went to Chicago to talk with Ralph Van Vechten of the Continental & Commercial National Bank of Chicago, a bank that had already loaned Lincoln $500,000.[15] A tentative plan was put before Mr. Van Vechten which involved the issuance of $8,000,000 in debentures. Assuming $6,000,000 could be raised by such an issue the proceeds would retire the outstanding bonds and pay about $2,000,000 to the merchandise creditors, leaving about $2,750,000 cash for working capital. There was also some discussion as to whether a receivership would eliminate the danger of a further income-tax assessment.

As to the refinancing plan, Van Vechten advised that it could not be carried through under existing depression conditions except on terms so drastic that they could not be accepted. He believed perhaps a million would carry the company to a position where it could be refinanced, or joined with some other company on a favorable basis. He advised against a receivership; such a course would cost money to protect the investors' interests, money that might be better employed in preventing receivership. Further a recent law precluded any protection from tax assessment in receivership.

When Van Vechten was asked if the banks would carry along

under the present conditions, even though business should be very quiet during the next few months, he stated that *with the guarantors standing by* he would put up pro rata with other banks the amount that would be required. So concerned was he about the straits of the company that he arranged for his attorney, Henry Russell Platt, to go to Detroit and sit in on some of the meetings.[16]

Things were getting desperate now. Some of the larger creditors were very pressing. Already certificates for $500,000 in the mortgage-bond issue had been set aside for the Anderson Company (bodies) and $200,000 for the Timken Axle Company to stop any action by the Cleveland banks in their behalf. The lawyers worriedly discussed how to transfer the temporary mortgage from Dr. Murphy to the bank. This transfer if just before receivership evidently entailed some fine legal points and some fear of the censure of the Michigan securities commission. Dr. Murphy, discouraged by the Chicago trip, had been unwilling to go farther afield for aid. Only the Lelands traveled about trying to find a sympathetic ear and a helping hand. G. Herman Kinnicut of Kissell & Kinnicut, New York investment bankers, who had handled the public offering of Lincoln stock, attended some of the directors' meetings and finally notified the Lelands that his firm had been in touch with some of the creditors and had hopes of working out a plan.

At the meeting of November 3 when the mortgage transfer had been arranged and the controlling directors were already contemplating a petition for receivership before some creditor got there, Mr. Platt took the floor and arranged an armistice. Negotiations were under way in New York with responsible people who had asked the Lelands, their attorneys, Mr. Emmons and Mr. Platt, to come to New York on November 7. If the Lincoln board would wait until November 8 before acting, the plan could be presented to them for consideration and thereafter they could take whatever action they wished on a receivership.

Mr. Leo Butzel, attorney for Mr. Boyer, asked:

> If during the absence of Mr. Henry Leland or Mr. W. C. Leland or Mr. Nash, or any one of our men, if an attachment was made, not originating or brought about by our instigation, would they, or whichever director is here in their absence, at once cooperate with us to get the property?

Mr. Platt answered:

> We will co-operate with you in holding the meeting and forming a quorum. If Mr. Nash or Mr. Leland was necessary to form a quorum, he will attend and vote whichever way he wants, but he will as I say to you gentlemen, go on record—as they sincerely are—as opposed to the receivership, but there will be no hostile tactics adopted outside.[17]

Butzel's phrase, "to get the property" remained in the Leland mind as one more evidence that the whole purpose of the receivership was to *get* the company for Dr. Murphy and his cohorts.

But hope was running high now. To Wilfred, at least, the call to come to New York meant "Come and get your money." With the $10,000,000 hoped for they could pay off all the creditors and have sufficient working capital left to carry their operations until the better times which were surely now just around the corner. They would be free of the carping criticism of supervisors who knew nothing of automobile manufacturing, free to make the success which they never doubted was within their grasp.

The four men went to New York, arriving on the morning train on November 7. As Wilfred entered the room reserved for him at the Belmont the telephone was ringing. It was his secretary calling from the Lincoln office in Detroit. The government had again presented a tax claim—this time for $4,500,000.

This claim then was the hard fact which in all honor had to be presented to the bankers before any further discussion of Lincoln affairs began. It followed inevitably that, with this 4½-million tax lien hanging over the Lincoln Motor Company, no rescue proposition was possible, and the meeting adjourned without its presentation. Wearily the defeated Lelands and their attorneys returned to Detroit on the evening train.

Now at last the dread day was upon them. When Henry Leland arrived at the factory he knew that the wrecking of his business was inevitable. But before he went into the board meeting he entered his private office and closed the door. He read from his worn pocket edition of the Psalms, "I will lift up mine eyes unto the hills from whence cometh my help. My help cometh from the Lord."[18]

At 12 o'clock noon November 8, 1921, all the directors and their attorneys assembled in the board room at the Lincoln plant. John

Trix, who had not talked with the Lelands for weeks, now mumbled to Henry that he had been convinced that it would not do the Lelands or anybody else any good for him to vote their way. The proceedings were more formal and quieter than in the past. Mr. Emmons presented the income-tax notice. Mr. Platt stated that he had gone to New York with Mr. Emmons and the Lelands "but after using their best efforts, they found themselves unable to command any financial aid from those sources." [19] Filed was a telegram from G. Herman Kinnicut urging the board to continue seeking working capital. Placed on record was the letter from the distributors protesting receivership; it meant their ruin. Other remarks were entered in the record—declarations and opinions which had been stated before but must now be repeated for the last time. Henry Leland's report showing the progress in sales was written into the minutes. During the twelve months ending September 30 Lincoln had built 2494 cars and was 20th in sales in the industry. Wilfred made three proposals, one after another, moving that the three parcels of real estate be sold and the proceeds used for working capital. These were promptly voted down. Dr. Murphy also felt obliged to make a statement for the record. "An inference in these protests should not go unchallenged. Receivership is not something one wants; there is no other way. It is not a matter of election . . . it is the end of the trail."

Then W. A. C. Miller offered the fateful resolution:

> WHEREAS, the condition of this company is such that the further continuation of its activities are impracticable unless it be immediately equipped with a large amount of fresh cash; and
> WHEREAS, its manufacturing operations have been and are now being conducted at a substantial loss and the company is unable, upon its own resources or upon its own credit to obtain the needed capital or credits: and
> WHEREAS, the company owes large sums of money which it is unable to pay and has heavy obligations maturing in the very near future, which it will also be unable to pay; and the property and assets of the company are under the laws of the state of Michigan subject to be levied upon and seized under writs of attachment, in advance of judgment of claimants: and
> WHEREAS, it is believed that the best interest of the corporation, stockholders, and creditors will be served by the conserva-

tion, so far as is practical, of the property, assets and business of the corporation by the administration of its affairs through a court of equity.

The legal phrases went on and on pronouncing sentence on the great corporation brought into being as the culmination of Henry Leland's skill and craftsmanship. Now its proud head would be brought down in shame and disgrace, betraying the trusting souls who had believed in Henry Leland.

The vote was as expected.

Ayes: William H. Murphy, Joseph Boyer, W. A. C. Miller, Charles H. Murphy, Fred T. Murphy, John Trix — 6

Nays: Henry M. Leland, Wilfred C. Leland, William T. Nash — 3

It was left to John Bourne, H.M.'s secretary, to record the closing scene.

> When the door opened at the termination of that final board meeting, the first to come out was Mr. Leland, upstanding as a patriarch and still with fire in his eye. Closely following came the snappy young directors and attorneys, chatting as they passed out with their briefcases. Mr. Leland stood at my desk, as with his hand he gestured a silent response to those who said, "Well, goodby, Mr. Leland," as they hurried out.
>
> Then together from the directors' room came his three historic friends. These white-haired allies of many a successful undertaking during the long years, were far from the cheerfulness of their young relatives, as they approached the silver-haired Mr. Leland at my desk. Tears were streaming down the face of John Trix and fell from his long beard to the floor; the face of Mr. Boyer was flushed by the conflicting emotions within him and upon his countenance was the confession that he was not proud of his part of the proceedings. Words were beyond these two; but perhaps Mr. William H. Murphy spoke the feeling of their hearts when, after brushing away the tears from his eyes with his handkerchief, he took Mr. Leland's hand and sobbed out: "Uncle Henry, I'm sorry to do it, but I had to vote with my family." Then the three went out. Mr. Leland closed the door of his private office and was alone. This indeed was the end of the trail.[20]

Chapter XVIII
Henry Ford Listens

"IT WAS TRAGEDY; tragedy to trusting investors and more. It was the tragedy of unrealized hopes, the feeling that one experiences at the passing of a young life of promise; or the gashing of a masterpiece by some uncouth vandal." [1]

Thus wrote Henry Leland's secretary, and undoubtedly this was the way the old master craftsman felt about the Lincoln car when the Lincoln Motor Company went into receivership. Many sorrowed with him. One reporter wrote, "Lincoln-like to the last, Detroit's grand old man battled for his convictions in his endeavors to carry the Lincoln Motor Company through stormy seas. . . . He has stood alone before. . . . He makes a more familiar figure battling single handed for survival of the institution in which he has put his uncapitulating soul. May our townsmen, assisted by the receivership to which he did not take kindly, see the fulfillment of his hopes. For is it not written: 'Seest thou a man diligent in business. He shall stand before kings.' " [2]

The press was uniformly kind and most dispatches expressed genuine regret at this reverse to Henry Leland, who was widely recognized as the nation's master automotive artisan and a man of unquestioned integrity. Prayers were said for him in the churches.

The receiver appointed by Judge Tuttle was the Detroit Trust Company. Ralph Stone, the president, immediately declared that everything would be done to keep the business going throughout the receivership and reorganization. The assets of the company according to the books were $14,800,000 and the liabilities $8,237,000. Henry Leland wired the distributors, "We are starting with undaunted courage to build a greater and more united organization to carry the enterprise to complete success."

So the Lelands set out again, trying to interest capital in the purchase of the plant and to prevent the interests, which they believed had brought about the catastrophe, from taking the final step of wiping out both the stockholders and creditors and securing for themselves the assets of the company which had cost $16,000,000— and were worth they believed $50,000,000—for a paltry two or three million dollars. Trips were made between November 11 and December 18 to Chicago, New York, Pittsburgh and Worcester.

On July 8 when Wilfred had approached Henry Ford with regard to the sale of the Holden Avenue plant and talked with him about the Lincoln's need for money, Ford had observed that he would not lend a nickel. But when Wilfred went on to say that unless financing could be arranged the directors would apply for a receivership, Ford answered, "After they do, come and see me." So now the Lelands decided to go again to Ford.[3]

When Wilfred went first on November 14 and talked with Henry and Edsel Ford together, he reported that Mr. Ford was impressed with the unprecedented opportunities which would result from the combination of his resources and the Leland organization.[4] At the close of the interview Ford said he would be out of town for about a week but would send a man to see the Lelands when he returned. Instead Henry Ford himself called Wilfred the next day by telephone and asked him to bring his father and come right out to the Dearborn plant. This was an augury of serious interest. In the conference room Mr. Ford had assembled what he was pleased to call "the men who do things in the Ford organization," Charles Sorensen, William B. Mayo, E. C. Kanzler, P. E. Martin, Ernest G. Liebold and others.[5]

Remembered Wilfred: "While the general discussion was in

progress, Mr. Ford took me aside and asked how much money it would take to clean this thing up. Would $10,000,000 do it? I then told him the 10 million would take care of the bank and merchandise indebtedness but would not take care of the stockholders."

The discussions went on at other times and places. On one occasion Wilfred went to Fairlane, the Ford home, entering by the back gate in secrecy, as Ford did not want the negotiations publicly known. Even Henry Leland was not apprised of their progress. Wilfred believed the Ford decision to buy was virtually taken as early as November 21 [6] and was in accord with the terms set forth by the Lelands, which were that creditors and stockholders would be paid, the dealer's franchises would be continued, and the Lelands would be retained to manufacture the Lincoln cars.[7] There was some discussion of the payment of the stockholders and their classification as good or bad stockholders, and whether all deserved to be repaid. Meanwhile, the Lelands were still traveling about trying to find other capital interested in restoring the Lincoln Company to independence. Some of the consultations of this period were with King, Hoagland Company of Chicago, Mr. Heeny Evans of Providence, R.I., and Mr. Elisha Walker of Blair and Company.[8] The Lelands were still obsessed with the idea that their late directors were planning a reorganization which not only would wipe out the equity of the stockholders, but also would discard the Leland management. While they were hopeful about the Fords, they were earnestly canvassing other possible sources of help.

Meanwhile, the receiver's inventory was completed and the appraisal of the financial status of the Lincoln Company was filed with the court on December 19. The buildings, machinery, plant equipment, tools, etc. showed a heavy deflation. Strangely enough the real estate was revalued at a higher figure than it had been carried on the books, from $1,452,743 to $1,709,401.[9] All in all, the valuation of the assets was reduced by $5,500,000 to a toal of $9,490,811 with liabilities, exclusive of the tax claim and the capital stock, listed at $9,073,105.[10] This great deflation in value would tend to support the fairness of the amortization allowed on the plant and equipment at the war's end.

Almost from the first the receiver had been optimistic about the tax lien and believed that when the receiver's appraisal had been made, the proper representation would cause the government to at least scale down the claim.[11] The receiver was also considerate and co-operative. It was realized that the business had real value only as a going concern and that its great asset was the Lelands. So they and their executives were retained and the purchasing, assembling and advertising proceeded.[12] Plans were made to exhibit a few cars at the New York and Chicago shows. Sales held up pretty well during November—only 200 cars had been scheduled—but they slumped badly in December.

The receiver announced on December 29 that the federal government had found no fraud in the Lincoln income-tax matter and that the claim would probably be reduced to about $500,000.[13] This news had come the day before, too late to inform the creditors, who had met earlier that day with the receiver. The Lelands received this news with mixed emotions. They had hoped for a public hearing in which they might defend their figures rather than compromise the settlement. However, the receiver advised and the Lelands agreed that litigation might cost more than a settlement in the end. The important thing was to get the creditors taken care of and the business going again as promptly as possible.

A stockholders' protective committee had also been organized and had advertised about the middle of November requesting that holders of A stock deposit their shares with the committee. Among the names signed as members of the committee were G. Herman Kinnicut and Robert K. Cassatt representing the investment firm which had sold the stock to the public initially.[14] George F. Fuller of Worcester, Mass., also a member of the committee, was the largest holder of A stock. Together with Sybil H. Fuller, he held 7500 shares. The second largest holders of the preferred stock were the Murphys—5400 shares in the names of Fred T., William H. and Rebecca Murphy.[15] Not one of the Murphy names appeared on the stockholders' committee.

Nor did the Murphy name appear on the creditors' committee although here too they were among the larger claimants. However, the Murphys sent out an independent call for a creditors' meeting on January 3 at the Penobscot Building.

In the meantime, Henry Ford had called Wilfred Leland to another conference on December 19. Almost at once Ford stated that as far as he was concerned there was no reason for any longer keeping secret his decision to purchase the Lincoln Motor Company. Wilfred should tell his father. Ford agreed that an early transfer of the plant would be of great advantage to the distributors, who were now holding on by the skin of their teeth. The figures appertaining to the Lincoln liabilities were again gone over verbally, and it was Wilfred who suggested that a written memorandum of them be sent to Edsel Ford the next day. Wilfred left the Fords convinced that the understanding between the conferring parties was complete on all the important points—reimbursement of the creditors and stockholders, continuance of the distributors, and retention of the Leland management.

The Lelands were believers. In this case, of course, the Ford offer was extremely fortuitous. Sore and defeated as they were, the Ford proposal was balm to their long-tried souls. It seemed logical to them that an experienced automobile manufacturer not only could appreciate the virtues of the Lincoln car and the excellence of the factory organization, but also could better foresee its certain brilliant future than the mechanically ignorant, money-conscious capitalists of the former Lincoln directorate. Given their parental pride in the Lincoln, it did not seem strange to them that the "king of the flivver" might also have yearnings toward a more sophisticated motor. There was another bond of understanding between the Lelands and Henry Ford besides an interest in things mechanical, and that was a certain distrust of coldly calculating financiers. Furthermore, holding fast to the popular image of Henry Ford's wealth, they felt his cavalier indifference to financial reports or contracts to purchase was but another evidence that he need not count the cost of anything he wanted. This transaction was directly between father and son and father and son, all honorable men, and there was no need to consider the careful dispositions of the financial world.

There was also the fact that the Lelands were no longer the owners or managers of the Lincoln Motor Company and could not legally dispose of it. All that Wilfred had to sell to Henry Ford was an idea and a plan of action. Certainly the fact that he was able to sell these intangibles for such a great sum was evidence of a high skill in salesmanship as well as testimony to the basic generosity of Henry Ford. Just as certainly at this point in this whole quixotic adventure, Wilfred Leland was in no position to insist on written signatures on dotted lines.

The Leland attorney, Harold Emmons, was summoned to Fairlane on December 22. Wilfred drove him out, going over again the terms he had discussed with the Fords. Emmons was slightly suspicious of such generous terms, but after he had finished his talk with Mr. Ford he reported to Wilfred that all was as he had understood.

Now that Henry Ford had made up his mind, he was in a hurry. The Lelands conferred with the receiver, who could give no assurance that a sale would be promptly ordered even though a reliable bidder could be found. Also they were a little suspicious of the Detroit Trust Company since the Murphys had stock in it. Hence it was decided to have an interview with the supervising judge. Judge Arthur J. Tuttle was persuaded to stop by the Henry Leland home on the morning of December 29 on his way to work. Present there were Edsel Ford, Harold Emmons and the father and son Leland.

Since there was afterwards much discussion and controversy over the verbal agreements between the Fords and the Lelands, it might be well here to review the only outside testimony to these understandings at the time, or soon after they were completed. Judge Tuttle made a statement concerning what he was told on that day of December. Emmons presented to the judge the purpose of the conference and the basic agreement. Tuttle thus remembered Emmons' presentation:

> After efforts in various directions to raise the necessary money to reorganize and refinance the Lincoln Motor Company, Mr. Henry M. Leland went to his old friend Henry Ford for the purpose of getting financial assistance and he has finally interested Mr. Ford, and Mr. Ford is willing to help him and furnish the necessary money, provided it can be done in such a manner as will meet with Mr. Ford's approval. One of the things Mr. Ford insists upon is that although his name is not to be known or appear in the matter at the present time, he does insist that you be fully advised relative to his part in the transaction. . . .

If the property can be sold now at a judicial sale, free and clear from all incumbrances, Mr. Ford will pay $5,000,000 in cash for it. He wants you to know, however, that ultimately he is going to pay every just claim against the Lincoln Motor Company, a hundred cents on the dollar. He is hoping that some way can be worked out to even do a little something for those stockholders like school teachers and people of that kind who put their money into the stock of this company as investments and have lost it. Of course, he would not expect to do anything for the speculators who have bought this stock at a cheap price or as a gamble, and at this time he does not know what will be the outcome relative to the stockholders, and the definite plans at the present time do not involve the stockholders, although Mr. Ford and Mr. Leland both hope that something can be done which will help those who have been stockholders from the beginning.

We want you to know that if you fix the upset price in the decree for sale at $5,000,000 and Mr. Ford is the purchaser at that price, he is going to pay all of the honest creditors in full. Mr. Ford's motives are to help Mr. Leland to save his financial situation and to save the industry for Detroit and the automobile world and Mr. Leland has urged Mr. Ford to do it and Mrs. Ford has urged him to do it, and it is not a moneymaking scheme on Mr. Ford's part.

Another thing which Mr. Ford and all of us are very anxious and want you to have in mind is that one of the very important and valuable assets of this concern is the sales organization. This is not only of value to whoever buys it, but it is a matter of great concern to the individual sales agents themselves. They have been hanging on for months, trying to sell an orphan car. . . .

Surely if Mr. Ford is to put money into this enterprise and go ahead with it, it is very important, and fairness demands that these sales agents should have some assurance for the future and know that the company is going to be reorganized and placed on a firm, sound financial basis. Now, these are the reasons which have induced Mr. Ford to agree to enter into this matter and purchase the property, provided he could do it in this way and handle it in this way. It would be necessary to have the sale take place next month.

We think the upset price ought to be $5,000,000 so that Mr. Ford can buy the property at that price and then later on, in his own way and at the proper time, he can pay the balance due to these different creditors.[16]

So it would seem that as Judge Tuttle remembered it the discussion brought forth all of the points on which the Lelands had placed special emphasis except that Mr. Ford had agreed to retain the Leland management. If the statement on the hope of paying the stockholders was not without reservation, this was not the place in which to go into details. Certainly the Lelands were anxious for the little stockholders to be paid; they were not sure themselves that some of the others deserved to be paid.

Judge Tuttle responded to this presentation by turning to Edsel Ford: "So long as your father is planning to pay these creditors in full, so long as the total amount of claims now known, is more than $8,000,000 and somewhere near $9,000,000, I hardly see why the upset price in the decree and the purchase price by your father should not be more than $5,000,000."

To this Edsel replied, "I shouldn't think it would make so very much difference."

So on December 30, 1921, Mr. Emmons made his written offer of $5,000,000 to the receiver, asking that the sale take place on or before January 24, 1922. With his letter he sent a deposit of $250,000. On December 31, the receiver filed a petition advising the court of the offer and asking the advice of the court relative thereto. The hearing was set for January 3. The hearing was attended by Attorney Henry M. Campbell, representing the stockholders' protective committee, and Leo Butzel counsel for the endorsers of the bank notes. Butzel put up several arguments against the sale. He said that Emmons, who had been counsel for the Lincoln Company, could not now represent an unknown bidder. He also protested that the proposed sale date did not give sufficient notice and the price bid was too small and would wipe out all the shareholders and only partially repay the creditors. Emmons wanted an early sale so an announcement could be made on the last day of the Chicago automobile show. Judge Tuttle fixed February 4 as the date of the sale and the upset or minimum price at $8,000,000, whereupon Mr. Emmons immediately raised his bid to that amount. Then he went on to state that if his bid was accepted the Lincoln Motor Company would be under the management of the Lelands.[17]

January 3 was also the date set for a creditors' meeting at the Penobscot Building where Fred Murphy was to present a plan for the reorganization of the Lincoln Company. The assembled creditors waited a long time for Fred Murphy to arrive and meanwhile they talked among themselves. At length one of them asked for an informal vote as to whether they would rather settle their claim for 75 cents and go forward with the Lelands or hold on for 100 per cent and take some other management. The Lelands won handily.

At length Mr. Murphy, Mr. Emmert and Mr. Butzel came in looking dejected and carrying a newspaper. They apologized for their delay and Murphy read from the newspaper, "The Lincoln plant will be sold on February 4 by the receiver at an upset price of not less than $8,000,000." He continued, "The water has gotten too deep for us. We have no plan to offer you today." Questions developed that he had planned to offer $2,000,000 for the Lincoln plant. The creditors were to be persuaded to accept small payments on account, and claims safeguarded by the issuance of junior securities, to be paid off from the earnings of the company. Compared with the $8,000,000 offer, this Murphy proposal looked like very small potatoes, and the whole plan was scorned. Wilfred would not have been human had he not felt some satisfaction at this demonstration.[18]

On January 6 the federal government advised that the tax claim would be settled for $610,274, and some weeks later Judge Tuttle ruled that this tax was to take priority over any other creditors' claim.[19] Adding this to the other liabilities the total figure went up well over 9½ million. But this burden no longer rested on the Lelands and the Lincoln Motor Company and what did a half million more or less matter to the purse of Henry Ford?

Gossip and rumor flew thick and fast over Detroit, swirled across country and through the financial centers in New York. On January 10, the whispers were put into print. "Rumors are that Ford interests are entering the Lincoln situation by backing the Lelands in the eight million bid made for the latter's property last week in Detroit. The blending of Leland craftsmanship with Ford genius at quantity production would be a combination of undoubted power." [20] The story went on to state that Ford would cooperate with the Lelands to realize one of their staunchest principles—that none of the original investors should lose through the receivership. This premature scoop stole some of the thunder from the surprise which Henry Ford was preparing for the public. As early as January 6 he had called in James Sweinhart of the Detroit *News* and given him an exclusive story of the Fords's rush to the rescue of the Lelands. But there were some difficulties about clearing the story with the Lelands, and some modifications had to be made which delayed the publication of the Sweinhart article until the January 11 issue of the paper.

The trend of Sweinhart's story must have been somewhat of a surprise to the Lelands, who had believed that Ford saw good business as well as charitable reasons for investing in the Lincoln Company and retaining the Leland management. However, the headline was FORDS SAVE LELANDS, and the gist of the announcement that followed was that the Fords neither wanted nor needed the Lincoln, but through the intercession of Mrs. Ford and her kind heart, and because of the constant pleading of the Lelands, Henry Ford's own kind heart was touched and he decided to help. Some praise was given to Wilfred for his able presentation of the Lincoln situation and his command of all pertinent facts. Mr. Ford got off some homilies on the coming of a new business era when there would be more consideration and human feeling between industrialists and less cut-throat competition. But along with these sentimentalities was the plain statement that "The Ford Motor Company will endeavor to work out some plan by means of which those stockholders, who in the opinion of the company, actually invested cash in Lincoln securities with the idea of sustaining the project and making it a going concern, may hope for some substantial return on their investment." There was also the statement that "The car will be marketed through the existing Lincoln sales organization."

Other newspapers reported with less froth and more fact. The Detroit *Free Press* stated bluntly that at eight million even the debts would not all be paid, but if Ford should go as high as $11,000,000, as town talk said he might if necessary, there would be a little left over for the stockholders. However, the press was quite uniformly adulatory.[21] "Absolutely splendid," said one, and another, "The romance of the winged wheel continues, thanks to Henry

Ford's capacity for doing magnificent things."[22] Speculators too took Henry Ford seriously and the Lincoln stock enjoyed a flurry on the stock exchange, rising from 2-3/8 to nine before going back down to five.[23]

The great excitement of the automobile world centered on what a merger of Ford and Leland capacity would mean in that very competitive field.[24] Speculation turned to the possibility that other industrialists might bid for the Lincoln to prevent such a strong combination. Durant, Studebaker and even the Du Ponts were all eyed as prospective bidders. For a time, however, no one but the Ford representative brought in the $250,000 deposit attesting an intention to bid. Then, when it was so late as to be legally questionable, two more bidders appeared, and the press was off again with a buzz of conjecture. Mr. Henry Ford continued to make statements to the newsmen stressing the necessity of keeping Henry Leland active in automobile circles.

"It would be a stain against the motor-car industry and against Detroit to permit outsiders to secure control of the Lincoln plant merely because the Lelands have been caught in a financial pinch. Henry M. Leland is one of the great motor-car men of America."[25] It is ironic to remember in the face of so much adulation that initially Henry Leland had almost spoiled the deal. At the second meeting of the Lelands and Fords when H.M. was present, he had been engrossed in telling the assembled Ford executives about the Lincoln troubles. Ford became bored and tried to stop the recital, actually saying once sharply, "We've enough of that." Finally, looking annoyed, Ford got up and left the room when H.M. persisted. Wilfred followed him out and talked with him, bringing him back into the room and directing attention and conversation back to a discussion of what the Fords could do with the Lincoln. Henry Leland did not attend any of the later conferences and did not again speak with Ford until the deal had been closed.

As the days passed the press continued to worry about the stockholders—their reimbursement was not so sure but rather qualified as to whether they were bona fide investors or speculators. The continued activity of the Lincoln stock on the market underlined the fact that some speculators were involved, else why should this stock continue to be traded?

The Fords with Pete Martin, one of their superintendents, visited the Lincoln plant on January 18 and observed everything most respectfully, Martin pointing out certain arrangements he had noted in his previous visits. Conferences from that time on centered on plans for getting things going as soon as the sale should be consummated and setting the scene for the day of the sale.

During this period all relations between the principal participants remained harmonious, Mr. Ford playing his role of respect and benevolence with much zest. In the general chorus of approbation, however, there was here and there a dissenting voice. Most of these pessimists spoke privately to the Lelands, who were in no mood to listen or believe. They had just surmounted what had seemed to them an impassable barrier to their continued business life and they glowed with gratitude to their deliverer. Although the newspaper poppycock about the deep old friendship of the two families, *et cetera*, was just publicity dressing, the help was real and solid enough. Only one journalist had the courage, or conviction, to put his doubts in print and he was a rather consistent heckler of Henry Ford, refusing to forget Ford's vindictive campaign against the Jews and the Ford failure to turn the profits of his war-time contract back to the government as he had publicly promised. Such a chronic critic did not receive much attention. He wrote, "Ford wanted himself pictured as the good angel of the Lelands, that is what he got in the papers, and the Lord knows we hope it will come out that way, but to us it looks like the passing of the Lelands. . . . The deal, however, looks to us like one in which Ford saw a chance to pick up a good plant and something of a going concern at a bargain and he is going into it on that basis—it rather grates to see the venerable Henry Leland pictured in the role of a mendicant to satisfy Ford in another of his advertising stunts." [26]

The consummation of the sale had been set for eleven o'clock on Saturday, February 4. It was a typically gray winter morning, and the air was raw and chill. Yet two hours before the time of the auction the lawn in front of the Lincoln building was filled with spectators, probably three thousand. Among them were hundreds whose employment depended on the outcome, faithful men and women who had been idle for months; hundreds of stockholders, whose only apparent hope lay in the Ford purchase; and hundreds of well-wishers, who were irresistibly drawn to the scene of action.

Promptly on the hour, a court officer took his position at a table on the wide entrance landing and commenced reading the long order of sale. At his side stood the three competing bidders. Every telephone in the neighborhood of the factory had been leased to reporters who were anxious to speed the news of the contest. The waiting multitude shivered during the preamble. Then just as the reading ended the sun broke through the clouds and bathed the gathering in golden light. Was it a sign?

The special master in chancery then called for bidders and Attorney Emmons threw up his arm and said: "I bid eight million dollars for Henry Ford." Other bids were called for but the two men standing by, who had made deposits, declined to bid.[27] As the auctioneer brought his gavel down on the table there was a shout, "Ford's got it," and the crowd broke into jubilant cheers. A band planted in the crowd began to play "Hail to the Chief." As the attorneys retreated into the lobby and up the stairs the crowd poured after them and would not leave until Henry Leland came and shook hands with about a thousand of them. These people too believed the things Ford had promised and wanted to congratulate their old friend.[28]

Then the Fords arrived, Mr. and Mrs. Henry with Edsel in a raccoon coat. Mrs. Wilfred Leland was there with her husband; the Fords and Lelands came downstairs preceded by two enormous baskets of red roses and posed together on the front steps.* As they stood there a great flag was unfurled down the front of the building. The affair had all the appearance of a festival or wedding. Indeed, the official statement issued rather wordily described the affair as an affiliation. "On one end the tremendous Ford institutions turning out 1,000,000 or more motor vehicles a year, and on the

* This was Blanche Dewey Leland, who died in 1929. Mrs. Henry Leland (Nelle) had passed away in 1914.

other end the Leland-built Lincoln which in a comparatively short time has forged its way to the front as probably the finest constructed car the world has ever seen." [29]

The editor of the Manufacturer's *Record* wrote a lilting verse describing the happiness of Leland friends.

> Out from the jungle of finance
> Where bankers and leeches abound
> Into the open of business
> A way of relief has been found,
> And the friends of the Lelands, wide scattered
> Rejoice that once more they are free
> To work out their plans for rebuilding
> The "Lincoln"—to all it should be.[30]

Chapter XIX
Betrayed

IN THE COURSE of the conversations between Wilfred Leland and Henry Ford preliminary to the acquisition of the Lincoln Motor Company by Ford, Wilfred finally ventured, "Mr. Ford we have come to no definite understanding regarding our personal remuneration."

Replied the benefactor, "Mr. Leland, you just leave that to us. We are going to do what is right by you."

Wilfred, grateful and tactful too, responded, "Mr. Ford, in view of what you have already agreed to do, and of the spirit which you have manifested in these negotiations, we are willing to place ourselves in your hands."

So although always before the Lelands had worked under a definite contract, in this instance as well as in more important matters the Lelands trusted Henry Ford and placed themselves in his hands.

On January 24 before the receiver's sale of the Lincoln Motor Company, Wilfred Leland, all unknowing, made what was to be his last public announcement regarding the management of that company. The sale to friendly interests, he said, would make possible the carrying out for the first time of the complete Leland policy.

Under the old régime clashing elements in the directorate had made it impossible to put those policies into effect. Prices would be lowered; the production schedule for 1922 would be 6000 to 8000 cars. The sales organization would be continued, but markets would be widened and standards maintained.[1] The factory organization would be strengthened but in the main would continue as formerly. On February 4, when the sale had been completed, Henry Leland announced price reductions of $800 to $1200 per car and thus brought Lincoln prices right down to the level of Cadillac prices.[2]

On Monday morning after the sale, dawn found several thousand workers at the door of the plant and five thousand came before the day was done. Six hundred were employed according to the wage scales and employment practices of the Ford Motor Company.[3] At nine o'clock the Fords arrived bringing with them Charles E. Sorensen, superintendent of the Ford Rouge plant; G. W. Walker, Ford purchasing agent; and William B. Mayo, chief Ford engineer. The group went for a prolonged inspection of the plant. Orders totaling $1,000,000 came in on that first day.[4] The old Lincoln stock continued to sell on the exchange until Wednesday when it was cut from the list by the board of governors.[5]

On Saturday, exactly one week after the auction, a check for $8,000,000, signed by Henry Ford, was handed to the receiver of the Lincoln Motor Company by Attorney Emmons. On hand to witness this event were all the members of the Ford and Leland families together with Ford friends, Mr. and Mrs. Harvey Firestone. Within two hours the check for $610,000 in payment of the federal government tax claim was in the mail. Such was the exhilarating speed and power of the Ford money! The receiver announced that the first mortgage bonds amounting to $1,882,000 would be paid next and then would come the local taxes and the expenses of the receivership. About five million dollars would be left for the creditors.[6]

On February 16 the era of good feeling still persisted, and a birthday party celebrating Henry Leland's 79th birthday was held at the Lincoln plant. On that occasion Henry and Edsel Ford presented the elderly Leland with a Ford Motor Company badge, No. 79, and an investment certificate for $363,000 representing the par value of Leland's B stock in the old company.[7] Everybody was happy, and the news of the certificate went through the factory in a flash to spread even more cheer, for it encouraged all the employee investors to hope that they too would soon get reimbursement for their stock.[8]

The Detroit newspapers and the automobile journals speculated a great deal about this coalition of a quality product and a quantity method. Some thought the two incompatible. Others conceded that a car of "practically" the same quality could be turned out at lower cost by the elimination of "construction refinements and tests which have been insisted on hitherto by Henry Leland."[9] The vast Ford purchasing facilities would admittedly lessen costs and if the car should be sold through the Ford outlets that alone would soak up 8,000 units.[10] But speculation turned mainly on the run Henry Ford would give Cadillac and General Motors: "When he [Ford] introduces production on his favorite basis, turning out cars as a baker does biscuits, he will make the other fellows hustle."[11] Little of this speculation took account of the fact that the Lincoln was not intended to be as common as biscuits; its problem had been sales, not production; and systems designed to put out thousands of cars a day might not be so efficient when producing 50 cars a day. However, there was in all this comment one correct basic assumption which was that the Ford ideas and pattern would be dominant in this affiliation. Stated the Detroit *Times* on February 7, "Before the end of the week, the Ford Lincoln Motor Company will be operating as far as possible under the same set of economy and efficiency rules as are now in effect in all other Henry Ford enterprises."

When the Ford executives came into the plant after the sale it was said that they came to look at the Lincoln layout, methods and processes with the view of improving them or, if worthy, of adopting them for other Ford plants.[12] They found plenty to be improved, judging by their subsequent actions, but little worth copying. The very next day they came with a squadron of men and began tearing down walls and rearranging the plant. One of the walls first demolished was that of Henry Leland's private office. Certainly the Lelands had not envisioned such an extensive remodeling of what they had believed to be a fine automobile plant and one they had already adapted to the manufacture of the Lincoln car. Still the drastic rearrangement was apparently taken in good part. On the day of the birthday party Henry Ford gave a press interview. He was, he said, devoting practically all his time to laying the ground work for the application of his manufacturing ideas to the Lincoln plant. First it was being given a thorough cleaning and painting inside. A hundred men with scrubbing brushes had been turned loose in the plant a week before and they were still moving debris. Other men were knocking down partitions between offices and in shops.

If the Lelands did not actively oppose the remodeling of the plant, they did resent the manner in which the new directors of the work went at the job. They invaded the premises without prior notice and when they needed assistance they ordered the regular Lincoln employees to the task without reference to the Leland management or other executives whose domain they invaded. In fact the newcomers over-ran the factory, gave directions indiscriminately and often countermanded Leland orders. The very first time Pete Martin came in he ordered the call system torn out, and this order was given not to H.M. but to a minor executive. Another day he found the gate man with his hands in his pockets, a posture Martin thought offensive for some reason, and he roughly ordered the man to go get his time—he was fired. Sorensen too made a practice of similar arbitrary actions. He kicked a stool from under a man seated at work, admonishing him to "Stand up." The fact that the man was an employee of the Detroit Edison, who got up and took a swipe at Sorensen, in no way affected the warning the action gave to Lincoln employees. This kind of conduct on the part of Ford go-getters could for a time be overlooked as mere rudeness and bad manners, but when despite protests the offenses continued, repetition took on the character of studied insult and challenge.

Certainly Henry Leland began his employment with Henry Ford in a cooperative mood, understandably eager for success in this last chance to save the Lincoln and end his career on a successful note. But he was also a man of independent spirit, and he resented the contemptuous indifference to his authority, the continued calculated insult to his position. So he fought back. He countermanded orders which had been given without his knowledge; he fired men installed in place of his employees. One day when Sorensen paused to question a heap of cylinders thrown aside by the inspector and after a cursory review said to the workman at hand, "Use them!" H.M. came along with a sledge hammer and smashed every one of them beyond use or repair. When one night the Ford renovators had come into the tool department and in the progress of their work had thrown out on the floor indiscriminately the fine tools the mechanics had kept in the drawers of their benches, blunting and breaking delicate pieces, Henry Leland had an open quarrel with the Ford men. When the elderly man in charge of the reception desk and the Lincoln exhibit room at the plant entrance was abruptly dismissed by a Ford representative, H.M. took the matter clear up to Henry Ford to get the man reinstated.

Though neither the Lelands nor many others knew it at the time, this kind of behavior by Ford supervisors was not uncommon at Ford plants and with Ford's knowledge and approval. Men were not allowed to sit down at all, if they so much as leaned against a machine they were liable to be fired.[13] Strange and devious ways were used to discipline men. "If the work of certain clerks in the shop is not wanted, why tell them so? Smash their desks. . . . Expensive tools of skilled workmen are scattered over the floor. Foolish? Insulting? Humiliating? Not at all. It takes the conceit out of a man who prides himself on his work." [14]

Perhaps Sorensen and Martin behaved just as arbitrarily in the Ford plants where their own authority had been established and maintained by such methods. When remonstrated with, Sorensen retorted, "The general impression is that you think yourselves exclusive; you are no different from me or anyone else—no different from any Ford plant."

As a matter of fact the Lelands thought some of their methods were different and superior. When Scovell-Wellington made the survey of the Lincoln Motor Company in June and July 1921, they made this statement of the Lincoln management:

> The whole organization, it appears to us, is unusually harmonious and uniformly competent. We do not see, however, any individual of great distinction in *management,* that is, in the close and firm organization of a great business, operated under rigid

and exact supervision. Mr. H. M. Leland undoubtedly has distinction as a craftsman, a manufacturer and a pioneer in certain important developments in the automobile industry, and Mr. W. C. Leland has shared in this distinction; but their management today is, in our opinion, characterized more by leadership than authority.

As far as we could judge from our short contact with the organization, important decisions are either made in conference or rather speedily referred by the conference method for the approval of all executives concerned. Operations on this plan naturally develop loyalty, co-operation and harmony, provided the individuals concerned are capable of displaying those qualities; and, as noted above, we believe these qualities are effective in the Lincoln Motor Company. This is the strength and the weakness (as far as it is weakness) of the present organization.

The Ford method of management was the antithesis of this method. Said Henry Ford, "The Ford factories have no organization, no specific duties attaching to any position, no line of succession or authority, very few titles and no conferences." [15] Positions of power were fought for, maintained and enlarged by eternal vigilance and constant assertion. Ford delighted in setting one man against another; he thought competition made them more alert. As he put it, "The spirit of crowding forces the man who has the qualities for a higher place eventually to get it. . . . We have no cut-and-dried places—our best men make their places." [16] By the same token Ford seldom gave instructions, expecting his men to divine his will in most instances. If he gave an order or voiced a desire, he expected quick and thorough accomplishment. He did not care much how a thing was done, so it was done.

In contrast here were the Lelands, who led and did not drive. With them were men, many of them employees from L&F days. They expected to talk things over with their executives before coming to decisions and then, by the same process, explain to the men under them the reasons underlying the decision and thus secure co-operation. To the swiftly moving Ford bosses such a method seemed ridiculously slow and cumbersome. In fact the whole Leland organization seemed clumsy to the Ford people.[17] Manufacturing was to them a matter of logistics, lay-outs and systems, not human engineering.

This different approach to all problems seemingly underlay the reaction of Henry Leland to other Ford proposals for change in the Lincoln production process. When Ford told Sorensen to use AAA Ford steel in Lincoln axles, H.M. was said to have been outraged. But after a visit to the Ford laboratory and a demonstration he agreed to the change.[18] It is quite probable that he balked or temporized at other suggestions because he was given no time for investigation or the matter was not given a logical and convincing presentation. Undoubtedly he feared any cheapening of the quality and excellence of the Lincoln design. He had reason for caution. Ford had certain blind spots mechanically at this time which even his own engineers and designers deplored. He instructed his designer, Eugene Farkas, to work out a thermo-syphon system for the Lincoln motor though Farkas and all the other Ford engineers knew such a water-cooling system to be out of date.[19] While this device is not known to have progressed to the point where it was pressed upon Henry Leland in the few months he was permitted to continue in the management of the Lincoln factory, it is evidence that H.M. had reason to question Ford ideas. Yet when he would not be rushed into immediate changes he was considered to be stubborn and uncooperative.

In the departments of the Lincoln organization under Wilfred's jurisdiction some changes had come quite readily. The Ford methods of accounting and purchasing were adopted as were the Ford wage and employment practices. But there soon developed a wide difference as to the handling of sales and advertising. One thing that had been of great importance to the Lelands had been the preservation of the Lincoln sales organization—those distributors who had stood by so loyally through the receivership and the reorganization. They had been mentioned again and again in that period of sweet accord when Henry Ford had seemed so readily, but so carefully, in oral agreement with the wishes of the Lelands. The Lelands also believed strongly that an expensive car like the Lincoln could not be advantageously sold in the same salesroom as the Ford Model T. Neither would gain by the presence of the other as their sales approaches were so different. Since Wilfred dealt with Edsel Ford and William Ryan, the Ford sales-manager, both more courteous and less calculatedly ruthless men, the controversy on that point was more prolonged but no less painful. For a time it seemed as though the Lincoln sales department would be kept intact and the promise made by Henry Ford would be honored. Wilfred kept a careful chronology of the discussions and decisions regarding Lincoln sales and advertising:

- Feb. 6. Sales organization and policy discussed with Edsel Ford.
- Feb. 7. Henry Ford assured W.C.L. Lincoln sales policy would be carried out.
- Feb. 14. Edsel Ford suggests tentatively trying out Ford dealers in Detroit.
- Feb. 15. Definite sales policy established and reduced to writing. Lincoln distributors to control sales for one year in 75 leading cities.
- Feb. 20. Advertising program (national) approved.
- Mar. 21. Ryan advises he had orders from Edsel Ford to cancel Lincoln distributors in 40 cities.
- Mar. 27. Insisted by Sorenson, Martin and Kanzler that sales and purchasing departments be transferred to Ford plant.
- Mar. 28. Edsel supports Lelands and over-ruled transfer of departments.
- Mar. 29. Rumor reported by New York distributor that Lincoln sales department to be supplanted.
- May 3. Conference with Edsel on combining departments. Written sales agreement cited by W.C. but brushed aside. Ford and Lincoln purchasing and sales departments must be combined and national advertising will be eliminated.
- May 29. Sales department moved to Highland Park.[20]

Meanwhile, troubles continued in the manufacturing departments. The workmen were unsettled and the work interrupted. Sorensen continued to ignore the Leland management. Wilfred Leland fought back, in what seemed to him the proper way. Henry Ford had made the promises, exuding good fellowship. Surely he did not know what was going on in his plant. Ford was elusive but Wilfred persisted, going in by the back way to Fairlane and braving the armed guard posted to keep out unannounced callers. Ford was sympathetic. His advice on encroaching executives was to fight back, "Whack 'em. Don't let them do it." He would come over and look after things. He came one morning and again promised his full support. Then he came no more and it was impossible for Wilfred to make contact with him again.

Ralph Getsinger (Lincoln salesmanager) talked to Edsel, stating that all the irritation could be resolved if only all the orders could be channelled through the management. Edsel agreed and gave such instructions. This was a futile gesture since Edsel himself had little real authority,[21] and by this time Henry Ford was tired of the whole situation. As the most recent history of the Ford company put it, "During the next few years Ford was to show a tendency to revoke his outright or implied promises. He would charge into a situation, gain favorable publicity by pledges of what he would do, find his role unexpectedly complex and difficult, and suddenly abandon it in stubborn disgust." [22]

On February 2 Ford had been quoted as saying, "It would be an industrial crime to wreck an organization like that [Lincoln] and have the work of Henry Leland and all that he stands for in the motor industry lost to further development of the motor car. Of all places in the world where a thing like that should not be done, Detroit can least afford to have such a blot cast upon its good name." [23]

The Lelands fought hard to avoid this industrial crime of wrecking the Lincoln organization, as Ford had put it. Perhaps they fought too hard for their own good. Historians may argue that the Lincoln organization was inefficiently organized and improperly run, that Ford only wanted to put it in order, and that Ford had a right to do what he wanted with his own property. It may be admitted that Ford, having bought the Lincoln, had a right to do with it as he pleased had he not made a solemn pledge to let the Lelands run it. It may even be admitted that the Lelands, secure in their own reputation and dedicated to a less ruthless form of management, were not quick to throw out old employees or tolerate being pushed about by men who had no official denomination as their superiors in the Lincoln management. This whole period was to them a confusion of spit-in-your-eye, hit-and-run tactics. Plenty of action but little consideration, conference or explanation! They had been placed in charge, but their authority was flouted, their orders were ignored or countermanded; all manifestations completely beyond any earlier experience. To the confusion was added the continued pious assurances of Henry Ford himself that they were in charge, that they must assert their authority. In comparison, the old Lincoln directorate and the glacially immovable Fred Murphy himself were great gentlemen who, while disagreeing and balking, left the actual precincts of the plant itself to the Leland management. In that controversy the Lelands were not humiliated before their own workmen.

Some historians, in writing of this period and relationship, have assumed that Henry and Wilfred Leland by their unreasonable resistance to change brought upon themselves the harassment that ensued.[24] Yet these same historians make plain that almost every other executive of stature in the Ford organization eventually became the victim of such harassment and the *modus operandi* was often the same. Ford remained pleasant, agreeable and reassuring, while Sorensen controverted the orders of the victim and applied the needle, sensing Ford's hostility toward anyone who resisted his authority. This attitude became more pronounced as Ford grew older; he would brook no criticism or even independence in his domain and, as history now records, in the bitter end he had no executives of stature. Therefore, it seems unreasonable to single out the Lelands as the only subjects of the Ford animus. They wore out their welcome more quickly than most, but they were by their very experience and accomplishment especially liable to the Ford resentment when they did not fall quickly into the established ways of the Ford Motor Company.

Bewildered, discouraged, and at his wit's end, Wilfred knew that this state of affairs could not continue. So he wrote several letters to Henry Ford, stating the impossible conditions and proposing that the Lelands buy back the Lincoln Motor Company. He wrote, in part:

> The experience in conducting the Lincoln business since February 4th may have demonstrated that it is not possible for a separate organization to function in cooperation with the Ford interest due to your methods of operation, which methods have, of course, been eminently successful in your business. If this is the case, we have little hope that we could influence you to alter these methods and if, for this reason or for any other reason, the

assurances given and the understandings cannot be carried out, we believe that we should be privileged to buy back from you all the assets of the Lincoln Company at the price you paid for same, plus a reasonable interest rate.

Wilfred believed that with the now demonstrated ability of the Lincoln Motor Company to produce and earn he could get a loan from Kissel-Kinnicut with which the Lelands could buy back the Lincoln Company. When his letter was ignored he wrote again, specifying some of the things that had been done to injure the quality of the car:

Your representatives have recommended that certain inspection operations be omitted; that defective parts be used which it has been our policy to reject; that our employees be less particular about the quality of parts which they assemble; that operations which would not give quite as accurate results, but are less expensive, be substituted.

A third letter proposed that Ford with his great resources develop a car of his own, "There will be greater glory for you to develop such a superior car from the ground up and have the entire credit and prestige." He pleaded, "Turn the Lincoln plant back to us . . . allowing us to go on in our one-horse way producing and improving the Lincoln car." [25]

As Wilfred said in his letters, the situation was impossible as it was and Ford agreed rather more decisively than was his custom and sent Ernest G. Liebold and William B. Mayo to end the Leland association. "You better go over," said Ford, "and tell Wilfred we don't want him any more." They went the next day, June 10, and told the Lelands to go that afternoon and take their personal belongings with them. Wilfred and Henry Leland had now finally and irrevocably lost their Lincoln car.

This bitter association with the Ford Motor Company had not been the only nightmare to disturb the Leland days and nights during those last months. A fourth government tax claim was again hanging like a vulture over the Lelands. Scarcely a week after Henry Ford's check had been so triumphantly handed to the receiver, and the receiver had that very day *settled* the tax claim, the report came seeping out of Washington that another claim would be filed.[26] This news effectively stalled further action by the receiver in settling creditors' claims and liquidating the receivership.

John W. Weeks was now U.S. Secretary of War and Harry M. Daugherty was Attorney General. Weeks had taken the Lincoln tax claim together with others and brought them back into the War Department. They were being studied. On April 11, 1922, on the floor of the House, Roy O. Woodruff, Representative from Michigan, made a scathing attack upon "graft and fraud in the conduct of the War Department." He claimed that under the pressure of influential persons a number of cases of fraud against the government during the war were not being prosecuted. He threatened that unless Daugherty immediately proceeded to protect the government's interest in the Lincoln Motor case he would move his impeachment.[27] Under this fire Daugherty held a conference attended by all interested parties, the banks, the receiver, the creditors and the indorsers, and the Lelands. Pressured by Woodruff's fulminations, Daugherty decided to push the claim for $9,188,561.98 and filed action in the district court at Detroit on April 14.[28]

Sensational accounts of the case continued in the newspapers. Criminal action as well as civil was mentioned. Woodruff and Daugherty continued to made daily headlines and Senator Couzens added his voice to the accusations. The whole Lincoln episode was hashed over and over, and what had seemed simple and straightforward at the time now assumed sinister aspects. One newspaper listed the fraud under 14 points, some of which were:

> That the profits of the company on its war contracts amounted to 700 per cent on the money actually invested.
> That instead of erecting cheap, temporary buildings for this purpose, the Lincoln Company constructed the finest automobile factory in the world at government expense, although it is claimed the government was not consulted as to either character or cost.
> That one of these buildings was a permanent office building, costing $500,000 and another a restaurant costing $107,000.
> That although the company used only 18 acres of a 52-acre tract, all the land was amortized.
> That Henry Leland and Wilfred Leland received compensation of $100,000.[29]

No one stepped up to say that in the end the government paid the Lincoln Company exactly the same price per motor that had been paid all the other manufacturers of Liberty motors. Although the plant had been expensive its cost, except for the amortization allowed, had been returned to the government. Had the noncancellable contract not been cancelled the entire cost would have been returned to the government. The plant and its equipment had been acquired at greatly inflated war-time prices, and much of the equipment was so specialized as to be useless later; hence the amortization, in view of the price deflation since, was not exorbitant. Nor did anyone come forth to say that $100,000 a year was actually a cut in salary for the Lelands.

So it came about while the Lelands were finishing out their last uneasy days at the "finest automobile plant in the world," their reputation was being smeared almost daily in the public press. All their hopes and plans for their car and their own financial future had come to nothing. They had but one hope left and that was that Henry Ford, who had not hesitated to revise his promises respecting them, might still keep his pledges to the creditors and stockholders. Only one factor in their whole plan had been successful. In spite of the indignities of Ford manufacturing, the Lincoln was doing well.

Production had risen steadily from 166 units in February to 722 in June. It would rise further in July and fall somewhat toward the end of the year. All in all 5626 cars were shipped in 1922.[30] From the beginning of the year, orders were well ahead of production.

In a brochure, not dated but evidently issued soon after the Lelands had been retired, the Ford Motor Company tried to convince the public that the car was unchanged. "Fundamentally, the mechanism of the Lincoln is the same today as when it won the enthusiastic approval of the automobile public. The Lincoln was immediately recognized for its wonderfully smooth operation at all speeds, its riding comfort over all roads, its quick acceleration upon demand and its instant response to all controls." But the Ford genius had added something and in the telling of this addition there is an echo of the Ford scorn for the Leland factory organization. "No expense has been spared in fitting the plant throughout for efficient production of the very finest product. Work has been routed through the plant as efficiently as the arrangement of buildings permitted. . . . Innovations quickly appeared after the purchase. A new order prevailed. Work began to be routed through the plant along different lines, departments were transferred to new locations; machines within departments were re-grouped. Standards everywhere were raised and even more stringently enforced. . . . Rapidly, but without interruption to production, the plant became more efficient, more modern, more productive." [31]

When the Lelands were discharged Mayo told them that a settlement would be made with them the following Monday, but Ford did not appear then or later. Representatives came with a statement for distribution to the press, but since the substance of this release was that Henry Leland, on account of his age, did not feel up to the responsibility of the large plant, he refused to put his name to it; and so the firing of the Lelands could not be entirely glossed over. Harold Emmons finally made a diplomatic statement that "The overwhelming demand for this automobile has grown to such proportions that it is entirely beyond the production capacity of the present plant. A readjustment of manufacturing facilities and relationships thereupon has become necessary. . . . The management and conduct of the business will be transferred from Henry M. and Wilfred C. Leland to the combined Ford and Lincoln organization and under the control of Ford executives." [32]

Conjecture appeared in every news source, and the break was agreed to have been caused by the Leland unwillingness to conform to Ford production methods. One of the trade magazines implied that it could come closer to the truth by hinting that the break was due to the failure of the plant under Leland guidance to make satisfactory returns on the investment. Prices established in February had been based upon the ability to speed production to 50-60 cars daily and the best had been 30 cars a day.[33]

As a matter of fact the production in April, May and June had been 622, 535, and 722 respectively.[34] Production for the Lincoln Company was never a problem under the Lelands; it was the sales which held the production down. The same was to be true under the Fords. Even after the whole process had been integrated into the Ford Motor Company and was presumably operating under

Ford efficiency there was little necessity for a higher rate of production because the Lincoln car never attained the popularity envisioned by its creators in 1920 or its foster parents in 1922. Both had envisioned a production of 12,000 in the second year. By that time the depression was over and the Cadillac which had produced only 5250 cars in 1921 came back to make 26,296 in 1922. But in 1922, the Lincoln, now in the same price range with the Cadillac and a competitor, produced 5626 cars. In the following years Lincoln produced:

1923—7875 units	1926—8858 units	1929—7672 units [35]
1924—7053 "	1927—7141 "	1930—3515 "
1925—8380 "	1928—6362 "	1931—4329 "

From 1932 on the production declined as the depression deepened. In 1937 only 844 units came off the line and the Lincoln Motor Company is said to have lost in all $16,000,000 through the years of economic depression.[36]

However, it is not fair to say as did Keith Sward in *The Legend of Henry Ford* that the Lincoln car was a white elephant which never earned its own way.[37] Earnings figures are not generally available though one government inquiry reveals that the Lincoln earned over $2,000,000 in 1929 on sales of 6399.[38] Hence its manufacture was undoubtedly profitable up until the '30's. It is conceivable that, given the chance, the Lelands might have, under similar circumstances, worked off the debt that lay on the Lincoln Motor Company in 1921.

Chapter XX

The End of Hope

FOR A TIME AFTER their dismissal the Lelands hoped to have some discussion and settlement with Henry Ford. They received two weeks' advance salary as terminal pay and that ended their association with the great Ford Motor Company. They were not to talk with either of the Fords again.[1]

They had one bit of solace through this period of frustration and defeat. Just before the final break Wilfred had offered to buy back the Lincoln Motor Company. He had no money but he now had proof that the company could pay its own way. Freed by the receivership from the threat of the creditors, the Ford Motor Company had to put only $250,000 of working capital at the organization's disposal. From that point on, the Lincoln earned its own way and up until June 10 its profits had been a modest $200,000. In this period too production had gone up to 30–35 cars a day. Another set of statistics brought some comfort to the Lelands. Orders had run high all through the early part of that year of 1922. Orders received in the ten days from June 1 to June 10 had totalled 455, or an average of 53 a day. From June 12 to 29, after news had spread that the Lincoln was no longer to be Leland-built, orders totalled 147, or an average of only nine per day.[2] To the Lelands this statistic meant that the public which bought fine cars attached some value to the Leland name. Why else had the orders fallen off so abruptly right in the middle of the season?

All the while the clamor over the war-fraud cases continued in the press and from the platform. Politicians who in the campaigns had lambasted fraud in war contracts were now trying to find the graft. The Leland case was on every tongue. The Lelands were defended by the hometown newspaper.

> The Lincoln Motor Company which is one of the concerns involved, is known in Detroit to have reached a settlement [1919] with the government which was considered fair. . . . The men who were behind that company are among the best known and most highly honored business men in this community. It is safe to say that something more than a speech in Congress will be required to alter their standing in Detroit.[3]

Finally, however, after weeks of black headlines, Attorney General Harry Daugherty filed a claim with the receiver of the Lincoln Motor Company for $9,188,561.98. From that time on the records of the old company were at the disposal of the representatives of the Department of Justice. The investigation went on for a long time, and the lurid accusations kept pace. Senator James Couzens made a speech in Philadelphia on January 28, 1923, which now makes strange reading.[4] Couzens invested a few thousands in the Ford Motor Company and came out with many millions. But in his speech he stressed the fact that the Lelands had invested so little of their own money and made such a great profit. He questioned the salaries paid the Lelands. "Now the reason I am pointing this out is to try to indicate to you that public officers in any political subdivision anywhere in the United States could not pull a thing like this; in fact they would not have the temerity to try it." Senator Couzens shouted that there were possible grounds for criminal proceedings. But the Lelands had not been public officers, they were private businessmen with a government contract. At the end of the war when the contract had been terminated, their agreements had been arrived at readily and openly.

Henry Leland, when asked to discuss the matter, said he could not do so with the case pending. He hoped, however, to be able to tell his story in court. "I have been ready for seven months to go into court and tell our side of the story. The sooner the case gets into court so that everything can be cleared up, the better it will suit me." [5]

But Henry Leland never got the chance to go into court and explain either to the court or to the press. The case was compromised for $1,500,000 on January 31, 1923, by the receiver and the government representatives. It came into the district court before Judge Tuttle, and the court concurred in the settlement—there was no hearing. The report filed states: "This Court now finds as a fact that this compromise is based upon questions of law affecting overpayments of money by the United States to the Lincoln Motor Company on certain war contracts, and that the inducement for this settlement is the absence of fraud as disclosed in the investigation by officials of the Department of Justice preliminary to the filing of the stipulation agreeing to the amount provided for in the settlement agreed upon today." [6]

Earl J. Davis, U.S. attorney, said for those officials acting for the government who had handled the contracts, "We still credit them with making an honest legal mistake." So the mistake was rectified by taking back $1,500,000, a settlement very favorable for the government, said Davis, inasmuch as, when the old Michigan corporation merged into the Delaware corporation, "It took to the new concern only $1,500,000 and this was all that the government could have made a claim on." [7]

With the government claim out of the way the receiver now proceeded to pay off creditors of the old Lincoln Company at the rate of 47½% of each claim. Following that came negotiations with regard to Ford's paying off the remaining 52½%. Attorney Emmons was the go-between, and his reports of the progress of the various conferences were interesting.[8]

The Fords did not seem to have a very clear rememberance of their promises to pay. Mr. Mayo suggested that perhaps the creditors would be willing to settle for less than 100% of their claims. Emmons, prodded by W.C., reminded the Ford representatives that

Edsel had on the occasion of the meeting with Judge Tuttle agreed that every creditor was to be reimbursed 100 cents on the dollar. It was then suggested that a conference be held with the judge. Judge Tuttle declined, on the score that he should not discuss the matter further with any of the interested parties.

Then the argument was advanced that although such a statement relative to the payment of creditors had been made in connection with the offer of $5,000,000 for the company the judge had not accepted that offer. When he increased the price to $8,000,000 the fundamental condition of the proposition was changed and Ford was therefore quit of his promise to pay the creditors. Emmons denied that Mr. Ford had ever

> . . . repudiated his promise to pay the creditors, and insisted that if there had been attempts to evade the liability, they had come from Mr. Ford's advisers rather than from Mr. Ford himself. He said however, that the unanimous opinion of businessmen, including the president of a trust company, now deceased, was that Mr. Ford had been legally released from his liability to pay creditors.[9]

There was also the theory that Mr. Ford had no obligations for the government claim—that the introduction of the tax claim succeeded his promise to pay creditors and thus altered the situation. Here again Wilfred Leland was quick to point out that the third federal-tax claim for $4,500,000 was at the time of the negotiations hanging over the Lincoln assets and Mr. Ford had been apprised of it. When Wilfred was asked, "Ford knew it was pending?" he replied, "There is no question about it. Ford advised us to fight it, never to pay a penny. He had me call Emmons when he was down in Washington negotiating. He told me to have Emmons fight this thing to the last ditch." [10]

There was also an interval when the Ford representatives claimed they had no obligation to pay the endorsers, who were in a credit class by themselves. But this reluctance too was successfully overcome since the banks were the real creditors, not the endorsers. Finally, it was agreed that Ford would pay but that each creditor must sign an agreement that the payment was to wipe the slate clean and that the creditor would not press any further claim upon the Ford Motor Company. This agreement meant, of course, that any creditor who was also a stockholder would give up his claim as a stockholder to collect as a creditor. The Lelands against the advice of their attorney refused to so waive their claims. Finally on March 9, 1923, the checks were sent out by the Ford organization paying the creditors in full, including 900 merchandise creditors and the notes signed by the seven directors. Altogether Ford paid out for the Lincoln Company $12,018,699.21.[11]

With this payment to creditors accomplished, there was a pause. Stockholders hoped that payment for them would soon follow; but nothing happened.

Ford's promise to the stockholders had been indefinite. As with all the other negotiations this agreement had been an oral one, through private conversation. However, Wilfred Leland had urged it repeatedly and Ford had acquiesced. There were public statements which supported this fact. In the process of assembling and pinning down these instances of Ford promises Wilfred Leland made a written statement from which this account is taken. And it was in pressing these promises upon Mr. Ford that the Lelands came at last to the parting of their ways from those of Attorney Harold H. Emmons. In the beginning of the negotiation it will be remembered that Mr. Emmons had been called in to settle the details. In the days when all was euphoria and good feeling, Emmons' efforts seemed most acceptable to both sides, and his advice greatly facilitated the legal aspects of the purchase of the Lincoln Company. In retrospect it seemed to the Lelands that Emmons had even then been looking after the Fords in some respects rather than the Lelands, and particularly in this matter of paying the stockholders. There was that instance reported by the *Free Press*, on February 5, 1922.

> There had been rumors for the past weeks that if the company was purchased by Ford he would reimburse the original stockholders, but not those who had traded in the stock. Mr. Emmons was asked, after the sale, if there was any truth in the rumor. He replied, "The only announcement made by Mr. Ford was that nothing would be considered until after the sale."

THE END OF HOPE 257

"Now that the sale has been made is there any likelihood of Mr. Ford's adopting such a policy?" he was asked.

"I do not think there is the slightest chance of it," was the decided answer.

When Mr. Ford had made up his mind to buy the Lincoln plant and was in great haste to announce his philanthropy to the public, he gave a long interview to his favorite newspaperman, James Sweinhart, of the Detroit *News*, but the publication of this article was deferred until Emmons could get back from Washington to approve it. In it a reference was made to the payment in full of creditors and stockholders. Cautious, as a lawyer should be, Emmons insisted that the reference to payment of creditors be omitted and the reference to stockholders be modified. Sweinhart objected, saying that the piece had Ford's approval and, as it was Ford's business, not the Lelands', he could not see why such changes should be made. Mr. Emmons, who had been in Washington conferring on the tax claim, replied only that such promises might have an adverse effect on the Washington situation.[12] He had had high hopes of compromising the claim, but as soon as the government officials heard of the Ford offer the compromise was refused. Hence, through his objections, the article in the *News* came out on January 11, 1922, without any reference to the creditors and this modified note on the stockholders:

> The Ford Motor Company will endeavor to work out some plan by means of which those stockholders who, in the opinion of the company, actually invested cash in Lincoln securities, with the idea of sustaining the project and making a going concern, may hope for some substantial return on their investment.

At the time of the interview with Judge Tuttle on the purchase of the Lincoln Company by the Fords, Emmons advised the conferees in advance that the judge and the receivership were interested mainly in the creditors. He did, however, mention later that a plan would be worked out to do something for the deserving stockholders like school teachers, who had suffered great hardship.[13]

Emmons represented the Lelands throughout the conferences with the Fords about the business of paying the creditors, but he appeared to Wilfred Leland to be slow in pressing the creditors' claims as strongly as the Lelands would have liked. Emmons seemed fearful that if they asked too much they would jeopardize their chance of getting anything. When the creditors were paid and the stockholders claims due to be considered, Emmons bowed out of the picture. He had wanted to press Ford to do something for the Lelands personally but this they refused. Perhaps he felt some responsibility for the fact that there had never been any formal written agreements. Surely this lack indicates some negligence on an attorney's part.

When other lawyers were questioning Wilfred later about the agreements one question was: "Did Emmons ever discuss with you the advisability of putting these things in writing? It is unbelievable . . . that any lawyer would not insist on writing up an agreement." And this same point is bound to occur to anyone hearing the story. When the attorneys pressed Wilfred, for "Somewhere we must have a definite promise to pay stockholders," he answered, "Ford is notorious for saying he doesn't want to put things in writing. In some of the earlier statements he said, 'I'll do these things but I won't put anything in writing.'" [14]

There was the further fact that the Lelands really had nothing tangible to sell Ford except their own skill and experience. While they were eager to go along with the company they were not emphasizing that phase of the transaction. They sold him the Lincoln Motor Company although it was not actually theirs to sell. They could not convey it to him. He could have gone out on his own and bought it of the receiver without the help or approval of the Lelands. And he could then have bought it much more cheaply without promising to pay the creditors 100% and the stockholders in any part.

In retrospect it appears that Edsel Ford wanted the fine car; Henry Ford wanted the glow that comes from a good deed—the publicity and acclaim that saving the Lelands would bring to him. Wilfred Leland had sold him a great idea—the idea of saving a fine automobile, saving the great contribution of Henry Leland to the industry, saving the savings of many deserving little people. But as time went on the great, glowing, beneficent idea evaporated under the everyday abrasion of differing business concepts, and the vision dimmed. In the clarity of Henry Ford's lapse of interest he felt he had paid more for his whistle than he should have, and he decided he would not pay any more. Some slight attempt is said to have been made on a list of stockholders, but all action was soon given up and the matter rested. The Ford attorneys would contend later with regard to the stockholders, "Hope alone was promised."

However, the Lelands were determined not to let the matter rest there. After some months, during which they hoped against hope, they had the case studied by other attorneys. On March 19, 1924, Wilfred Leland wrote Henry Ford a long letter setting down the facts of their agreement and some history of subsequent developments including the erroneous reports that he *had paid* the stockholders. The Lelands were especially angered by an article written by Dr. William L. Stidger and published in the *Y. M. C. A. Magazine* which erred particularly as to amounts paid to the Lelands. As has been stated, the Lelands received two weeks' salary, and when the investment certificate given H.M. on his birthday was presented March 22, 1923, it was paid, $363,000, with approximately four months' interest at 6% amounting to $6957.50.

When no reply was received to Wilfred's letter it was published on April 5 in the Detroit *Saturday Night,* a weekly newspaper. By such an open presentation, the Lelands hoped to bring the pressure of public opinion to bear upon Henry Ford. But the great automobile magnate was not to be pushed; he made no answer and he did nothing.

Hence it was that the Lelands engaged two attorneys, William Henry Gallagher and Kenneth Stevens, who believed in the validity of the case and with the support of 1800 stockholders initiated a suit on November 16, 1927, in the Oakland County Circuit Court in Pontiac, Michigan. The complaint asked $6,000,000 to pay the stockholders of the Lincoln Motor Company. The letter was also printed in a separate pamphlet and sent to all the Lincoln stockholders. It included a letter from Henry Leland to Henry Ford, "I cannot but feel certain that you intended to keep those pledges when you made them to me personally and, while I cannot understand the long delay on your part, I still hope and trust that you will not shake my life-long faith in humanity. . . ."

Before discussing this suit, it might be well to go over once more the discussions the Lelands had had with Ford on this matter. Wilfred's statement follows:

> On November 21st [1921] we discussed the situation regarding stockholders in detail. I gave Henry Ford the detailed figures and told him about the class B stockholders and the class A stockholders, and we discussed the Murphy relationship and that in our judgment it would not be necessary to pay the Murphy and the Boyers who were responsible for wrecking the company. As that discussion developed, Ford took the stand that we must repay every stockholder, "that means the good and the bad stockholders, even those who have wrecked the company" and he went on to amplify that by saying that in doing so it would be the best way of punishing them, that it would "heap coals of fire on their heads, that those coals would burn in and hurt as nothing else would."
>
> We discussed the profits of the company. Then we discussed the question as to the possibility of selling 50 cars a day . . .
>
> Then we got back to the discussion of stockholders and we explained that we couldn't do absolute justice to all the stockholders, that there had been so much interchanging of stock that we couldn't follow it all, but that we believed we could do substantial justice to perhaps 80 or 90 per cent of the stockholders and we explained that the thing to do would be to study the records as carefully as we could, get all the data possible, and try as far as human beings could to repay every stockholder that we could get information on regarding an amount which would return to him every dollar he had lost because of the receivership. Mr. Ford agreed that that would be the final procedure.
>
> The thing we discussed was that we would take up the merits of each case. We were going to weigh into that problem the demoralizing effect of the Murphys in throwing the company into receivership, and if that man was an honest-to-goodness investor but felt that matters as they were would wreck the company and so cause a complete loss to him and he sold his stock, we would pay him his loss. He was a straight-forward investor, he had confidence in the company, and he should be reimbursed.
>
> At about the time of the receivership stock was being sold at from 2 to 3 dollars per share. Mr. Ford's reference to speculators seemed to voice a firm determination that he would not allow shrewd speculators to make a profit at his expense. Ford always said, "That doesn't mean the speculator" and we said, "No." [15]

THE END OF HOPE

When the December 19 interview took place Henry Ford was eager for Wilfred to go to the Judge and put forth the proposition to buy while Edsel wanted to wait and lay more specific plans. It did not seem wise to Wilfred for him to go to Judge Tuttle by himself and tell the Judge what Henry Ford wanted to do.

Seeing Edsel holding back, I said, "I understand that you are going to do these things; that the Lincoln will be an absolutely independent organization under our management; that the Lincoln and all it stands for will be preserved; that the Lincoln Sales organization will be maintained and the only part the Ford selling organization will play will be to reach out into the small localities where it would not be feasible to maintain Lincoln dealers; that every creditor will be paid 100 cents on the dollar, and that every Lincoln stockholder will be repaid his investment in Lincoln stock."

Ford said, "Yes."

And I went over the amount of money that would be required —17 to 18 million dollars—to do the trick. That morning I didn't have my papers with me but I gave him the figures from memory and I made that an excuse for saying, "Perhaps before I actually see the Judge, I better hand Edsel a list showing these figures so there will be no misunderstanding thereafter." And I did later give Edsel that list.[16]

A day or two before the sale in February the subject of the stockholders was again mentioned.

The first time anything was said to me to limit it in any way was when Edsel said, "My idea would be to put in about $12,000,000 now and then let the balance be paid out of the earnings of the company." I said, "Well as far as I am concerned that would be quite satisfactory because I am confident that within one year the earnings of the company will justify that payment and it will take some time to get all the data in and determine what is due the stockholders." That is the first and only time any limit was suggested. That was not decisive or final, but that it would be his idea to do it thus and so.[17]

The matter of payment to the stockholders was again mentioned on the day of January 18, 1922, when Henry and Edsel Ford came over to make a trip through the Lincoln plant. Before the trip

Henry Ford had a discussion with Henry Leland in the latter's office. This was the first time the two had talked since the first interview on November 15. H.M. spoke again of the fact that up to this time no person had ever lost a dollar by investing in a company which he controlled. He reiterated his determination that every creditor and every stockholder should be repaid in full. He went on to say that the investigations he and his son had made had convinced him that they could obtain the money to buy the plant and reimburse all these people. Henry Ford replied, "I know you can, Mr. Leland. I know you can get all the money you need to buy the plant and do these things, but you let me have it. I will pay the creditors and stockholders right away. It may take you a long time to pay them out of the profits of the company. We will pay the creditors and stockholders. . . ."[18]

It was upon these statements showing the agreements made between the Fords and the Lelands that the case for reimbursement of the stockholders rested. The attorneys hoped to put the Lelands on the witness stand and the Fords as well. The newspapers reported the allegations:

> The Lelands assert that in an oral contract before the purchase [of Lincoln Motor] they agreed to remain in the employ of the new company and to cease their activities in seeking a purchaser or new finances for the old company in return for which Mr. Ford agreed to meet all the old company's debts and to reimburse all stockholders except brokers and those who purchased the stock at less than $3 a share and those who bought after receivership.[19] The Fords obtained the Lincoln properties by virtue of their promises to us. To retain these properties and to break their promises to us is a species of fraud.[20] It was contended that the tangible assets of the plant had a value of $12,000,000 but that the reputation and skill of the Lelands brought the value up to $25,000,000.

To this the defendants replied, without admitting the contract,

> The alleged contract shows a failure to observe the ordinary legal obligations and duties owed by the Lelands to the stockholders of their company, and shows a direct endeavour on their part to contract secretly for their own benefit for the purpose of feathering their own nest, first by creating jobs for themselves, second, by preserving their reputation at the expense of others.

What right did the Lelands, as directors, officials and stockholders have to trade away this enormous value which they estimate between the junk value of the corporate assets and $25,000,000 without the consent of all the stockholders? [21]

Thus with evasion and distraction did the Ford attorneys avoid the main issue—that the Fords had not kept a contract made in good faith. Without arguing the case they asked that it be dismissed on the grounds that the agreement as set up in the bill was invalid and unenforceable:

1. Because against public policy in that it was made for the advantage of the Lelands especially, and of a part only of the stockholders and excluded other stockholders from its benefits,
2. That it was within the statute of frauds in that the defendant's promise if made, was one to answer for the debt, default or misdoings of another, and
3. That it was a contract to stifle bidding at a judicial sale. [22]

The motion to dismiss was over-ruled by the trial judge, Frank L. Covert, on March 15, 1928, whereupon the case was appealed to the Michigan Supreme Court by the Ford attorneys on June 7, 1928.

The supreme court handed down its decision on February 1, 1929, four judges concurring and three dissenting.* On the second point it held that the contract was not within the statute of frauds since the alleged promise by the Fords to pay the stockholders was a direct promise not conditioned by the promise of another; on the third point it held that the contract was not void because it stifled competition in bidding, for, in instances where large sums were necessary to purchase assets at a receiver's sale, preliminary negotiations were necessary to raise the large sums of money. On the first part, the court stated,

What we do hold and it is all that the purposes of the case require, is that after they (the Lelands) publicly announced that they were going to look after the interest of the stockholders, if they acted at all their duty required them to act for all, not for a portion of the stockholders. A contract for the reorganization of a corporation which contemplates the taking care of a portion

* The dissenting judges were Justices Nelson Sharpe, Howard Wiest and George M. Clark. Justice Grant Fellows wrote the majority opinion.

only of the stockholders, and the exclusion of another portion from the benefits of reorganization, is fraudulent and cannot stand. The man who bought a share of stock for $3 acquired the same interest in the company as the man who paid $50 for his share of stock.[23]

The court recommended, however, that the defendants of the motion to dismiss be given the opportunity to amend their bill. They did so, claiming that the Lelands had acted in a private capacity in making the contract. They no longer had any legal control over the Lincoln corporation, nor had they made any public announcement that they were acting for its stockholders. They could not therefore be held responsible as Lincoln officials acting for the stockholders in a reorganization. The case went back for a re-hearing. However, both Judge Covert and the supreme court refused a re-hearing, holding that the defect of the bill was not cured by the amendment and the contract was recognized as one void and unenforceable.[24] So after almost four years of litigation the Lelands had to notify the stockholders that all efforts had been exhausted in their behalf.

On September 1, 1931, Henry Leland wrote this last letter to the stockholders of the Lincoln Motor Company:

> I am eighty-eight years of age; on the threshold of the exit from life; ready to meet my Maker. And I am unwilling that this case be ended without my putting myself on record.
>
> I have followed every step of this three-year fight to obtain our day in court. To me this case has meant the fulfillment or the failure of the agreement I obtained from Henry Ford for those individuals who suffered loss directly because of their faith in me. This suit was not brought in my own behalf, for Mr. Ford paid me personally the amount agreed upon. I have brought, and together with my son, Wilfred, entirely financed this suit in behalf of those others for whose benefit this agreement was made. . . .
>
> We have no further recourse to law. There is no step we can take at this time to gain for you the day in court to which every American citizen is entitled. But the equities and the Ford obligations have not changed. Henry Ford by the terms of his agreement, owes you the amount of your stock investment in the Lincoln Motor Company.[25]

There came in answer, personally and by letter, sympathy and appreciation. One stockholder wrote to Henry Leland:

> I am just in receipt of my copy of the form letter which you addressed to the stockholders of the Lincoln Motor Company, as I only yesterday returned from a trip to J——! I want to thank you for it. I was a very small stockholder in your company having invested between one thousand or $1100 in it. I cannot recall the exact figures.
>
> I learned to drive on your splendid car the Cadillac and I knew the Lincoln was going to be a great achievement as well. So I went in to it with what little I had. . . . My father, the late Otto K—— of Detroit was an admirer of yours. I once met you at father's house when I was making him a visit. I *know* the account of what you say took place between you and Henry Ford is *true,* and I feel grateful to you for the long and bitter fight you have made to obtain justice for your old stockholders. I wish I could say don't worry about it any more! I can say so for myself and I do.[26]

But there were others who, when they met the Lelands, did not fail to condemn them and accuse them of losing their money. They evidently considered, as had Henry Leland himself, the investment a personal transaction and the failure not a cold business proposition but just cause for anger and reproach. These recriminations, too, the Lelands bore with what patience they could muster.

One consolation alone remained. They had tried. Perhaps it had been a fragile chance from the beginning, but they had not turned it away. In a measure, while they had lost their case, they retained their reputation for personal integrity and responsibility. The business and industrial world was the better for this attempt to keep an obligation, no matter what the cost in failure, ridicule and slander.

But the time was not long for Henry Leland. He had fought his last fight, finished the course and kept the faith as best he could. When he wrote he was "on the threshold of the exit from life," he had but six months more, including another birthday. With his son Wilfred at his side, as always, he died March 26, 1932.

Notes

Chapter I

1. British Information Service, New York City (information about Brooklands); "Cadillac Cars," Royal Automobile Club Year Book 1909, p. 248 (account of test). Brooklands was first opened June 25, 1907, less than a year before the Standardization Test.
2. See Chapter VI for discussion of American and European cars.
3. Letter from F. S. Bennett to W. C. Leland, May 7, 1953. This letter is among the Leland Papers which are in the possession of Mrs. Wilfred C. Leland, Detroit.
4. *The Autocar* (British automobile magazine), October 18, 1913, p. 711.
5. Pamphlet, *The Romance of the Cadillac Car*, by Old Stager, Undated. This work seems to have been produced about 1920, and was written by a friend or perhaps by Bennett himself. It is among the Leland Papers.
6. *Ibid.*
7. "Cadillac Cars," *RAC Year Book 1909, loc. cit.*

Chapter II

1. Leland Family Record; John Bourne Manuscript, p. 29. This manuscript of 243 typewritten pages is preserved in two loose-leaf notebooks. Inserted are loose pages entitled, "Correction to my Biography," written by Henry Leland and dated February 25, 1926. John Bourne was Mr. Leland's secre-

tary for many years. The manuscript is the principal source of information on the family and early life of Henry Leland.
2. Thomas Babington, Lord Macaulay, *Works*, II (Speeches, Poems, and Miscellaneous writings), London, 1898, "Epitaph on Henry Martyn" (1812), p. 443.
3. Memorandum in Henry Leland's writing, Leland Papers.
4. Sherman Leland, *The Leland Magazine or a Genealogical Record of Henry Leland and His Descendants*, Boston, 1850, p. 162.
5. Bourne Manuscript, p. 21; Leland Family Record.
   Leander Leland, born Mar. 2, 1803; died Nov. 18, 1881.
   Zylpha Tifft Leland, born May 20, 1810; died Jan. 15, 1876.
   The children, who lived to maturity, were:

Sylvia M.,	born,	Sept. 26, 1829: married William H. Young, 1846.
Richard Frank	"	March 2, 1833.
Mary Ann,	"	April 1, 1836; married Charles F. May 1857.
Thomas Edison	"	June 4, 1840; died Sept. 12, 1862.
Henry Martyn	"	Feb. 16, 1843

6. "Open Letter from Henry M. Leland in Reply to Henry B. Joy," *Manufacturer's Record*, Feb. 8, 1926, Baltimore, Maryland; Bourne Mss., p. 21-38.
7. Bourne Manuscript, p. 38.
8. Bourne Manuscript, p. 43.
9. William Lincoln, *History of Worcester, Mass.*, Worcester, 1862, p. 333.
10. Victor Clark, *History of Manufactures in United States*, New York, 1929, Vol. I, p. 390.
11. Bourne Manuscript, pp. 56-70.
12. Charles Nutt, *History of Worcester*, New York, 1919, p. 857.
13. Bourne Manuscript, p. 57.
14. Bourne Manuscript, p. 63.
15. Charles R. Fitch, *Report on Manufactures of Interchangeable Mechanisms, Report of U.S. Census*, 1880, Vol. II, Manufactures, p. 4.
16. Roe, *op. cit.*, pp. 109-238; Clark, *op. cit.*, Vol. I, pp. 402-422, 1515-27; Fitch, *loc. cit.*; George Soule and Vincent Carosso, *American Economic History*, New York, 1957, p. 114; Harold Williamson, ed., *The Growth of the American Economy*, New York, 1946, Chap. 12, Constance M. Green, "Light Manufactures and the Beginnings of Precision Manufacturing before 1861."
17. Roe, *op. cit.*, pp. 184-215.
18. Clark, *op. cit.*, p. 444.
19. Bourne Manuscript, p. 66.
20. Ellen Hull to Henry M. Leland, undated; Leland to Ellen Hull, May 3, 1866. Leland Papers.
21. Bourne Manuscript., pp. 66-67.
22. Roe, *op. cit.*, pp. 222, 226. Both the Loring Coes Wrench Company and the Lucius W. Pond Tool Co. remained active up to modern times. The Pond Tool Co. is now a part of Niles-Bement-Pond Co.

23. Leland Family Record: Martha Gertrude Leland was born June 8, 1868, Wilfred Chester Leland, November 7, 1869. The nephew, son of Frank, was William Henry Leland born February 22, 1866. This William Leland became a tool manufacturer. (Nutt, *op. cit.*, p. 791.)
24. Bourne Manuscript, pp. 71–78.
25. Burlingame Manuscript, 20 pp., entitled, "Henry M. Leland Conference with L. D. Burlingame, August 24, 1929," sent to Mrs. Wilfred C. Leland by Henry D. Sharpe, June 3, 1960.

   Luther D. Burlingame served an apprenticeship at Brown & Sharpe and for twenty-six years thereafter he was chief draftsman, holding that position when Henry M. Leland also worked there. Later Burlingame became industrial superintendent of the company. *Machinery*, June, 1915, p. 777.
26. *Representative Men and Old Families of Rhode Island*, J. H. Beers & Co., Chicago, 1908, Vol. II, p. 693.
27. Burlingame Manuscript, p. 5.

Chapter III

1. Richmond Viall, born 1834, an apprentice in the jewelry trade, came to Brown & Sharpe in 1863 as a machine hand at $1.50 a day. In 1864 he became foreman on machine castings, having 37 men under him. In 1872 he was put in charge of all the sewing machine work; in 1878 he became superintendent of the entire plant, remaining so until after 1908. *Representative Men and Old Families of Rhode Island*, J. H. Beers & Co., Chicago, 1908, Vol. II, p. 656.
2. Burlingame Manuscript, p. 7.
3. This clipper story was published in the *American Machinist*, June 28, 1939. It also appeared at various times in Detroit newspapers, in the Bourne Ms., p. 93 and in the Burlingame Ms., p. 7–9.
4. *Representative Men, op. cit.*, p. 694.
5. Roe, *op. cit.*, p. 213; Bourne Ms., p. 90; Burlingame Ms., p. 10.
6. Leland, "Grinding Machines."
7. Williamson, *op. cit.*, p. 208. "Under this (contract) arrangement, a competent master workman entered into a contract with the shop whereby, supplied with raw materials, tools and power, he underook to turn out the product of his department for a settled sum. He engaged his own workmen and set his own wage rates. The contract might run a year or until the completion of a given job."
8. Bourne Manuscript, p. 81.
9. In preparation for writing a book about his father's work Wilfred Leland had dictated to his wife many of his memories. These remain among the Leland Papers and will hereafter be cited as the Wilfred C. Leland Memoirs.
10. Lord Macaulay *Works, op. cit.*, p. 349.
11. Bourne Manuscript, p. 82.
12. Henry Leland, "The Art of Manufacturing."

13. Richard Bayles, *History of Providence County, R.I.*, 1891, Vol. I, p. 475.
14. William Lincoln, *History of Worcester, Massachusetts*, 1862, p. 333.
15. Bourne Manuscript, pp. 81, 88.
16. Washington Gladden (1836–1918), Congregational clergyman, graduate Williams College, teacher and minister. He was of a practical rather than a philosophical turn of mind. Among his books were *Working Men and Their Employers, Tools and the Man. Dictionary of American Biography*, Vol. 7, p. 235.
17. Bourne Manuscript, pp. 91–92.
18. "Grinding Machines."
19. Henry Leland to Wilfred, October 16, 1887, Leland Papers.

Chapter IV

1. *The Detroiter*, September 5, 1927.
2. Unidentified clipping in Henry M. Leland file, Burton Historical Collection, Detroit Public Library.
3. Charles A. Strelinger, born 1856, began his business career in 1870 in the employ of various Detroit hardware merchants, among them, T. B. Rayl & Co. He went into business for himself about 1884. Clarence M. Burton, *City of Detroit*, 1922, Vol. III, pp. 515–16.
4. George B. Catlin, *The Story of Detroit*, the Detroit News, 1926, p. 651.
5. Detroit *Journal*, 13th Anniversary Edition, August 1895.
6. J. W. Leonard, *Industries of Detroit*, Detroit, 1887, p. 25, 38, 52.
7. George B. Catlin and Robert B. Ross, *Detroit Landmarks*, Detroit News Association, Detroit, 1898, pp. 612–13.
8. Burlingame Manuscript, p. 14.
9. Detroit *Saturday Night*, July 8, 1932, p. 2.
10. When he went to Europe in 1896 Wilfred Leland carried letters of introduction from Brown & Sharpe, whose machines were already well-known in Europe. These letters are in the Leland Papres.
11. Wilfred C. Leland Memoirs.
12. Bourne Manuscript, p. 98.
13. The business affiliations of the new stockholders were as follows:
    William H. Strong, Strong, Lee & Co., Wholesale Dry Goods.
    Rufus W. Gillette, President Preston National Bank.
    William K. Anderson, Treas., Michigan Car Co.
    Edward Y. Swift, Attorney.
    Henry K. Lathrop Jr., Dentist.
14. Records of Annual Meetings of Leland & Faulconer, still owned by the Cadillac Motor Car Co. and loaned to Mrs. Wilfred C. Leland.
15. Bourne Manuscript, pp. 104–05.
16. Wilfred C. Leland Memoirs.
17. Hartford (Ct.) *Daily Courant*, March 29, 1899. This newspaper clipping was one of a number pasted in a scrap book in the Leland Papers.

18. Bourne Manuscript, p. 111.
19. Wilfred C. Leland Memoirs.

Chapter V

1. This story has been published in numerous newspaper articles and at least four books. These are:
   Ford, *The Times, op. cit.*, pp. 211-13.
   McManus, *op. cit.*, p. 2.
   William A. Simonds, *Henry Ford*, Indianapolis, 1943, p. 62.
   Reginald M. Cleveland & S. T. Williamson, *The Road Is Yours*, New York, 1951, p. 36.
2. Ford, *The Times, op. cit.*, pp. 212.
3. *Automobile Trade Journal*, December 1, 1924, p. 358.
4. John Bourne Manuscript, pp. 128-30.
5. Detroit *Free Press*, April 14, 1904.
6. Detroit *Journal*, October 28, 1905.
7. John Bourne Manuscript, p. 132.
8. E. D. Kennedy, *The Automobile Industry*, New York, 1941, p. 24.
9. Ford, *The Times, op. cit.*, pp. 284-322; William Greenleaf, *Monopoly on Wheels*, Detroit, 1961.
10. John Bourne Manuscript, p. 133.
11. Ford, *The Times, op. cit.*, p. 644. Since the Ford production figures were not compiled by the calendar year, only an estimate can be given.
12. Detroit *News*, December 13, 1937.
13. Ralph C. Epstein, *The Automobile Industry*, Chicago, 1938, p. 81.
14. Cadillac Sales Manual 1905, Automotive History Collection, Detroit Public Library.
15. Cadillac Sales Manual 1908, Automotive History Collection.

Chapter VI

1. Pamphlet, *The Romance of the Cadillac Car*, by Old Stager, undated, in the Leland Papers.
2. *Ibid.*
3. *Ibid.* This story is also told in *Autocar*, October 18, 1913, p. 712.
4. *Royal Automobile Club Year Book 1909*, p. 248.
5. Leaflet in Leland Papers.
6. *Romance*. Also *Motor Age*, July 16, 1908. The French car noted was the Zedel.
7. Frederick A. Talbot, *Motor-Cars and Their Story*, London and New York, 1912, p. 108. "I have heard many British motorists describe the American production as cheap and nasty."
8. *Autocar*, October 18, 1913, p. 711.

9. *Autocar, op. cit.*, p. 713.
10. *Veteran Car Club Gazette,* Winter 1953, Vol. III, No. 43, p. 504.
11. From F. S. Bennett to Wilfred Leland, May 7, 1953.
12. David R. Cohn, *Combustion on Wheels,* New York, 1944, p. 94.

Chapter VII

1. The Cadillac engine numbers by years are given in *Horseless Carriage Gazette,* Nov.–Dec., 1961.
2. Detroit *News,* October 23, 1952.
3. Epstein, *op. cit.*, pp. 76–80; Ford, *The Times, op. cit.*, p. 275.
4. Detroit *News,* July 9, 1909.
5. William A. Simonds, *Henry Ford,* Indianapolis, 1943, p. 37.
6. *Motor World,* July 15, 1909, p. 629.
7. Wilfred C. Leland Memoirs.
8. Kennedy, *op. cit.*, p. 38.
9. Ford, *The Times, op. cit.*, p. 282.
10. Cleveland and Williamson, *op. cit.*, p. 36.
11. Alfred P. Sloan Jr., with Boyden Sparks, *Adventures of a White Collar Man,* New York, 1941, p. 37–39.
12. Detroit *Free Press,* February 16, 1927.
13. *Motor World, loc. cit.*
14. Arthur Pound, *The Turning Wheel,* Garden City, 1934, pp. 111–14.
15. Detroit *Journal,* July 8, 1909.
16. Detroit *News,* July 9, 1909.

Chapter VIII

1. Arthur Pound, *The Turning Wheel,* Garden City, 1934, p. 51.
2. Ford, *The Times, op. cit.*, p. 238, which gives the figure $28,000. After publication of the book it was discovered that $1500 more had been invested.
3. Detroit *News,* July 9, 1909. This figure of $178,000 is given as the amount the Cadillac stockholders had put into their automobile promotions up to 1904.
4. John B. Rae, *American Automobile Manufacturers,* Phila., 1959, p. 36.
5. Pound, *op. cit.*, pp. 111–12.
6. *Ibid.*, pp. 68–78.
7. Rae, *op. cit.*, p. 18.
8. Pound, *op. cit.*, p. 90. Although Buick's output was 8487 it may not have been the largest. The Ford production of 1907–08 was only 6398 but for 1908–09 it was 10,007. If the Buick figure is for the calendar year there is no real comparison. It was in this very year that Ford with the model T

began that tremendous surge forward which left production figures of all other manufacturers in the rear.
9. Lawrence H. Seltzer, *A Financial History of the American Automobile Industry*, Boston, 1928, pp. 145–63. The story of the founding of General Motors and the acquisition of the various units is told in detail in Pound, *op. cit.*, pp. 111–130; Rae, *op. cit.*, pp. 86–90; and *Federal Trade Commission, Report on Motor Vehicle Industry*, 76th Congress, 1st Session, House Document No. 468, Washington, 1939, pp. 421–24.
10. Alfred P. Sloan, Jr., *My Years with General Motors*, Garden City, 1964, p. 4.
11. *Ford, The Times*, pp. 412–14; Detroit *News*, July 13, 1909.
12. Pound, *op. cit.*, pp. 109, 223.
13. Seltzer, *op. cit.*, p. 30.
14. Pound, *op. cit.*, pp. 123–27.
15. Wilfred C. Leland Memoirs.
16. Wilfred C. Leland Memoirs.

Chapter IX

1. Bourne Manuscript, p. 145.
2. Seltzer, *op. cit.*, pp. 162–63.
3. Ralph C. Epstein, *The Automobile Industry*, Chicago, 1928, p. 164.
   The members of the committee were:
   James V. Wallace, Central Trust Co., New York
   Frederick Straus, J. & W. Seligman & Co., New York
   James J. Storrow, Lee, Higginson & Co., Boston
   William C. Durant, Vice-Pres., General Motors Co.
   Anthony Brady, a large stockholder.
4. *Ibid.*
5. Henry Greenleaf Pearson, *Son of New England, James Jackson Storrow*, Boston, 1932, p. 144.
6. Pound, *op. cit.*, p. 133.
7. E. D. Kennedy, *The Automobile Industry*, New York, 1941, p. 77.
8. Pound, *op. cit.*, p. 269.
9. Pearson, *op. cit.*, p. 133.
10. Letter, Lloyd F. Blunden to Mrs. Wilfred C. Leland, February 16, 1961.
11. *Automobile Trade Journal*, December 24, 1924, p. 245.
12. Wilfred C. Leland Memoirs.
13. Walter Chrysler, *Life of an American Workman*, New York, 1937, p. 126.
14. Kennedy, *op. cit.*, p. 79.
15. Seltzer, *op. cit.*, p. 171.
16. Sloan, *op. cit.*, p. 9.
17. Kennedy, *loc. cit.*
18. Seltzer, *loc. cit.*
19. Pound, *op. cit.*, pp. 145–49.

Chapter X

1. Eugene W. Lewis, *Motor Memories*, Alved Pub. Co., Detroit, 1947, p. 57.
2. "The Young Man and Business," an address delivered in the Westminster Presbyterian Church, Detroit, October 30, 1910 by Henry Leland. A copy is in the Leland Papers.
3. 1915 Catalog, *Cadillac School of Applied Mechanics*, Automotive History Collection, Detroit Public Library.
4. *Ibid.*
5. *Ibid.*
6. Interview with Samuel F. Wilson, July 20, 1960.
7. Interview with Lot A. Merrill, June 18, 1960.
8. 1915 Catalog, *Cadillac School of Applied Mechanics.*
9. Conversation with Sydney Handyside, August 3, 1960.
10. Ford, The Times, *op. cit.*, p. 452.
11. For an account of the Henry Ford Trade School see Nevins & Hill, *Expansion and Challenge*, New York, 1957, pp. 341-44.

Chapter XI

1. *The Automobile*, April 25, 1912, p. 984.
2. *Motor World*, September 21, 1911, p. 896.
3. *Motor World*, November 30, 1911, p. 665.
4. *Automobile Topics*, October 4, 1913, p. 577.
5. Letter, Ralph Lewis to Wilfred C. Leland, undated, Leland Papers.
6. Charles Kettering in *Prophet of Progress*, Edited by T. A. Boyd, New York, 1961, p. 54.
7. T. A. Boyd, *Professional Amateur*, New York, 1957, p. 54.
8. *Automobile Trade Journal*, December 1, 1924, p. 82.
9. *The Automobile*, September 9, 1909, p. 455.
10. John C. Glover and Rudolph L. Lagai, *Development of American Industries*, New York, 1959, p. 654. *Automobile Trade Journal*, December 1, 1924, p. 342.
11. *The Automobile*, August 31, 1911, p. 304.
12. *Motor World*, December 14, 1911, p. 802.
13. *The Automobile*, November 23, 1911, p. 917. Howard Coffin was a past president (1910) of the Society of Automobile Engineers.
14. *Automobile Trade Journal*, December 1, 1924, p. 82.
15. C. B. Glasscock, *The Gasoline Age*, Indianapolis, 1937, p. 169.
16. Manuscript of a speech of Wilfred Leland before the Houghton Study Club, Detroit, September 4, 1936. Leland Papers.
17. *The Automobile*, November 23, 1911, p. 918.
18. *The Automobile*, March 28, 1912, p. 786.
19. *The Automobile*, July 4, 1912, p. 20.
20. *The Autocar*, October 25, 1913.

21. *Horseless Age*, December 2, 1914, p. 942.
22. *Motor World*, December 14, 1911, p. 810.
23. *The Autocar*, November 1, 1913.

Chapter XII

1. Report on Motor Vehicle Industries, *op. cit.*, pp. 17–22. *Automotive Trade Journal*, December 1, 1924, p. 54.
2. In *Ford, The Times, op. cit.*, p. 483–87, there is an interesting account of the movement for better roads.
3. Epstein, *op. cit.*, pp. 105–10.
4. *Motor World*, August 24, 1911.
5. *Ford, The Times, op. cit.*, pp. 461–76.
6. *The Automobile*, July 4, 1912, p. 48; Glover & Lagai, *op. cit.*, p. 649.
7. *Automobile Trade Journal*, December 1, 1924. In this silver anniversary issue, the progress of the automobile industry is given year by year.
8. Wilfred C. Leland Memoirs.
9. *Horseless Age*, August 26, 1914, p. 303.
10. *The Automobile*, September 17, 1914, p. 524.
11. Reminiscences of Charlie Martens given to Mrs. Wilfred C. Leland.
12. Lloyd Blunden to Mrs. W. C. Leland, February 16, 1961.
13. Bourne Manuscript, p. 151. Apparently Henry Leland delighted in such detail.
14. Pound, *op. cit.*, p. 224.
15. The Old Guard was composed of Cadillac agents, who had been with the company since 1905. *The Automobile*, August 25, 1910, p. 335.

Chapter XIII

1. Bourne Manuscript, pp. 216–17.
2. John C. Lodge, *I Remember Detroit*, Detroit, 1940, p. 79.
3. William P. Lovett, *Detroit Rules Itself*, Boston, 1930, p. 76.
4. Lodge, *op. cit.*, p. 84; Lovett, *op. cit.*, p. 80.
5. This story is also reported in Lodge, *op. cit.*, p. 86–87 and in Malcolm Bingay, *Detroit is My Home Town*, New York, 204–07.
6. Lovett, *op. cit.*, p. 86.
7. *Ibid.*, p. 83.
8. *Ibid.*, p. 133–34.
9. *Ibid.*, p. 63.
10. *Civic Searchlight*, November 1916.
11. *Ibid.*, March 1914.
12. *Ibid.*, August 1914.
13. Lovett, *op. cit.*, p. 89.
14. *Searchlight*, November 1913.
15. *Searchlight*, May 1914.

16. Detroit *Journal*, June 26, 1918.
17. Detroit *News*, July 9, 1918.
18. *Searchlight*, August 1918.
19. Robert Y. Ogg in the Detroit *Journal*, July 11, 1918.
20. Bulletin of Detroit Citizens League, undated, but about 1960.
21. Lovett, *op. cit.*, p. 155. ". . . afterward President Leland also resigned. The League entered a new regime under the presidency of Divie Duffield, in which it became more broad and democratic in method and control."
22. Letters in the Leland Papers, mostly of the period prior to the Detroit residence.
23. Henry Leland to A. L. Munger, March 14, 1918, Leland Papers.
24. Ford, *The Times, op. cit.*, p. 513.
25. Arthur Pound, *Detroit, Dynamic City*, New York, 1940, p. 283; Ford, *The Times, op. cit.*, p. 515.
26. *The Lincolnian*, published by the Lincoln Motor Company, November 1918 to December 1919.
27. Bourne Manuscript, p. 219.

Chapter XIV

1. Frederick Bennett to Wilfred Leland, May 19, 1952.
2. Pliny Marsh to Wilfred Leland, March 26, 1952.
3. See Note 1.
4. *The Automobile*, June 21, 1917, p. 173. Henry Leland conferred with Lord Montague, Lord Sydingham, Sir Albert Stanley, etc.
5. Isaac F. Marcosson, *Colonel Deeds, Industrial Builder*, New York, 1947, pp. 234–41.
6. Marcosson, *op. cit.*, p. 237.
7. George O. Squier, *Aeronautics in the United States 1918*. An address before the American Institute of Electrical Engineers, Jan. 10, 1919, p. 58.
8. *The Literary Digest*, July 13, 1918, pp. 21–22. "The Truth about the Liberty Motor," by Theodore Knappen from the New York *Tribune*.
9. Theodore M. Knappen, *Wings of War*, New York and London, 1920, p. 88.
10. *The Literary Digest, loc. cit.* This source gives July 3 as the date of the test, most other sources give July 4.
11. The Detroit *Journal*, June 18, 1917.
12. This discussion comes in general from a presentation of the "Lincoln Motor Company, before the Commissioner of Internal Revenue in the Matter of 1918 Income and Profit Tax Return, Exhibit IV," p. 12. This book consists of photographs and printed text on the activities of the Lincoln Motor Company during the war period. Hereafter, this will be cited as "1918 Profit Tax Return."
13. *Judge Charles Evans Hughes' Report and Recommendations on the Aircraft Production Investigation*, Congressional Record LVII Appendix A, 65th Congress, 883. Hereafter this will be cited as the *Hughes Report*.

Chapter XV

1. Information by LeRoi Williams on September 26, 1918 at the Myers Inquiry. This investigation was carried on at the Lincoln plant in September 1918 by T. P. Myers representing the Government and concerned manufacturing problems. The transcript of the testimony covers 554 typewritten pages and is in the Leland Papers.
2. George O. Squier, *Aeronautics in the United States 1918*. An address before the American Institute of Electrical Engineers, Jan. 10, 1919, p. 56.
3. Squier, *op. cit.*, p. 55.
4. *Automobile and Automotive Industries*, October 25, 1917, p. 743.
5. 1918 Profit Tax Return, p. 3.
6. Letter, Pliny Marsh to Wilfred Leland, March 26, 1952.
7. Hughes Report, *op. cit.*, p. 899.
8. Reminiscences of Charlie Martens.
9. 1918 Profit Tax Return, p. 18.
10. John Bourne Manuscript, p. 172.
11. 1918 Profit Tax Return, p. 18.
12. *Ibid.*, p. 19.
13. Myers Inquiry. *See* Note 1.
14. 1918 Profit Tax Return, p. 12–14. A detailed discussion of all the Leland contracts with the Government is given in this presentation.
15. For this story *see Literary Digest*, July 13, 1918, pp. 21–22; *Current Opinion*, May and June, 1918, pp. 302, 374; Marcosson, *op. cit.*, p. 258.
16. *Literary Digest*, September 7, 1918, p. 18.
17. John Bourne Manuscript, p. 176.
18. Hughes Report, *op. cit.*, p. 905.
19. *Ibid.*, p. 907.

Chapter XVI

1. Transcript of Myers Inquiry, p. 432.
2. *Ibid.*, p. 551.
3. Annual Report of the Lincoln Motor Company, 1920.
4. A 36-page letter written by Wilfred Leland on October 4, 1922 to the stockholders and creditors of the Lincoln Motor Company. Hereafter this source will be cited as Letter to the Stockholders, 1922.
5. 1918 Profit Tax Return, p. 14; Letter to the Stockholders, 1922, pp. 6–7.
6. John Bourne Manuscript, p. 177.
7. Annual Report of the Lincoln Motor Company, 1920.
8. *1920 Lincoln Presentation Catalog*, Book of Advance Information. Automotive History Collection, Detroit Public Library.
9. Annual Report, Lincoln Motor Company, 1920.
10. *Wall Street Journal*, December 2, 1921.

11. *The Lincolnian*, December 1, 1919, p. 9. This was the employees magazine published throughout the year 1919.
12. Letter to the Stockholders, 1922, p. 8.
13. Letter, Lloyd Blunden to Mrs. Wilfred C. Leland, February 16, 1961.
14. Letter to Stockholders, 1922, pp. 16–17.
15. John Bourne Manuscript, p. 183. The reference is to Exodus I, 8, "Now there arose a new king over Egypt which knew not Joseph."
16. Annual Report, Lincoln Motor Company, 1920, read at the Annual Meeting, March 10, 1921.
17. This phrase was used by Dr. Murphy at the Directors' Meeting of July 11, 1921. Directors' Minutes in Leland Papers.
18. These sales figures come from the report of Scovell, Wellington & Co. on the Lincoln Motor Company, June 23, 1921.
19. The Dent Act passed by Congress early in 1919 allowed that any contract could be re-opened by the War, Navy or Treasury Departments up to March 1, 1924.

Chapter XVII

1. Transcript of Wilfred Leland's testimony in Hughes Investigation, pp. 21–22.
2. The original prices are taken from a 1920 Lincoln catalog in the Detroit Automotive Collection, Detroit Public Library. The 1921 prices are from the magazine, *Automotive Industries*, February 9, 1922, p. 294.
3. Memo on June 18, 1921 Conference. The record of this conference as it remains in the Leland Papers seems to have been a personal one made by W. C. Leland.
4. *Ibid.*
5. Executive Minutes, Board of Directors, Lincoln Motor Co., Oct. 6, 1921.
6. Ralph Getsinger, Lincoln sales manager, is said to have stated that the first bodies were unattractive and the dealers condemned them unanimously. He then arranged for others. (Nevins & Hill, *Ford: Expansion and Challenge*, p. 176) Wilfred Leland remembered some disappointment over the first Lincoln bodies but added no detail on the matter.
7. Minutes of Executive Committee, July 21, 1921.
8. The preliminary report of Scovell, Wellington & Company, dated June 23, 1921, is in the Leland Papers. The final financial report is not. The information on its findings is taken from later quotations in the minutes regarding it.
9. Directors' Minutes, October 10, 1921.
10. Minutes of the Executive Committee, October 3, 1921.
11. Minutes of the Executive Committee, September 29, 1921.
12. Many of these companies and their difficult position at the time are discussed in John B. Rae, *American Automobile Manufacturers*, Phila. and N.Y., 1959, pp. 133, 146, 148, 184.
13. Minutes of the Board, October 10, 1921.

14. Minutes of the Executive Committee, October 12, 1921.
15. Minutes of the Board of Directors, October 19, 1920.
16. Minutes of the Board, October 21, 1921.
17. Minutes of the Board, November 3, 1921.
18. John Bourne Manuscript, p. 230. The quotation is from the 121st Psalm.
19. Minutes of the Board, November 8, 1921. Wilfred Leland in his Letter to the Stockholders, 1922, relates this part of the story in much the same terms.
20. John Bourne Manuscript, p. 191.

Chapter XVIII

1. John Bourne Manuscript, p. 191.
2. Detroit *Times*, November 10, 1921.
3. Letter to the Stockholders, 1922.
4. Chronology of events by Wilfred Leland. This table of dates and events was prepared in 1924. Hereafter it will be cited as Chronology.
5. Letter to the Stockholders, dated March 8, 1923. This letter also prepared by Wilfred Leland will hereafter be cited as Letter to the Stockholders, 1923.
6. Chronology.
7. Letter to the Stockholders, 1923.
8. Statement of W. C. Leland, July 3, 1924.
9. Detroit *Free Press*, January 12, 1922.
10. *Automotive Industries*, December 22, 1921, p. 1246.
11. *Automobile Topics*, December 3, 1921; *Wall Street Journal*, November 28, 1921.
12. Detroit *News*, December 14, 1921.
13. Detroit *Times*, December 30, 1921; *The Automobile*, December 29, 1921.
14. Detroit *Journal*, November 12, 1921.
15. *Automotive Industries*, December 8, 1921, p. 1140.
16. *Pipp's Weekly*, February 3, 1923. *Pipp's Weekly*, a small pamphlet of sixteen pages, was published in Detroit for three or four years beginning in June 1920. E. G. Pipp, the editor, had been the first editor of *The Dearborn Independent* and knew Henry Ford well, in the days of his political activity. Pipp became disillusioned, left Ford and began a crusade against him in the little weekly.
17. Detroit *Free Press*, December 31, 1921.
18. Letter to the Stockholders, 1923.
19. Detroit *Journal*, January 25, 1922.
20. *Wall Street Journal*, January 10, 1922.
21. *Wall Street Journal*, January 12, 1922; Chicago *Journal of Commerce*, January 12, 1922.
22. Detroit *Times*, January 12, 1922.
23. Detroit *Free Press*, January 12, 1922.
24. *Automotive Industries*, January 19, 1922, p. 145.
25. *Automotive Industries, loc. cit.*

26. *Pipp's Weekly*, January 21, 1922.
27. One of these gentlemen was later described as a Ford stooge, as the other was probably also. Detroit *News*, February 4, 1922; Detroit *Saturday Night*, February 11, 1922.
28. All the Detroit newspapers reported the auction in great detail. The account used here comes mainly from the John Bourne Manuscript, pp. 202–03.
29. Detroit *Journal*, February 4, 1922.
30. John Bourne Manuscript. p. 209.

Chapter XIX

1. *Automobile*, January 26, 1922; *Chicago Motor Age*, February 2, 1922.
2. Detroit *News*, February 4, 1922.
3. Detroit *Journal*, February 6, 1922.
4. Detroit *Times*, February 7, 1922.
5. Detroit *News*, February 7, 1922; Detroit *Saturday Night*, Feb. 11, 1922.
6. Detroit *Free Press*, February 12, 1922.
7. Chronology, February 16, 1922. This investment certificate was comparable to non-voting preferred stock in the Ford Motor Company. Any employee could buy such certificates and hold them as long as he stayed on the payroll. They yielded 6% interest.
8. Statement made by Wilfred Leland July 3, 1924 regarding conversations and other contacts with Henry Ford.
9. *Automotive Industries*, January 19, 1922.
10. Detroit *News*, January 29, 1922. Ford had about 8,000 distributors.
11. Detroit *Journal*, February 11, 1922.
12. *Ford: Expansion and Challenge, op. cit.*, p. 184.
13. *Ibid.* p. 514.
14. Samuel S. Marquis, *Henry Ford, An Interpretation*, Boston, 1922, p. 143.
15. Henry Ford, *My Life and Work*, New York, 1922, p. 62.
16. *Ibid.* p. 97.
17. *Expansion and Challenge, op. cit.*, p. 183.
18. *Ibid.* p. 184.
19. *Ibid.* p. 410.
20. Wilfred Leland Chronology.
21. *Expansion and Challenge, op. cit.*, pp. 276–77.
22. *Ibid.* p. 84.
23. Detroit *News*, February 2, 1922.
24. *Expansion and Challenge, op. cit.*, p. 184. *See also* pp. 168, 275, 280–81, 293–94, 349–50, 440 and 620.
25. Copies of these three letters, dated May 23, 26, 27, 1922 remain in the Leland Papers.
26. Detroit *Journal*, February 22, 1922.
27. Detroit *News*, April 11, 1922. Senator Truman Newberry is said to have been the person who threw his influence against the tax claim.

28. Detroit *Times*, April 14, 1922.
29. Cleveland *News*, April 24, 1922; *Automotive Industries*, May 4, 1922.
30. This figure is from a record of Lincoln shipments by months, found in the Leland Papers. It differs slightly from other sources.
31. This brochure entitled, "What Ford Resources Mean to Lincoln" is in the Automotive Collection, Detroit Public Library.
32. *Automotive Industries*, June 15, 1922.
33. *Ibid.*
34. List of Lincoln shipments in Leland Papers.
35. Allan Nevins and Frank Ernest Hill, *Ford, Decline and Rebirth*, New York, 1963, Appendix I.
36. Federal Trade Commission: *Report on the Motor Vehicle Industry, op. cit.*, pp. 653–54.
37. Keith Sward, *The Legend of Henry Ford*, New York, 1948, p. 171.
38. *See* Note 36.

Chapter XX

1. Letter to the Stockholders, 1922.
2. This tabulation, together with other figures relating to the Lincoln operation, is in the Leland Papers.
3. Detroit *Free Press*, April 13, 1922.
4. Detroit *Saturday Night*, January 28, 1923. James Couzens was appointed Senator to complete the term of Senator Truman Newberry, who had resigned.
5. Detroit *News*, October 18, 1922.
6. Copy of court record in Leland Papers.
7. Detroit *Free Press*, January 3, 1923.
8. The account of these various negotiations is taken from a statement by Wilfred Leland before attorneys who were preparing the case for the stockholders against Henry Ford. It covers over 100 typewritten pages and is titled, "Statement of Wilfred C. Leland concerning Conversations with Henry Ford, July 3, 1924." Not all the pages are numbered. Hereafter this will be cited as Leland Conversations, 1924.
9. Memorandum of conference with Harold Emmons, July 30, 1924.
10. Leland Conversations, 1924, p. 20.
11. Detroit *News*, March 9, 1923; *Expansion and Challenge, op. cit.*, p. 194.
12. Emmons Memorandum.
13. *Pipp's Weekly*, February 3, 1923.
14. Leland Conversations, 1924, p. 50.
15. *Ibid.*, pp. 66–67.
16. *Ibid.*, p. 31.
17. *Ibid.*, p. 33.
18. *Ibid.*, pp. 101–02.
19. Detroit *News*, February 21, 1928.

20. Detroit *Free Press*, February 21, 1928.
21. Detroit *News, loc. cit.*
22. 245 *Michigan Reports* 599. A discussion, more easily understood by the layman, is to be found in Federal Trade Commission, *Report on Motor Vehicle Industry*, pp. 644–54.
23. 245 *Michigan Reports* 607.
24. 252 *Michigan Reports* 547. This decision was given on Mar. 29, 1929.
25. A copy of this printed letter is in the Leland Papers.
26. Leland Papers.

Index

Acme White Lead & Color Works, 111
Advent, doctrine of second, 45, 46
Albert, Prince, 19
Alexandra, Queen of England, 139
Alpena, Michigan, 52
Air brakes, 48
Aircraft Production Board, 176, 179; Bureau of, 188
Airplane industry in United States, 182
Airplane motors, 172; development of, 175, 176; testing, 186; difficulties, 188, 189; production scandal, 190
Amsterdam St., Detroit, 69, 71
American Automobile Manufacturers, 278
American Bridge Company, 183
American industry, 30
American Injector Co., 177
American Institute of Electrical Engineers, 276
American Institute of Weights & Measures, 169
American Judicature Society, 165
American Society of Mechanical Engineers, 105
American versus European cars, 79, 80
Anderson Company (bodies), 219
Anderson, William K., 57, 270

Anglo-American Motor Car Co., 15, 80
Anti-Saloon League, 158, 167, 169
Appomattox, Lee's defeat at, 29
Armory Building, Detroit, 62
Army and Navy Technical Board, 176
Art Institute, 66
Art of Manufacturing, 44, 45
Association of Licensed Automobile Manufacturers, 75, 144
Autocar, 69; Company, 75
Autocar, The, 267, 271, 272, 274, 275
Automobile, 274, 275, 276, 280
Automobile, bodies, development, 145; Club of Great Britain and Ireland, 80; clubs, 89; industry, rise 1910–15, 117; shows, 1901 Detroit, 62; 1903, New York, 69; 1907, New York, 89; 1908, New York, 91; 1920 and 21, New York, 215
Automobile Topics, 274, 279
Automobile Trade Journal, 271, 273, 274, 275.
Automotive Industries, 279, 280, 281

Back rest, 35
Backson, Jill, 28
Backus, Standish, 11, 121, 204, 209

Baker, Newton, Secretary of War, 198
Baldwin apples, 42
Ball, Mrs., ——, 94
Ballard, Charles H. Rifle Co., 32
Baltimore, Maryland, 268
Bankers, and automobile companies, 104; consider General Motors finances, 106-108; committee administers G.M., 109-110
Baptist church, 46, 50
Baptist Church, Pearl St., 46
Barthel, Oliver, 119
——, Otto, 68
Barton, Vermont, 19
Bates Street, Detroit, 53
Bayles, Richard, 270
Beale, Earle V., 56
Beam squares, 49
Beers, J. H. & Co., 269
Belle Isle, bridge, 52, 61; ferry, 51; park, 53, 129
Belmont Hotel, New York, 107, 220
Bennett, Frederick S., 15, 16, 17, 79, 80, 82, 84, 85, 87, 138, 171, 267, 272, 276
Berry Brothers, 53
Bible reading at plant, 31, 45, 74, 119
Bicycle craze, 53; chainless, 59; gears, 59
Black, Clarence A., 69, 71, 96
Blackstone Street, Detroit, 161
Blair & Company, 225
Blanchard lathe, 28
Blanchard, Thomas, 28
Blunden, Lloyd, 77, 112, 152, 201, 273, 275, 278
Bohuka, George, 161
Boston, Mass., 21, 109, 130, 273
Bourne, John, 156, 267
Bourne Manuscript, 269, 270, 271, 273, 275, 276, 277, 278, 279, 280
Boushaw, Billy, 159, 163
Boyd, T. A., 274
Bowen, Lemuel B., 66, 67, 72, 89, 96, 207
Boy Scouts, 167
Boyer family, 208, 260
Boyer, Joseph, 57, 177, 203, 204, 208, 209, 211, 217
Brady, Anthony, 273
Bribes to aldermen, 157

Briscoe Brothers, 99
Briske, Joseph F., 125
British Air Board, 173
British Information Service, 267
Brooklands, 15, 16, 82, 83, 267
Brown-Lipe-Chapin, 101
Brown, Joseph R., 30, 34, 39, 40, 49
Brown & Sharpe Manufacturing Co., 37-42 passim, 47, 53, 54, 55, 57, 58, 93, 114, 177, 269, 270
Brown University, 54
Browning, Elizabeth Barrett, 170
Brush, Alanson, 68, 76, 77
Budlong, Milton J., 200
Buffalo, N.Y., 60
Buick car, 112, 141; company, 70, 75, 89, 99, 100, 103, 106, 112, 181
Buick, David D., 99
Bureau of Aircraft Production, 188
Burlingame, Luther D., 37, 41n, 269
Burlingame manuscript, 269, 270
Burroughs Adding Machine Co., 57, 177
Burton, Clarence M., 163, 270
Butzel, Leo, 219, 220, 230, 231

Cadillac, Antoine de la Mothe, 69
Cadillac automobile, standardization test, 15; first models, 69, 70; in Great Britain and abroad, 79, 80; reliability trial, 81; No. 530, 80-85; body design, 88; at 1907 show, 89; "30", 91-94; closed bodies, 115; 1912 model, 133, 134; price field, 141; body lines, 145; noises in motor, 151, 180, 265; advertising, 76, 77, 79, 146, 150, 153; agents, 16, 69, 154, 175; car production, 1904-1905, 74; 1909, 94; 1909-10-11, 112; 1912, 137; 1915-16, 173; engineering division, 149; factory, 72, 73, 82, 87, 136, 137; sales manuals, 1905 and 1908, 271
Cadillac Automobile Company, 67, 69, 71, 72, 74
Cadillac Hotel, Detroit, 60
Cadillac Motor Car Company, organized, 74, 85, 88; financial depression, 89-90; sale to G.M., 94, 95, 96; saves G.M., 104-06; under bankers, 109;

INDEX

slogan, 114, 115, 122; electric starter, 133, 136, 137, 150, 169; V-8, 171, 173, 176; Lelands resign from, 177, 178, 181, 185, 186; contract for airplane motors, 207, 208, 216, 237, 251, 270
Cadillac Old Guard, 154
Cadillac School of Applied Mechanics, 122–126
California, 202, 215
Campbell, Henry M., 230
Candidate rating by Citizens League, 161
Cannon Street, London, 81
Card-setting machine, 32
Carnegie, Andrew, 172
Carter, Byron T., 129
Carter-car Co., 101, 112, 129
Cass Avenue, Detroit, 67, 69, 71
Cass school, Detroit, 166
Cassatt, Robert K., 226
Castings, iron, 58–59
Catlin, George B., 270
Census Report of 1880, 268
Center rest, 35; gauges, 49
Central Trust Co., 273
Chalmers cars, 137, 141; company, 135
Champion, Albert, 100
Champion Ignition Co., 100
Chandler company, 215
Charter commission, Detroit, 163
Chase National Bank, 106
Chevrolet organized by Durant, 117
Chicago, Ill., 46, 49, 51, 52, 103, 108, 224, 269
Chicago Pneumatic Machine Tool Co., 57
Chickahominy river, Va., 28
Chinese Catholic Mission Society, 167
Chinese Y.M.C.A., 167
Christmas Cove, Maine, 150
Chronology of Wilfred Leland, 244, 279, 280
Chrysler, Walter P., 18, 114, 115, 206, 273
Chrysler company, 114
Congregational Church, First, 66
Church of Our Father, 66
Church of Jahveh, 45, 46
Citizens League, 157, 158, 160, 165

Civic Searchlight, 160, 161, 162, 163, 164, 275, 276
Civic Uplift League, 157
Civil War, 27, 30
Clark, Justice George M., 263
—, Victor, 268
Clement, George, 150
Cleveland banks, 219
Cleveland, Ohio, 272
Cleveland *News*, 281
Cleveland, Reginald M., 271
Clippers, 38–39
Clutch, multiple disc dry, 151
Clyde, Ohio, 101
Coffee break, 169
Coffin, Howard E., 135, 136, 179
Cohn, David R., 272
Cole Motor Car Co., 135, 137
Colt Armory, 31
Colt Revolver Factory, 29
Columbia car, 69
Columbian school, Detroit, 166
Columbus Buggy Co., 71
Columbus, Ohio, 46, 47, 71
Colvin, Fred H., 191
Compote de trois, 83
Continental & Commercial National Bank of Chicago, 218
Contract system of manufacture, 40, 41
Conversations, Wilfred Leland with Henry Ford, 260, 261, 281
Cooper, James Fenimore, 26
Corrupt voting practices, 159
Couzens, James, 163, 164, 248, 253
Covert, Frank L., 263
Cowan, John, 160
Cranks, automobile, 128
Crittenton (Florence) Home, 169
Crompton, George, 25, 28
Crompton (George) Loom Works, 24, 25, 26, 27
Crompton, William, 25
Cross-licensing agreement, 148
Cunningham car company, 215
Current Opinion, 277
Cycle and Automobile Trade Journal, 79

Dame, Stoddard & Kendall, 38, 39

INDEX

Dance hall ordinance, 162
Daniels Car Company, 215
Daugherty, Harry M., Attorney General, 248, 253
Da Vinci, Leonardo, 148
Davis, Earl J., 254
Dayton Engineering Laboratories Co., 134
Dayton Metal Products, 177
Dayton, Ohio, 132, 133
Dearborn Ford plant, 224
Dearborn *Independent*, 279
De Dion-Bouton car, 130, 149
Deeds, Col. Edward A., 176, 179, 190
DeHaviland planes, 192
Delco, 133, 137
Dent Act, 278
Dequindre Street, Detroit, 56
Detroit, 16, 17, 51, 52, 53, 54, 56, 60, 61, 82, 96, 101, 111, 117, 124, 126, 129, 132, 134, 135, 153, 274, 276; board of aldermen, 155, 156; city hall, 149
— Automobile Company, 66, 67
— Bicycle Club, 53
— Citizens League, 157, 158, 160, 165, 276
— Employers Association, 167, 170
— Public Library, Automotive History Collection, 77, 271, 277, 278; Burton Historical Collection, 270; Symphony Orchestra, 66
Detroit Edison, 66, 240
Detroit *Free Press*, 69, 76, 232, 271, 272, 279, 280, 281, 282
Detroit Historical Museum, 78
Detroit *Journal*, 270, 271, 272, 276, 279
Detroit National Bank, 96
Detroit *News*, 157, 162, 164, 165, 231, 257, 271, 272, 276, 279, 280, 281, 282
Detroit *Saturday Night*, 259, 270
Detroit *Times*, 239, 279, 280, 281
Detroit Tuberculosis Sanitarium, 167
Detroit Trust Co., 216, 224, 228
Detroit United Railway, 158
Detroiter, 270
Dewey, Blanche Molyneaux. See Leland, Mrs. Wilfred C.
Dewar, Sir Thomas, 17, 83
Dewar Challenge Cup, 82

Dewar Trophy, 17, 82, 139
Dime Building, 149
Dimmer, Frank J., 60
Distinguished Service Medal, 202
Dodge Brothers, 18, 62, 126
Dodge company, 206
Dodge, Horace, 55, 61
— John, 55, 61
Double wheel tool grinder, 55
Dow Rim Co., 101
Downey, ——, 103
Drive, left or right hand, 142
Drydock Street, Detroit, 150
Duffield, Divie, 156, 163, 276
Dupont, 18, 117, 233
Durant, William C., 18, 92; organizes Buick, 95; employs Lelands, 96; organizes General Motors, 98–101; relation to Lelands, 103, 118; search for money for G.M., 105, 106; bankers meeting, 106–108; deposed, 109; again in control, 116; organizes Chevrolet, 117; refuses war work, 174, 176; again leaves G.M., 205–06, 233, 273
Duryea, Charles, 17
Duryea, Frank, 17, 140

Ebelhare, William H., 196
Eddy, Sherwood, 167
Edison, Thomas Alva, 130
Eight-cylinder motors, 147
Election boards, 161; frauds, 159
Electric starter, 131–139
Elmore Manufacturing Co., 101
Elmwood Street, Detroit, 52
Emancipator, 200
Emerson, Ralph Waldo, 26
Emmert, John T., 203, 204, 231
Emmons, Harold H., 156, 179, 219, 221, 228, 230, 235, 238, 254, 255, 256, 281
Employees, Lincoln company, 168, 169
Employer's Association Employment Service, 188
Engineering Foundation of New York, 39
England, 15, 16, 55, 105, 138, 169
English cars, 80
English and American tool builders, 28
English workmen, 26

INDEX

Epstein, Ralph C., 271, 273, 275
Estabrook school, Detroit, 166
Evans, Mr. Heany, 225
Everitt car company, 135
Everitt-Metzger-Flanders, 114
Evolution of car bodies, 145
Ewing Automobile Co., 101

Factory life, 31
Fairlane, Ford home, 225, 228
Farkas, Eugene, 243
Faulconer, Robert C., 52, 53, 57, 58, 59
Federal Trade Commission, 273, 281
Fellows, Justice Grant, 263
Ferris, Frank E., 60
Ferry (D. M.) Seed Co., 52, 66
Finance committee, 136
Financing first auto companies, 98
Finsbury Pavement, London, 81
Fire companies, 32
First Congregational Church, 66, 68
First National Bank, Detroit, 91, 104, 208
Fish, Frederick A., 71
Fisher Brothers, 115
Fisher, Charles, 60
— Fred, 115
Fitch, Charles R., 268
— John, 26
Fiske tires, 81
Flint, Michigan, 95, 99, 100, 101, 103
Florence Crittenton Home, 167
Florida, 171, 172
Flowers, Charles, 160
Flynn, Alfred D., 39n
Foltz, Bill, 77, 129
Ford, Edsel, 224, 227, 228, 230, 235, 238, 243, 244, 258, 261
Ford, Henry, 18, 55, 63, 66, 67, 68, 70, 119, 120, 127, 138; approached by Lelands, 224, 225, 227; agreement with Lelands, 228-30, 232; buys Lincoln company, 235, 237, 245; discharges Lelands, 247, 252; tax claim, 255, 258; oral contract of, 260, 261; suit brought against, 259, 261, 262, 263, 264, 265, 279, 280
Ford, Mrs. Henry, 232, 235
Ford (Henry) Company, 66, 67

Ford, Model T, 76, 243
Ford Motor Co., 75, 76 89; smoking in factory, 125n, 126, 127, 164, 181, 191, 205, 206, 216; employee treatment, 238, 241, 242; sales policies, 244, 246, 247, 252, 256
Ford (Henry) Trade School, 127
Fort Sumter, 27
Foundry, L&F, 58; G.M., 103
Fox Trimmer, 55
France, 55, 169
Franklin car, 141, 145
Franklin, H. H., Manufacturing Co., 75
French cars, 80
Fuller, George F., 226
— Sybil H., 226
Fulton, Robert, 26

Gallagher, William Henry, 259
Gauges, 30, 113, 114
Gear, cutters, 30; generator, 60; grinding, 55, 60
General Electric Co., 136
General Motors Company, 18; buys Cadillac, 94, 95; organized by Durant, 98-101; in trouble, 105; bankers confer on, 106-08; under finance committee, 110-15; Durant again seizes control of, 117, 133, 136, 137, 177, 180; airplane motor contract, 181, 206, 273
Geneva, Ohio, 101
Germany, 55, 169, 172
Getsinger, Ralph C., 212, 245, 278
Gillette, Rufus W., 57, 270
Girls' Protective League, 161
Gladden, Washington D., 47, 270
Glasscock, C. B., 274
Glover, John C., 274, 275
Glover, Vermont, 20
Gnome plane, 182
Goo-goo League, 157
Gordon, ——, 25, 26, 27, 28
Goss, Arnold, 95
Government tax claim on Lincoln, 200, 226, 231, 247, 254
Grace Hospital Annex, 167
Grand Boulevard, Detroit, 52
Grease cups, 120
Great Britain, 79, 81, 83, 172

Great Lakes Engineering Co., 123
Green, Andrew, 157
— Constance M., 268
Greenleaf, William, 271
Greening apples, 42
Grimm, Ada, 169
Grinding machines, 39
Guy, William, 87, 116, 178

Hall, E. J., 176, 186
Haltske Company, 136
Handyside, Sydney, 274
Harlequin, 3, 17, 83, 84
Harris, Julian, 180
Hartford, Conn., 29, 31, 60
Hartford (Ct.) *Daily Courant*, 270
Haviland motors, 183
Hawes, Fred, 63, 130
Hayes (Rutherford B.), 47
Haymarket riots, 51
Headlights, tilt beam, 143
Healey, John, 60
Heany Lamp Co., 101, 112
Heaslet, James G., 179, 186
Hecker, Col. Frank J., 56
Hercules motor, 77
Hickory wood for wheels, 82
Hill climbing contest, 80
Highland, Michigan, 126, 127
Highland Park Ford plant, 127
Hill, Frank Ernest, 67, 274, 278, 281
Hispano-Suiza plane, 182
Holden Avenue (Lincoln) plant, 175, 179, 183, 189, 210, 216, 224
Hope, Lawrence, 78
Horatius, 43
Horse clippers, 38
Horseless Age, 275
Horseless Carriage Gazette, 272
Hot Springs, Arkansas, 167
Houghton Study Club, 274
House of Representatives, 181
Howard, Earl C., 131, 132
Howe, Frederick H., 30
Hudson car, 141; company, 137
Hudson, Joseph L., 156
Hudson Motors, 126
Hughes investigation, 195, 208, 278

Hughes report on airplane production, 192, 276, 277
Hughes, Charles Evans, 190, 197, 276
—, Mark B., 124
Hull, Elias, 23
—, Ellen. *See* Leland, Mrs. Henry M.
Hull farm, 42, 43
Hupmobile car, 141
Hupp Motor Car Co., 135

Ideal Manufacturing Co., 150
Ignition, electric, 133
Illinois, 184
Indianapolis, Ind., 71
Industrial revolution, 25
Information on candidates, 161
Initial investments of car companies, 98
Initiative law, 165
Inspection in factories, 44
Interchangeable parts, 15, 16, 29, 30, 83
Iowa Territory, 19
Iron castings, 58
Italy, 169

Jackson company, 137
Jahveh, Church of, 46
Jefferson, Thomas, 26
Jefferson Avenue, 61
Jerald, Rev., ———, 25
Johansson gauges, 113, 114
Johnson, Frank, 63, 77, 87, 130, 151, 178
Johnson, W. R., 178
Joint Thanksgiving Day sermon, 167
Jordan & Meehan, 46–47
Journal of Commerce, Chicago, 279
Joy, Henry B., 70, 91, 169, 268
Justice, Department of, 190

Kansas City, Mo., 200
Kanzler, Ernest C., 224, 244
Kappen, Theodore M., 276
Kennedy, E. D., 271, 273
Kettering, Charles F., 132, 133, 136, 137, 152, 177, 179, 274
King-Hoagland Company, 225
Kinnicut, G. Herman, 219, 221, 226
Kirby Avenue, Detroit, 210
Kissell & Kinnicut, 219, 247
Knox Automobile Co., 75

INDEX

Knudsen, William S., 152
Kresge, Sebastian S., 156
Kurth, Charles, 161

Lafayette car company, 215
Lagai, Rudolph L., 274, 275
Lake Angelus, Oakland Co., Michigan, 131
Lake District, Scotland, 84
Lake-shipping, 52
Lansing, Michigan, 61, 63, 69, 100, 103, 180
Larned Street, Detroit, 62
LaSalle Boulevard, Detroit, 77
Lathes, 30, 39, 49
Lathe center grinder, 55
Lathrop, Henry K., 57, 270
Layng, George, 178
Lee & Co., Wholesale Dry Goods, 270
Lee, Higginson & Co., 109, 273
Leland, (Thomas) Edison, 23, 24, 27, 28, 268
— (Richard) Frank, 23, 24, 32, 268
— (Martha) Gertrude, 32, 166, 212, 269
— Henry Martyn (1843-1932), parentage and childhood, 19-24; first job, 25; apprenticeship, 25, 26; first vote, 29; marriage, 32; fire fighter, 33; policeman, 34; Brown & Sharpe, 40-50; L&F, 54-74; meets William Murphy, 66; Cadillac manager, 73; Osceola, 77-78; talk with Sloan, 92-93; meets Durant, 97; advises G.M. units, 113-116; Johansson gauges, 114; lesson on grease cups, 120; school for mechanics, 122; self-starter, 130; 6-cylinder engines, 147; V-8 motor, 151; Citizens League, 155-165; family letters, 166; church affiliation, benevolences, 167; attitude towards labor, 167-69; honorary degree, 170; leaves Cadillac, 174; organizes Lincoln, 178, 179; machine tools for Liberty motor, 185; testing motors, 186; competency questioned, 196; Dr. Fred Murphy, 203, 211; financial crisis, 217, 218; Lincoln receivership, 222; sale of Lincoln, 235; 79th birthday, 239; Ford difficulties, 239-245; discharged, 247; paid off by Ford, 259; conversation with Ford, 262; letter to stockholders, 264-65; death, 265
— Mrs. Henry M. (Ellen Hull), 24, 31, 32, 42, 167, 170
— Joseph, 21
— Leander, 19, 21, 22, 23, 42, 268
— Mrs. Leander (Zylpha Tifft), 20, 23, 24, 27, 42, 268
— Mary Ann, 23, 268
— Miriam, 42, 167
— Sylvia M., 268
— Wilfred Chester (1869-1958), birth, 32, 42, 49, 50; mechanic, 54; salesman, 55-56; payroll L&F, 58-59; Olds motor at auto show, 62-63; first Leland car, 65; contact with William Murphy, 66-67; enters Cadillac, 73; marriage, 83; son in Dewar Trophy, 83, 86; 1907 depression, 89-91; negotiates sale of Cadillac to G.M., 94-95; sells G.M. stock, 96-97; goes with Durant to raise money, 105; saves G.M., 106-08, 110, 111, 112, 113; steel bodies for cars, 115; Durant shows G.M. stock to re-capture control, 117; country home, 131; Kettering and self-starter, 133; test of Cadillac electrical system, 136; baby car, 138; six-cylinder motor, 146; V-8 motors, 147-50; V-8 plaque presented, 154; married, 166; asks Durant to permit war work, 174; resigns from Cadillac, 175; Liberty motor contract, 178-181, 183; Hughes investigation, 195; Lincoln financial difficulties, 203-209; controversy, 210-222; executive committee, 209; search for money, 218, 220; vote on receivership, 222; first contact with Henry Ford, 224; meeting with Judge Tuttle, 228; agreement with Ford, 227-28; creditor's meeting, 230; second meeting with Ford, 233; sale of Lincoln, 235, 237, 242; difficulty with Ford management, 243-44; chronology, 244; discharged by Ford, 247; proposes to buy Lincoln back, 246, 254, 255; dissatisfied with Emmons, 257; negotiations for pay-

Leland (continued)
  ment of stockholders, 255, 258; letter on Ford's promises, 259; suit to make Ford pay stockholders, 259; testimony on Ford's oral contract, 260–61; loss of suit, 265, 267, 270, 272, 274, 278, 279, 281
— Mrs. Wilfred C. (Blanche Molyneaux Dewey), 83, 166, 235
— Mrs. Wilfred C. (Ottilie Masey), 77, 83, 269, 273, 275, 278
— Wilfred Chester, Jr., 83, 139, 166, 269
— William Henry, 269
Leland & Faulconer (originally Leland, Faulconer & Norton) organized, 53–54; type of work, 56; foundry, 58–59; bicycle gears, 60; Olds transmissions, 61; motors, 62, 64, 65, 67; Cadillac car, 69; merged with Cadillac, 74, 90, 102, 112, 113, 166, 167, 207, 270
Leonard, Arthur C., 96
— Everetta, 96
— J. W., 270
Leverenz Street, Detroit, 160
Lewis, Eugene W., 274
Lewis, Ralph C., 130, 131, 274
Liberty motor, first model, 176; costs of, 178, 179; Lelands sign contract for, 181, 183; difficulties in manufacturing, 185; cost of production, 189, 192; Hughes investigation and report of, 193, 195; settlement of Leland contract for, 197, 198
Libby prison, 28
Licensed Automobile Manufacturers, 89
Liebold, Ernest G., 127, 224, 247
Lincoln, Abraham, 27, 29; statue at Lincoln plant, 178, 200
Lincoln, William, 268, 270
Lincoln automobile distributors, 202, 221, 224, 225, 226, 227, 229, 243, 261
Lincoln collection and exhibit, 170, 241
Lincoln Highway Association, 140
Lincoln motor, description, 198–99
Lincoln Motor Company (Michigan corporation), stockholders, 177; organization, 178, 180; first contract signed, 181; plant built, 183–85; tools for plant, 184–85; labor turn over, 187; sabotage in plant, 188; financing of plant and contract, 188–89; investigation, 190; Hughes report on motor production, 192–93; end of war, 194; final settlement, 197, 198; Delaware corporation organization, 199; stock structure, 200; tax claim on war profits, 201; financial difficulties, 203–04; sales, 202, 205, 206, 214; directors, 204, 205; price cut, 209, 220, 221, 222; executive committee, 209, 219; real estate, 210; Scovell Wellington report, 212, 213; production, 205, 214; minutes of executive committee, 211, 212, 214, 278, 279; minutes of the board, 213, 220, 279; Chicago trip to raise money, 218; tax claim, 220; receivership, 222, 223; receiver appointed, 224; inventory of assets, 225; stockholders protective committee, 226; Henry Ford decides to purchase, 227; negotiations with Ford, 228–35; court sets upset price, 230; purchased by Ford, 234–35; Ford ownership, 237; Ford pays Leland for stock, 238; plant rearranged, 239, 240; difficulties of Ford and Leland management, 241–43; question of sales and distributors, 243, 244; Lelands ask to buy Lincoln back, 246–47; Lelands discharged, 247; tax claim revived, 248–49; Lincoln production under Ford, 249, 250, 251; creditors paid by Ford, 256
Lincoln statue, 170
Lincolnian, 276, 278
Literary Digest, 276, 277
Little, William, 103
Locomobile Company of America, 75, 141, 215
Lodge, John C., 156, 162, 275
London, England, 15, 79, 81, 82, 132, 133, 135
Loring Coes Wrench Works, 32, 268
Lormer, Dr. George, 50
Lovett, Robert, 276
Lovett, William P., 165, 275
Lucius W. Pond Tool Co., 32, 268
Lumbering industry, 52

INDEX

McCarthy, Father, 167
Macaulay, Lord Thomas Babington, 19, 43, 268, 269
Macauley, Alvan, 178
Machine shops in Detroit, 53
Machine tools, 18, 29, 30, 49, 90
Machinery, 269
Machinists' Union, 28
McCormack, Cyrus, 26
McFarland car company, 215
McGregor, Tracy, 156
McKinley, (William), 47
McLaughlin Motor Car Co., Ltd., 101
McManus, Theodore F., 68, 271
Magneto ignition, 85, 138
Maine, 21, 66, 184
Malcomson, Alex Y., 89
Maloney, M. J., 161
Manufacturer's Record, 169, 236, 268
Manufacturing, Art of, 44-45
Marcosson, Isaac F., 276
Marine boilers and engines, 52
Marine motors, 61
Marmon car, 145
Marquette Motor Co., 101, 112
Marquis, Rev. Samuel S., 162, 280
Marsh, Pliny, 156, 158, 159, 161, 165, 276, 277
Martens, Charlie, 62, 87, 151, 178, 186, 275
Martin, Pete, 127, 224, 234, 240, 244
Martyn, Henry, 19
Marx, Oscar B., 163
Masey, Ottilie. *See* Leland, Mrs. Wilfred C.
Mass production, 86, 143
Massachusetts, 20, 21
Maxwell car company, 215
May, Charles F., 268
Mayo, William B., 224, 247, 250, 254
Mayoralty election 1916, 163-64
Memoirs, Wilfred C. Leland, 269, 270, 271, 272, 273
Mendelsohn, Louis, 115
Merrifield estate, 23
Merrill, Lot A., 124, 274
Metzger, William E., 69
Michigan, 52, 53, 104
Michigan Auto Parts Co., 101

Michigan Ave., Chicago, 50
Michigan Car Company, 52
Michigan Motor Castings Co., 101
Michigan Reports, 282
Michigan Supreme Court, 263, 264
Michigan, University of, 170
Micrometers, 30, 49, 92
Middle West, 51
Midland Automobile Club, 80
Miles, Sam, 150
Miller, W. A. C., 204, 212, 213, 217, 218, 221, 222
Miller, William, 24
Milling machines, 40, 49, 55
Milwaukee, 50
Mississippi river, 55
Montague, Lord, 276
Montgomery, Col. Robert, 181, 189
Montreal, Canada, 20
Motor Age, 271
Motor World, 272, 274, 275
Motors, eight-cylinder, 147
Moving assembly line, 18
Mullins, William, 170, 201
Munger, A. L., 276
Municipal ownership, 162, 163
Murphy, Charles Edmond, 202
— Charles H., 222
— Dr. Fred, assumes supervision of Murphy estate, 202-04; warns Lincoln on deficits, 206; denies aid to Lincoln, 208; executive committee, 209-220; Lincoln company into receivership, 220-22; arranges creditors meeting, 226, 230-31; Lincoln stockholder, 226, 230, 231, 246
— Rebecca, 226
— Simon J., 66
— Walter, 202
— William H., first contact with Lelands, 66-68; church affiliation, 68; organizes Cadillac Automobile Co., 69; organizes Cadillac Motor Car Co., 73; treasurer of Cadillac, 74; sold Cadillac stock to G.M., 96; buys stock in Lincoln Motor Co., 177; recommends nephew as Lincoln dealer, 202; supports Lincoln notes at bank, 203; turns management of Lincoln

Murphy (*continued*)
  interest to Dr. Fred Murphy, 204, 208, 211, 217; votes for Lincoln receivership, 222; Lincoln stockholder, 226
Murphy family, 66, 228, 260
Myers inquiry, 195, 277
Myers, T. P., 277

Naphtha launches, 60
Nash, Charles W., 11, 112, 114, 115, 152
Nash, William T., 178, 180, 203, 219, 220, 222
Nash Motors, 206
National Automobile Chamber of Commerce, 133, 144, 147
National Cash Register Co., 132
National Foundries Association, 169
National Park Bank, 106
Neal House, 47
Neal, Thomas, 111, 112, 113, 115, 137
Nevins, Allan, 67, 274, 278, 281
New England, 18, 19, 21, 22, 58
New England Historical Society, 157
New Jersey, 100
New Testament, 46
New York, 69, 80, 89, 101, 106, 109, 147, 152, 224, 273
New York City Hospital, 28
New York *Tribune*, 276
New York *World*, 190
Newberry, Senator Truman, 280
Newspapers report scandals in war contracts, 248
Niagara Falls, 53
Niles-Bement-Pond Co., 268
Nobel prize, 17
Noble, George H., 32, 35
Non-partisan elections, 163
Nordyke & Marmon, 181
North Dakota, 124
Northern car company, 89
Northway Motor & Manufacturing Co., 101
Norton, Charles H., 40, 53, 56
Novelty Incandescent Lamp Co., 101
No. 1 Surface Grinder, 40
Nutt, Charles, 268, 269

Oak Power Co., 101
Oakland car, 112, 141; company, 112, 137; Motor Car Co., 101, 106
Oakland County Circuit Court, 259
Olaf, Prince, of Norway, 139
Ogg, Robert Y., 276
Old Guard, 154, 275
Old National Bank of Detroit, 104
Old Testament, 46
Olds, Ransom E., 17, 61, 63, 65
Olds company, 63, 67, 70, 71, 72, 89, 98, 103, 137; Motor Words, 75, 100; Vehicle Co., 61
Oldsmobile car, 18, 61, 65, 67, 69, 112; factory fire, 61; motors, 61, 62, 63
Oliver, James M., 55
One-inch plug and ring, 54
Oostdyke, Charles, 114
Open shop, 52
Oral contract, 256
Orchard Street, London, 82
Oregon, 19
Orleans County, Vermont, 21
Osceola, 77, 78
Osler, Rev. Lemuel, 46
Owen, Clair, 63, 133
Owen company, 145
Owosso, Michigan, 101

Packard car, 69, 91, 141; company, 70, 89, 101, 127, 137, 186, 191, 192, 206; Motor Car Co., 75, 175, 178, 181
Papers, Leland, 39, 267, 268, 270, 271, 274, 276, 278, 280, 283
Parry Brothers, 71
Patent pool, 134
Peace Palace at The Hague, 172
Pearl St. Baptist church, 46
Peerless car, 94, 137; Motor Car Co., 75, 215
Pearson, Henry Greenleaf, 273
Pelham Street, Detroit, 150
Penalty of Leadership, 153
Penobscot Building, Detroit, 66, 226, 230
Perry, Commodore, 19
Pershing, Gen. John J., 178
Petersburg, Illinois, 60

Pettee, Harry H., 96
Pharmaceutical products, 52
Phipps, Walter, 63, 113
Piece work, 40, 41
Pierce-Arrow car, 124, 141; company, 59, 89, 215
Pierce, George N., Company, 60, 75
Pike, Robert, 149
Pipp, Edwin G., 279
Pipp's Weekly, 279, 280, 281
Piquette plant, Ford Motor Co., 126
Pistons ground, 48
Pittsburgh, Pa., 48, 224
Platt, Henry Russell, 219, 220, 221
Policeman, 34
Politics in Ohio, 47
Pollock, R. T., 196
Pond, Lucius W., Tool Co., 32, 268
Pontiac company, 101, 103
Pontiac, Michigan, 259
Pope, Colonel, 60
Pope Manufacturing Co., 60
Pope Motor Car Co., 75
Pope-Waverly car, 69
Pound, Arthur, 133, 272, 273, 275, 276
Practical Christianity, 47
Pratt, Amos, 30
Pratt, Anthony, 156
Pratt & Whitney, 48
Pring, W. W., 68
Protestant churches, 156, 157
Prouty, Augustus B., 31, 32, 35
Providence, R. I., 34, 42, 43, 46, 49, 53, 54, 94, 225
Providence Tool Co., 30
Pullman company, 135

Quaker faith, 21
Quality versus quantity production, 86
Quantity manufacture, 30

Rae, John B., 272, 273, 278
Randall, Dwight T., 130, 178
Ranier Motor Car Co., 101, 112
Rapid 2, Volunteer Fire Co., 32, 33
Rapid Motor Vehicle Co., 101
Recall, 165
Recorder's Court, 165

Referendum, 165
Regal cars, 137
Reliability trial, 80–81
Reliance Motor Truck, 101
Reo cars, 137, 141; company, 89
Reports, newspaper, on Ford, Leland agreement, 231, 232
Resolution for Lincoln receivership, 221
Rhode Island, 21
Right hand or left hand drive, 142
Ripley, Mr. ———, 41
River Hill, England, 81, 82
Roads and highways, need for, 140, 141
Roe, Joseph Wickham, 28, 268, 269
Rolls Royce, 173, 178, 191
Ross, Robert B., 270
Rochester, N.Y., 150
Rouge plant, Ford Motor Co., 127, 129
Round Table Club, 168
Royal Automobile Club, 15, 16, 80, 83, 84, 139, 267
Russell House, 51
Ryan, William, 243, 244

Sabotage in Lincoln plant, 188
Saeger Engine Works, 101
Saginaw, Michigan, 101
St. Louis, Mo., 48, 57
St. Paul's Cathedral, 162
Salem, Ohio, 170
Salvation Army, 167
San Francisco, 176
Saturday Evening Post, 153
Sawsmith, 33
School (Cadillac of Applied Mechanics), 123–126
Schwartz, Walter, 63
Schwarze, Herman, 130
Scotland, 84
Scott-Flowers election law, 160
Scott-Hall Motor Co., 176
Scovell, Wellington & Co., 212, 213, 215, 241, 242, 278
Screw machines, 36, 49
Scriptures, 46
Seavers & Erdman, 115
Second Advent congregation, 25; doctrine, 24, 45, 46

Selden, George, 75
Self-starter, 130–135
Seligman, J. W. & Co., 109, 273
Seltzer, Lawrence H., 104, 273
Semet-Solvay Company, 157
Seminole Indians, 77
Senate committee, 190
Settlement of government tax claim, 254
Sevenoaks, England, 82
Seventh Street, Detroit, 157
Sewing machine department, Brown & Sharpe, 30, 35, 37, 39, 40
Sharpe, Henry D. Jr., 41n, 269
— Lucian, 30, 34, 39, 48, 53, 57
— Justice Nelson, 263
Shaw, James T., 111
— John T., 91
— Mrs. John, 208
Signal Corps, 175
Simonds, William A., 271, 272
Six-cylinder motors, 146
Sloan, Alfred P. Jr., 18, 92, 93, 101, 152, 272, 273
Slough, England, 84, 85
Smith, Fred L., 63
Smithsonian Institution, Washington, 153
Smoking in factory, 125, 125n, 168
Snell, Lyle, 63, 130
Social gospel, 47
Society of Automotive Engineers, 144, 169, 172
Sorenson, Charles E., 127, 224, 238, 240, 241, 243, 244, 246
Soule, George, 268
South British Trading Co., 81
Sparks, Boyden, 272
Split-tapered chuck, 49
Springfield Armory (Massachusetts), 28, 31, 34, 140
Squier, Gen. George O., 175, 179, 181, 276, 277
Standard sizes, nuts, bolts, etc., 144
Standardization test, 15–17, 82, 267
Stanley, Sir Albert, 276
Steam motors, 60
Stearns company, 89
Stec, Theodore, 125

Steel bodies for closed cars, 115, 174
Steenstrup, Peter, 92
Stevens-Duryea Co., 75
Stevens, Henry, 259
Stidger, Dr. William, 259
Stockholders, letter to (1922), 277, 278, 279, 281
Stone, Ralph, 224
Stones, Dr., ——, 50
Storrow, James W., 109, 111, 273
Straight edges, 49
Straus, Frederick, 111, 273
Strelinger, Charles A., 52, 53, 61, 270
Strong, William H., 57, 58, 270
Studebaker, John M., 71
Studebaker company, 71, 126, 137, 206, 233
Subtyposer, 56
Sunrising Hill, 80
Surface grinding machines, 49
Supreme court decision, 263
Sward, Keith, 251, 281
Sweet, Ernest E., 63, 73, 96, 113, 129, 130, 131, 133, 151, 178, 184
Sweinhart, James, 232, 257
Swift, Edward Y., 57, 270
Sydingham, Lord, 276

Talbot, Frederick A., 271
Tax Return, 1918 Profit (Lincoln), 276, 277
Tax claim. See U.S. government tax claim.
Test of Cadillac's electrical system, 136, 137
Test of Westinghouse air brakes, 48–49
Testament, Old and New, 46
Textile industry, 24, 25
Thanksgiving Day joint meeting, 167
Thomas, E. R., Car Co., 75, 89
Tifft, Zylpha. See Leland, Mrs. Leander.
Tiger Company No. 6, 33
Tilt-beam headlights, 143
Timken Axle Co., 120, 219
Tireman Street, Detroit, 210
Tolerances or limits on machined pieces, 45

INDEX

Tool makers, 30, 35, 55
Tooling for airplanes, 184
Torpedo body, 145
Trego Motor, 181
Trimmer sales demonstration, 55–56
Trix, John, 170, 177, 203, 204, 220, 221, 222
Trombly Avenue, Detroit, 56, 58
Turner, Jean, 78
Turret screws, 30
Tuskegee Institute, 167
Tuttle, Judge Arthur J., 224, 228, 229, 230, 254, 257, 261
Twenty-fourth Street, Detroit, 52
Tyler, John, 19

Uncle Henry, 32, 74, 87, 93, 121, 222, 267
Union Trust Co., 96
U.S. Armory, Springfield. *See* Springfield Armory.
U.S. Constitution, 169
U.S. government tax claim, 200, 201, 206, 220, 225, 226, 247, 254, 257
U.S. Rubber plant, 61
U.S. Treasury Department, 201, 206
Universal Grinder, 40
Universal milling machines, 49
Up-set price of Lincoln Motor Co., 229

Van Cleaf, J. C., 106, 108
Van Dusen, Charles, 156
Van Vechten, Ralph, 218
V-8 motor, 87, 148, 150, 152, 153
Velie car company, 135, 215
Verdict in Leland vs. Ford, 263
Vermont, 23
Vernier calipers, 30, 40, 49
Vernor, James, 161
Veteran Car Club Gazette, 272
Veteran Car Club of Great Britain, 85
Viall, Richmond, 38, 39, 40, 41, 48, 53, 54, 57, 93, 269
Victoria, Queen, 19
Vincent, Jesse G., 175, 176
Vlasek, Paul P., 124

Wabash Railroad, 157

Wages at Cadillac school, 125
Walbridge-Aldinger Company, 183
Walbridge, George, 183
Waldensians, 170
Waldon, Sidney D., 179
Waldorf Astoria, 138
Walker, Elisha, 225
Wall Street Journal, 279
Wallace, James V., 273
War Department (U.S.), 190
Warner-Cramton law, 160
Warren Avenue plant, 183
Warren, Ohio, 70
Washington, D.C., 180, 201, 257
Wayne Street, Detroit, 60
Weeks, John W., 248
Welch Motor Co., 101, 112, 122
Welch, Mr., ——, 48
Wellesley College, 167
Wells, W. H., 81
Westinghouse Air Brake Co., 48
Westinghouse Electric Co., 136
Westminster Presbyterian Church, 68, 121, 156, 167, 274
Weston-Mott Co., 100, 115
White, A. E. F., 69, 96
White car, 141, 145
White, D. McCall, 149, 151
Whiting, James H., 99
Whitney, Eli, 26, 29
— Francis A., 30
Wickham, Dr. A. B., 161
Widman, A. W., 178
Widman Street, Detroit, 56
Wiest, Justice Howard, 263
Wilcox & Gibbs, sewing machine company, 39
Williams College, 270
Williams, LeRoi J., 180, 277
Williamson, Harold, 260, 268
— S. T., 271, 272
Willys car company, 206, 216
Willys-Overland, 141, 206
Wilson, Charles E., 130
—, Clarence T., 196
—, J. J., 103
—, Joe, 113
—, M. W. H., 178
—, Samuel F., 123, 126, 274

Wilson, Woodrow, 173, 174
Wingo, R. T., 130
Winton company, 141, 145, 215
Winton Motor Carriage Co., 75
Wisconsin, 124
Woman driver stalls car, 129
Woodbridge, Angus, 166, 170, 212
— Mrs. Angus. *See* Leland, Gertrude
— Miriam, 78, 166
Woodbridge Street, Detroit, 61
Woodruff, Roy O., 248
Woodward Avenue, Detroit, 51
Worcester, Mass., 22, 23, 24, 25, 31, 35, 40, 42, 45, 224; Fire Department, 32, 33
World War I, 171, 172

Y.M.C.A., Detroit, 167
Y.M.C.A. Magazine, 259
Yagley, Joe, 168
Young-Man-Afraid-of-His-Car, 129
Young, William H., 268
Youth's Companion, 43

Zannoth, Herman, 130
Zeder, Fred M., 114